THE 4 KEYS TO PROFITABLE FOREX TREND TRADING

UNLOCKING THE PROFIT POTENTIAL OF TRENDING CURRENCY PAIRS

By Christopher Weaver

HARRIMAN HOUSE LTD
3A Penns Road
Petersfield
Hampshire
GU32 2EW
GREAT BRITAIN

Tel: +44 (0)1730 233870
Fax: +44 (0)1730 233880
Email: enquiries@harriman-house.com
Website: www.harriman-house.com

First published in Great Britain in 2012

ISBN: 978-0-857190895

British Library Cataloguing in Publication Data
A CIP catalogue record for this book can be obtained from the British Library.

Set in Minion, Bebas Neue and FrutigerMW Cond.

Printed and bound in the UK by CPI Antony Rowe.

Hh Harriman House

CONTENTS

PREFACE

What this book covers

This book covers four different approaches to trend trade the foreign exchange market. These four keys are:

1. Trend lines
2. Channels
3. Fibonacci retracements
4. Symmetrical triangles

We will explore the primary strength of each key, why it is useful, and the different variations of each key. We will then go through two practical strategies for each key and how to use them to execute successful trades.

It is worth noting that all of the strategies in this book can be described as continuation strategies. A continuation strategy is one that is traded in the direction of the trend on the assumption that the trend will continue.

As these keys are general concepts in technical analysis they are not limited to specific currency pairs. For example, one can trade using a trend line for a minor cross currency pair such as the GBP/AUD, with the same confidence as when trading a major currency pair such as the EUR/USD.

These keys and their corresponding strategies are designed to be traded in the foreign exchange spot market. But they are equally applicable to trading CFDs or spread betting.

Who this book is for

As this book does not cover such basics as general trading terminology, the process of placing a trade or navigating through a trading software package, it is assumed the reader is comfortable with trading in general and is therefore looking to enhance their overall trading experience by generating more profit. The application of the techniques in this book should be possible with any standard charting package.

Notes on charts

All the charts in this book were produced using © eSignal.

INTRODUCTION

The currency pairs which make up the foreign exchange market provide us with some of the most reliable trading trends. This is due to the high daily liquidity, or volume, of the market. The foreign exchange (forex) market as a whole trades around US$4 trillion every day - far more than all of the major stock markets in the world combined. All of this trading creates strong trends!

For instance, look at the EUR/USD currency pair.

Figure 0.1: major trends in EUR/USD

Of all of the currency pairs that make up the forex market, none is traded as heavily as this one. This means that whatever direction this currency pair is moving in, there is a huge amount of money backing it. It is believed that there is nearly US$1 trillion of trading volume per day on this currency alone. If it is trending up, it will require something dramatic to sufficiently turn the sentiment of the buyers into sellers and shift the trend.

Compare that to an obscure stock listed on a minor stock exchange. The smallest bit of news regarding the company, or the change of opinion by just a handful of stock holders, can turn an uptrend into a downtrend very quickly.

Liquidity is the key in providing reliability for trend trading - this is good news for the forex trend trader.

KEY 1
TREND LINES

A trend line is one of the most commonly used tools in technical analysis. However, while most traders know what this tool is, not so many know how to use it to implement an effective trading strategy. More often than not, traders draw a single trend line, which is used to highlight historic price action rather than to project a probable future.

Because of this, the trend line has come to play a minor role for many traders in setting market entries and exits. People have overlooked the simplicity of the trend line in favour of more complex indicators and systems. This is a shame as they are missing out on a powerful tool.

In this chapter, I am going to explain trend lines by defining their characteristics, by discussing different types of trend lines, and showing how they can be used to project future trading zones. We will also look at the power of using trend lines to pinpoint exact entry and exit prices.

THE THEORY

Primary strength: tells you whether to buy or to sell

A trend line shows which way the currency pair is trending and reveals the current market sentiment of the pair. The market sentiment is revealed by the direction of the trend line. If the trend line is moving up, then the market feels that the base currency (the first currency in the pair) is stronger than the terms currency (the second currency in the pair).

If the pair is trending up then we are likely to buy, if it is trending down then we are likely to sell. Knowing this up front, before considering the entry and exit points of the potential trade, puts you in a good position to effectively analyze a particular currency pair. Once your trend line is drawn and you are sure about your intention to either buy or to sell, you can move on with confidence and begin looking for possible places of entry into a position.

Another important benefit of trend lines is that they allow us to spot key turning points in the price action. A key turning point is a moment where the price action changes direction, forming either a peak or a trough. As we will see in this chapter, identifying these turning points creates effective entries in the market.

Some practicalities

In this book the price action, which is the plotted history of the exchange rate fluctuations, is shown by using candlesticks. The most basic of charting software will have a trend line option that can be used to highlight trend lines when they occur.

While it is true that each chart can present many different trend lines and can therefore be highly subjective, the goal for the trader is to identify the most obvious one. This is because our trading decisions must be based on information that the larger market moving traders, such as banks and large funds, are considering. The more eyes that see these trend lines, the more trading that takes place based on them and the more this happens the more likely they are to cause the desired reaction to the price action.

Trend lines can be drawn on any time frame. In this book, however, the shortest time frame chart we consider is the 15 minute chart and the longest is the daily chart. This is because trend lines drawn on anything less than the 15 minute chart tend to breakdown too often and are therefore unreliable to trade with. While charts longer-term than daily do not produce enough trading opportunities and can become outdated. The effect of being able to draw trend lines on a number of different time frames is that the amount of potential trading opportunities is very large.

Basic trend line characteristics

A trend line has two major characteristics,

1. it has a **minimum of three touches** with the price action, and
2. it is **angled** and not horizontal.

The requirement for three touches is a generally accepted rule in technical analysis. Two touches are more likely to be just a coincidence. With that in mind, the more touches there are the stronger the trend line.

The trend lines in the following charts demonstrate both of the required characteristics.

Figure 1.1: example of a simple, single-sided trend line

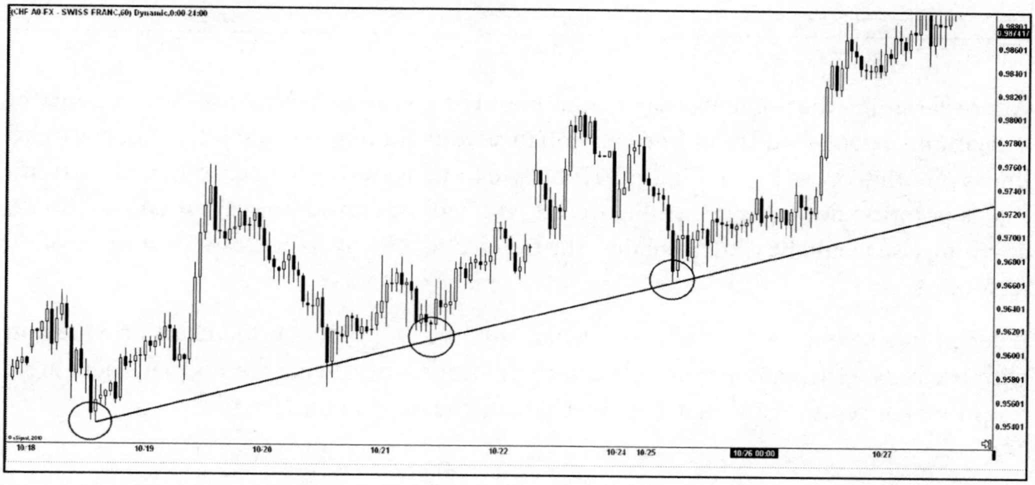

Figure 1.2: example of a simple, single-sided trend line

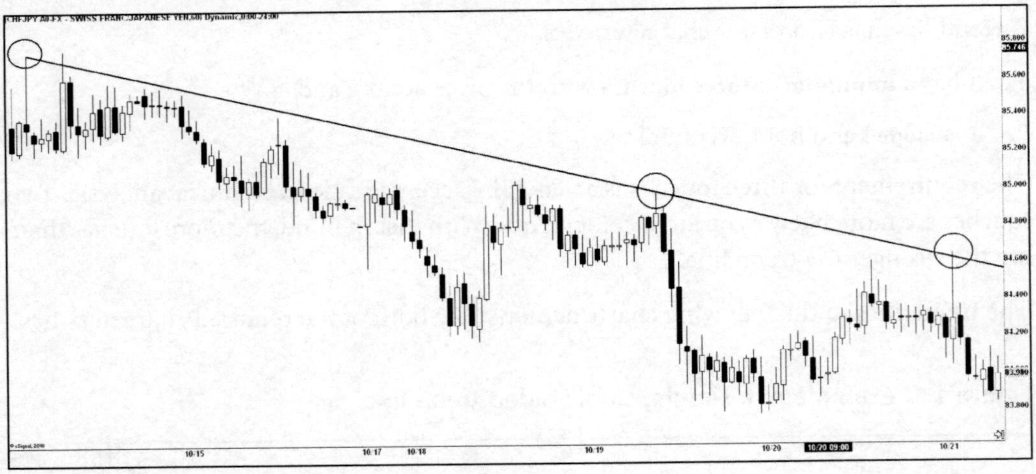

After examining the previous charts, you should be able to recognize how the presence of a clear and established trend line can enhance your trading profitability. When a trend line is pointing up, as it is in Figure 1.1, you will be considering long entries; when a trend line is pointing down, as it is in Figure 1.2, you will be considering short entries. To do anything else would be trading against the trend, and is likely to decrease your probability of success.

Later in this chapter we will identify which significant points on the chart provide you with the most efficient entry in relation to the trend line. Before we do that, there are a few more concepts regarding trend lines which you need to understand.

Trend line types

The basic trend line shown in Figure 1.2 is a simple concept which people generally find easy to identify. This basic approach, however, is insufficient, leaving you wondering how far back on the chart to go in search of trend lines and which trend line to use if you identify more than one.

Answering these questions is a matter of understanding the difference between major and minor trend lines, the impact that key moving averages have on trend lines and differentiating between the single-sided trend line and the double-sided trend line. The following sections of this chapter will do just that.

Single-sided trend lines

A single-sided trend line (like those in the previous figures) are called *single-sided* because the price action is only on one side of the trend line.

- If the price action is **going up**, the trend line is *beneath* it. One can think of the trend line as holding up the price action.
- If the price action is **going down**, the trend line is *above* it. One can think of the trend line as pushing down the price action.

Take a look at Figures 1.1 and 1.2 again, viewing them with this understanding of single-sided trend lines.

Double-sided trend lines

A double-sided trend line always runs through the price action, as opposed to running on just one side of it. The result is that there will be price action on either side of the trend line. A single-sided trend line connects only troughs or peaks depending on its direction, but a double-sided trend line connects both peaks and troughs. As with single-sided trend lines, the double-sided trend line must have three touches with the price action.

One problem that can occur with introducing the double-sided trend line to our analysis is that suddenly we can identify many trend lines. To address this we must understand two points:

1. The more touches the price action has with the trend line the more relevant the trend line is.
2. The most obvious trend line is the one to use. This is for the same reason as previously mentioned concerning single-sided trend lines – we want to use the trend lines that the majority of the market is also using.

Look at the following chart of the EUR/USD daily chart for the nine month period between March 2009 and November 2009.

Figure 1.3: example of a double-sided trend line

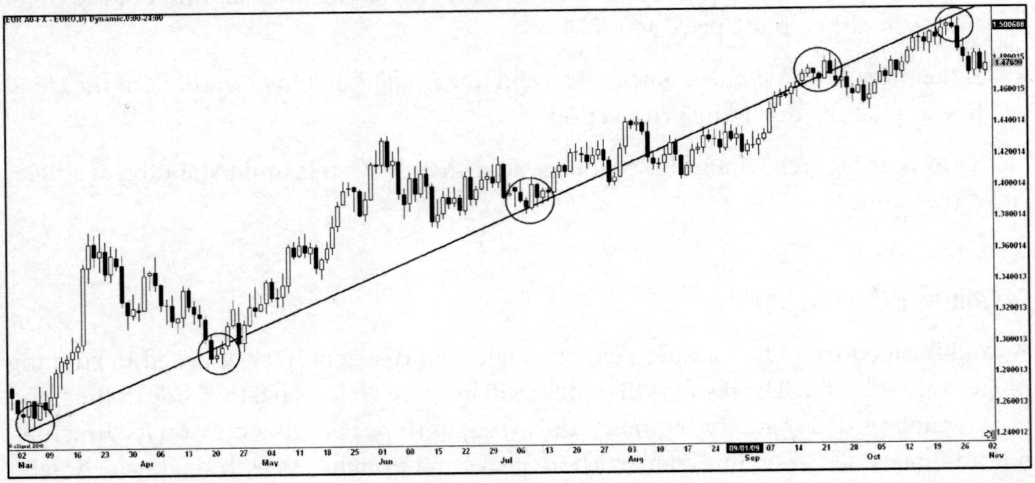

You can see that the overall trend for this time period is definitely up, but the price action jumps from one side of the trend line to the other. This is typical of longer-period trend lines, especially when viewed on the daily chart.

Let's look at another double-sided trend line. The following chart is the USD/JPY for the 18 month period between July 2008 and January 2010. The trend in this case is down.

Figure 1.4: example of a double-sided trend line

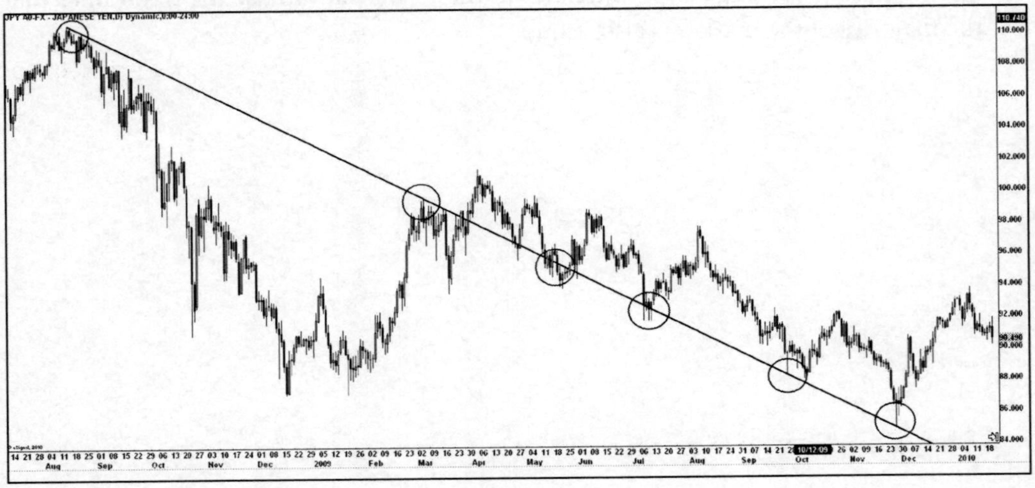

Although the overall trend is down, you will notice that between March 2009 and December 2009 the price action is bouncing off the top of the downward trend line. This is not a problem. Remember we are now considering more complex trend lines and the interaction which the price action has with them. In this example, the downward trend is further confirmed by the presence of another downward trend line. The following image reveals the second trend line and unveils more recent price action for the same currency pair.

Figure 1.5: example of multiple double-sided trend lines

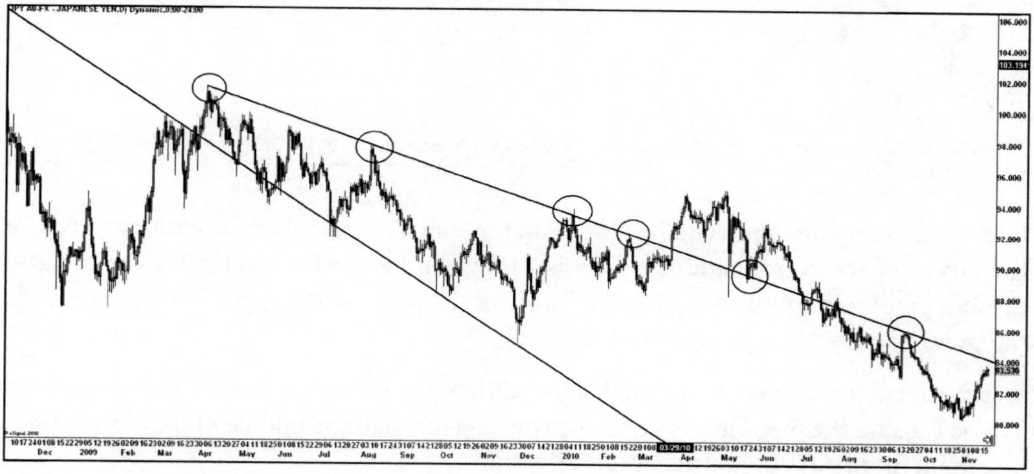

The direction of these two trend lines conveys the message of a very strong downward trend. From this chart we know that short setups are the only trades that we should be looking for. Long positions are completely out of the question. That is the discipline of trend trading - recognising the trend and trading with it.

Figure 1.6 is the daily chart of the AUD/CHF for the 12 month period from April 2009 to April 2010. It is another example of a double-sided trend line.

Figure 1.6: example of a double-sided trend line

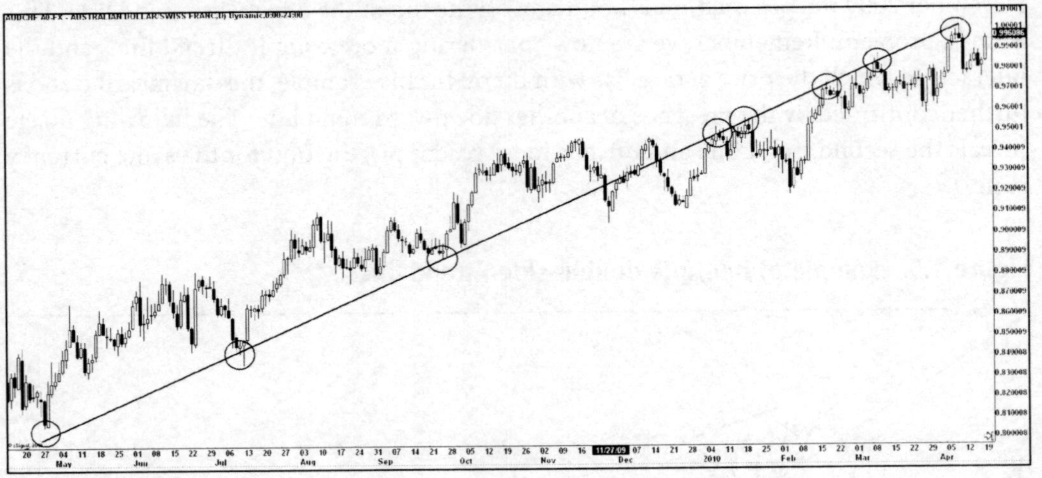

Notice the clarity that the trend line brings to the chart. You should be beginning to realize the power of trend lines and the way that they can be used to determine meaningful turning points within the price action. Think of the price action as being drawn towards the trend line and then pushed away from it.

Double-sided trend lines are normally more difficult to spot than single-sided trend lines. This is because the trend line is normally running through the middle of the price action, making it more difficult for the eye to discern.

A good way to discover these trend lines, however, is to use your charting software to project rays from significant peaks and troughs. Keep projecting these rays until you find the line that has the most touches with the price action over the longest period of time. Although this approach may sound like a fairly random way of doing things, you will be able to appreciate just how effective it is once you've tried it.

Double-sided trend lines normally occur when dealing with larger time frames such as months, or even years. This is because it is very difficult for the market to trade on, or to keep to, just one side of a trend line for an extended period of time. Remember that with double-sided trend lines it is the angle of the trend line that determines the direction of the trend, not the side of the trend line which the price is bouncing off.

Now that you understand the difference between single and double-sided trend lines, we can explore the concept of major and minor trend lines.

Major trend lines

In order to trend trade effectively you must understand the difference between a major trend line and a minor trend line. Note that both major and minor trend lines can be either single or double-sided.

A major trend line is defined as the primary trend line that is consistent with the *visual flow* of the chart. It is used to determine whether to trade a long or a short position.

When looking to spot the major trend line on a chart, you need to know if the price action is moving up or down. You can usually tell by a quick glance at the chart.

For example, look at the following 60 minute CAD/JPY chart and ask yourself whether the price action is moving up or down.

Figure 1.7: example of a downward moving currency pair

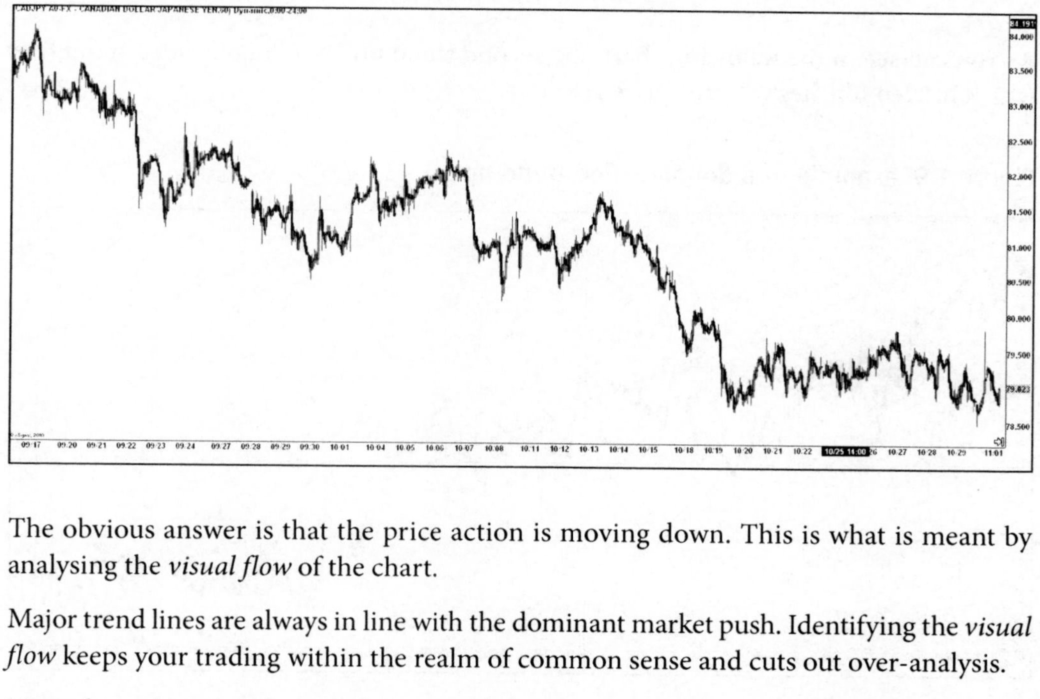

The obvious answer is that the price action is moving down. This is what is meant by analysing the *visual flow* of the chart.

Major trend lines are always in line with the dominant market push. Identifying the *visual flow* keeps your trading within the realm of common sense and cuts out over-analysis.

Next, draw the most obvious downward trend line that you can find. In this case, there are two trend lines worth considering. The first one is a single-sided trend line with three touches as shown in Figure 1.8.

Figure 1.8: example of a single-sided trend line

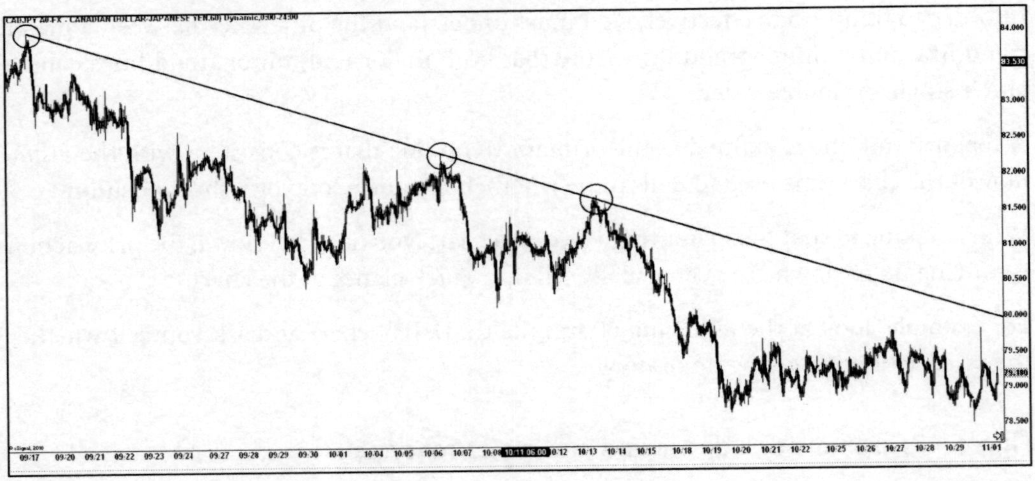

As you can see in the following chart, the second trend line is a double-sided trend line which has ten touches with the price action.

Figure 1.9: example of a double-sided trend line

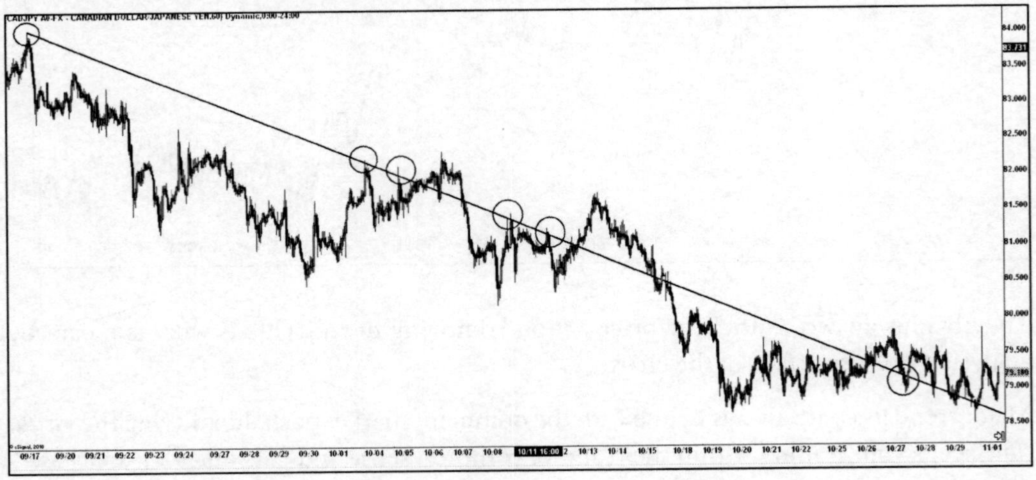

From this analysis we come to the conclusion that the major trend line for this particular chart is the double-sided trend line, which has more than three times the number of interactions with the price action than the single-sided trend line does. It is, therefore, this trend line that can be used to identify key turning points for the currency pair.

To summarise, the major trend line is the line which is congruent with the *visual flow* of the chart and has the most touches with the price action. If a trend is present, then the chart will have just one major trend line.

Minor trend lines

Minor trend lines are trend lines which either run counter to the *visual flow* of the chart or follow the *visual flow* but have fewer touches with the price action than the major trend line. While there can be only one major trend line, there can be several minor trend lines.

Using the example of the CAD/JPY 60 minute chart shown in Figure 1.7, you can see that the single-sided trend line which we considered first is a perfect example of a minor trend line. Although it is consistent with the *visual flow* of the chart, which is down, it has fewer touches with the price action than the major trend line. This does not mean that this single-sided trend line should be forgotten; it should simply be recognized as a minor trend line. It certainly holds value, as far as our trading opportunities are concerned, though not as much value as the major trend line.

If you refer back to the earlier images of the USD/JPY daily chart, you will find two trend lines there. One is a major trend line, while the other is a minor trend line. Both were valuable.

Make sure that you plot both the major and minor trend lines on your chart together, as shown in Figure 1.10.

Figure 1.10: example of a double and single-sided trend line on the same chart

This is a good example of major and minor trend lines bringing clarity to a currency chart and adding a certain level of discipline to your trading. Later in this chapter we will explore the price zones that major and minor trend lines create.

As we discussed, minor trend lines can either go along with, or counter to, the *visual flow* of the chart. The first minor trend line which we looked at was consistent with the downward move. It was only considered minor because it had fewer touches with the price action than the major trend line. Now we are going to look at a minor trend line which is counter to the *visual flow* of a chart, known as a *minor counter trend line.*

Looking at the Figure 1.11, I have indicated where these minor counter trend lines have formed.

Figure 1.11: example of double and single-sided trend lines with minor counter trend lines

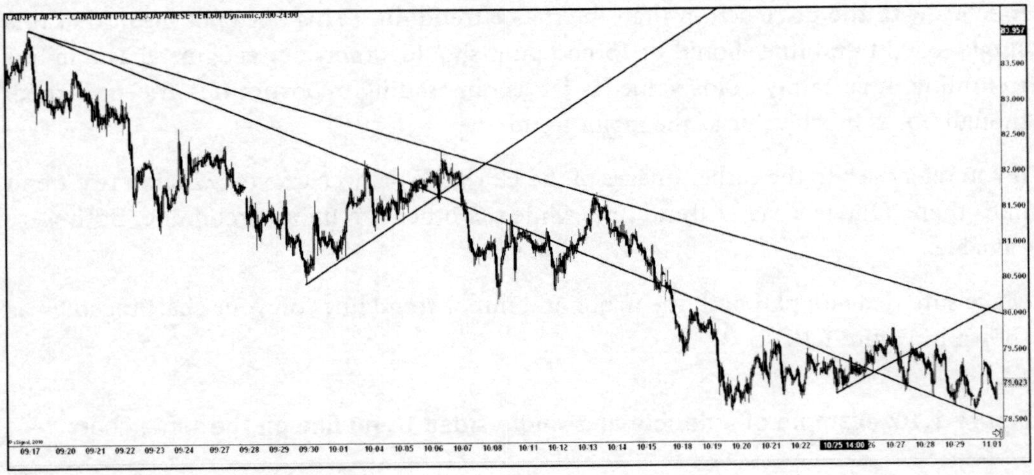

Notice that, as far as time is concerned, these minor counter trend lines have a much shorter life than either the major trend line or the minor trend line consistent with the *visual flow* of the chart. We therefore do not trade in line with these minor counter trend lines, as they are against the major trend of the chart. They only become useful once they have been broken, as this is an indication that the major trend is taking over again and we can be on the lookout for entries that are in line with this major trend. Notice the strong downward moves that occur once these minor counter trend lines are broken.

Let's walk through another example. First we will establish the major trend line and then we will locate any minor trend lines going along with the major trend. Finally, we will look for minor counter trend lines. Watch how the chart develops and becomes more informative as we draw each of these lines.

The following chart is the EUR/GBP 60 minute chart. Visually, we notice that the chart is pushing up.

Figure 1.12: example of an upward moving currency pair

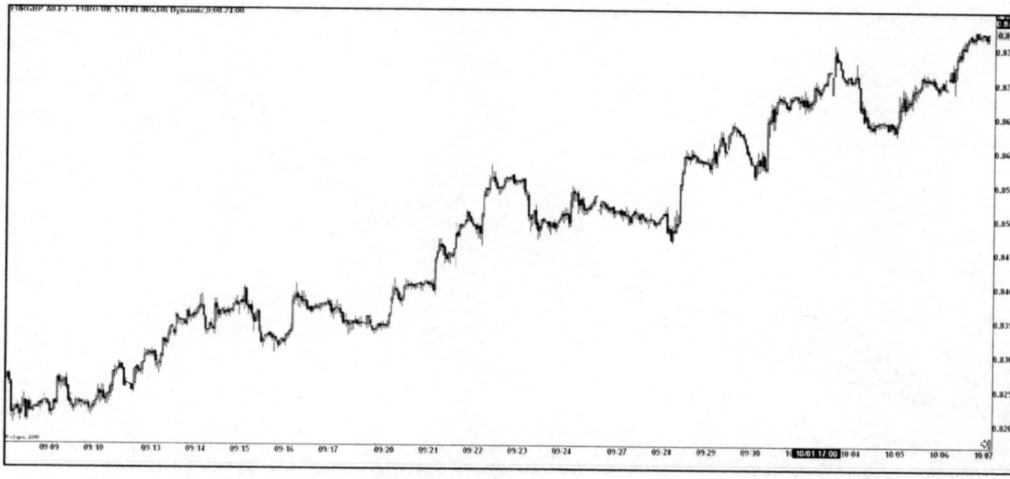

The first trend line that is likely to stand out is a single-sided, upward trend line. Figure 1.13 shows this trend line, which has five touches with the price action.

Figure 1.13: example of a single-sided trend line

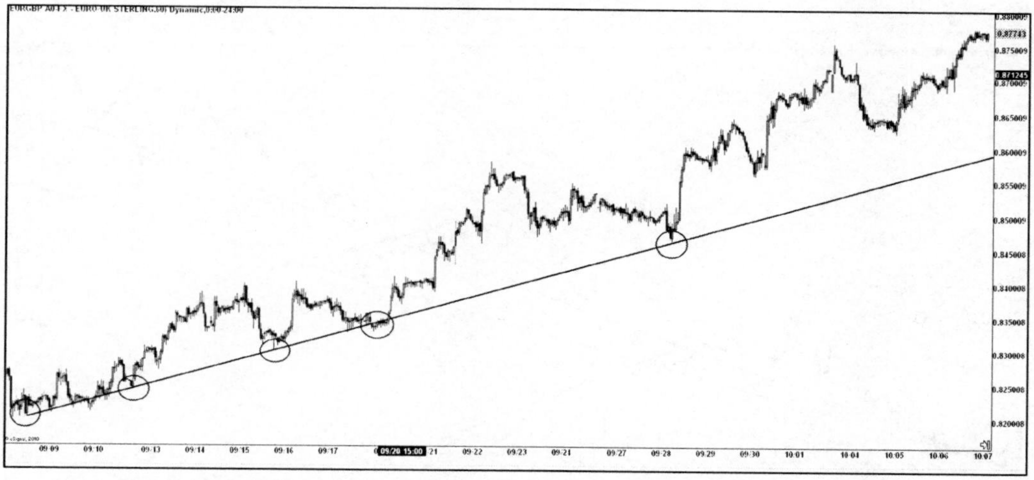

We also discover that there is a double-sided trend running through the price action. This trend line has five touches and would therefore be considered the major trend line.

Figure 1.14: example of a major, double-sided trend line

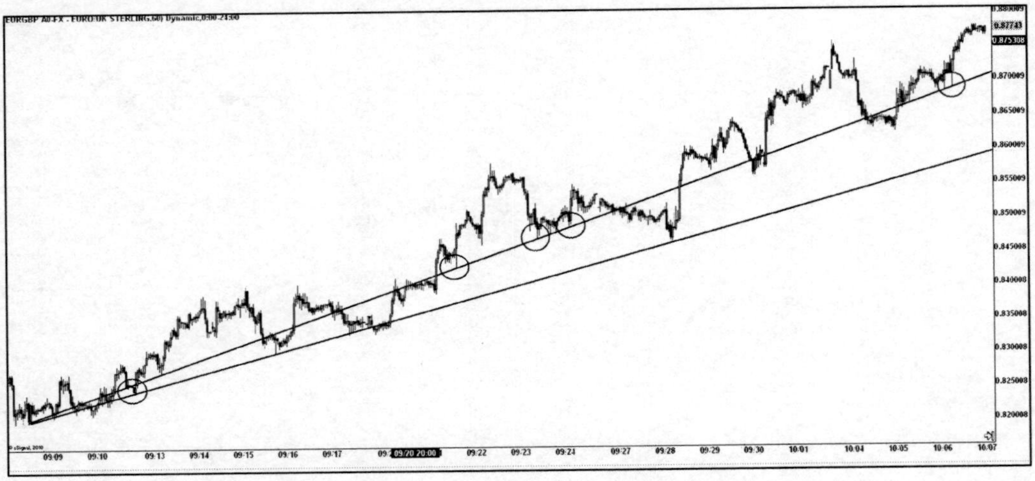

Within this upward trend, there are also a few counter minor trend lines, as seen in Figure 1.15.

Figure 1.15: example of double and single-sided trend lines with counter minor trend lines

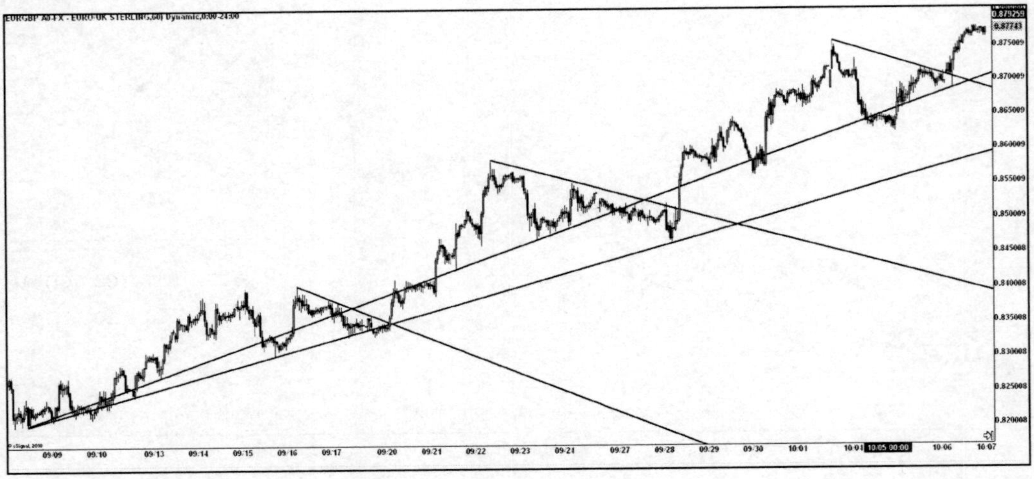

Once you begin plotting your major trend lines, minor trend lines and minor counter trend lines, your chart may become too busy. A busy chart is one that is so filled with trend lines that it becomes difficult to see which lines are important and which lines are not. Remember, the only reason that we are plotting these trend lines is to bring clarity and make sense of what we are looking at. A busy chart causes confusion and ultimately frustration. Frustrated traders are rarely profitable.

The following is an example of a busy chart.

Figure 1.16: example of a busy chart

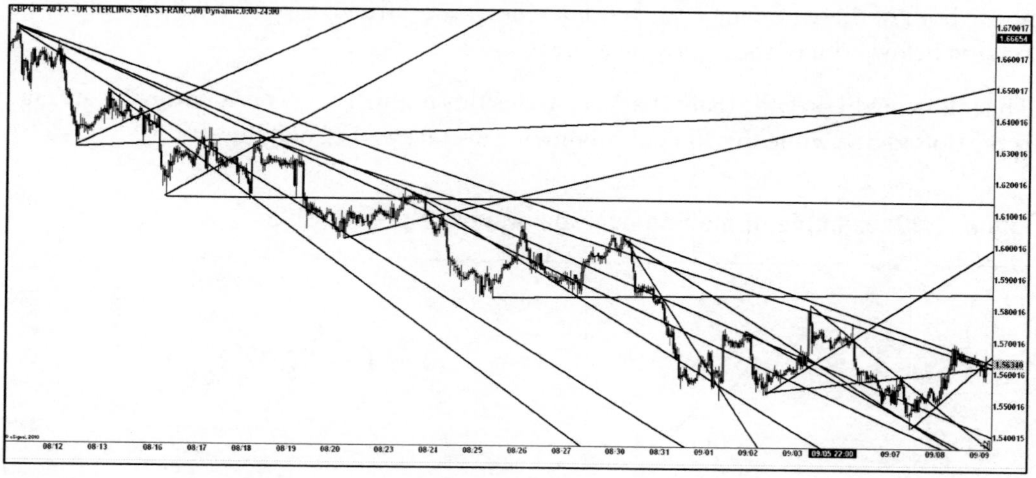

Ask yourself whether your trend lines have brought clarity or confusion. If the answer is confusion, then you have too many trend lines on your chart. The best thing to do is remove all of the trend lines and start again from a clean chart.

Traders who have busy charts fear missing a trade and are desperate to exploit every single minor trend line to get an edge in the market. This type of anxiety should not be part of your trading experience. The forex market provides plenty of opportunities for the patient trader.

Summary

In summary, the major trend line is the line with the most touches to the price action which runs in the same direction as the dominant *visual flow* of the chart. The minor trend lines are lines which, run in the direction of the flow of the chart but have fewer touches than the major trend line, or lines which run counter to the major trend line. If it is difficult to discern the *visual flow* of the chart, it is likely that no trend line of any value exists. When this happens we move onto the next chart in search of a better opportunity.

Moving averages

It is worth noting here that some technical traders use the location of the current price action in relation to the 50 and 200 period exponential moving averages (EMA) to confirm the trend. In theory any pair of moving averages may be used, for example the 10 and 20 period EMA, but in practice the most common pair used is the 50 and 200 period.

For price to be in an upward trend, for instance, the current price action has to be trading above both of these moving averages. For a downward trend, the price would need to be trading below both of these moving averages.

The following EUR/USD daily chart illustrates this point. The 50 period moving average is the dotted line while the 200 period moving average is the solid line.

Figure 1.17: example of moving average and price relationship

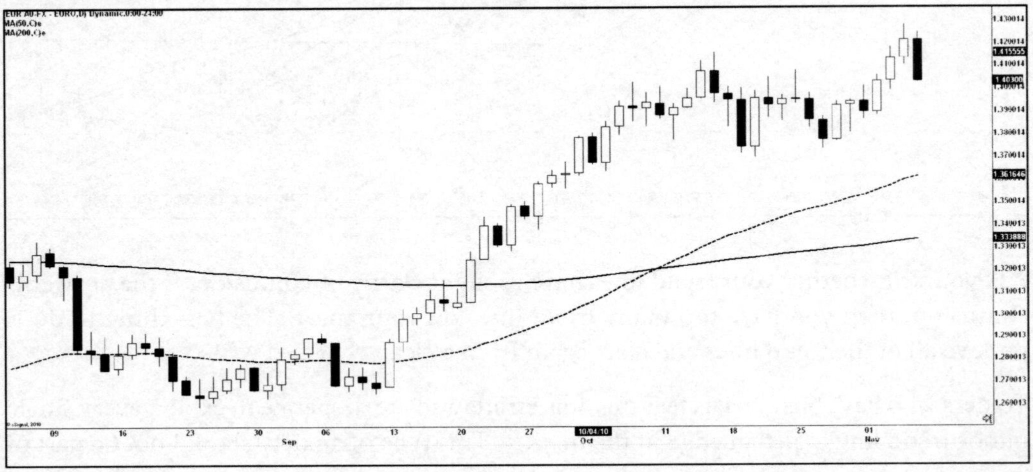

Notice how the current price action is trading above both significant moving averages. This indicates that, providing we have an established trend line, we would be looking for long setups. We can take this as a general rule.

In the following USD/JPY daily chart, we can see that the price action is clearly trading below both the 50 and 200 period moving averages. This is a strong confirmation of a downward trend.

Figure 1.18: example of moving average and price relationship

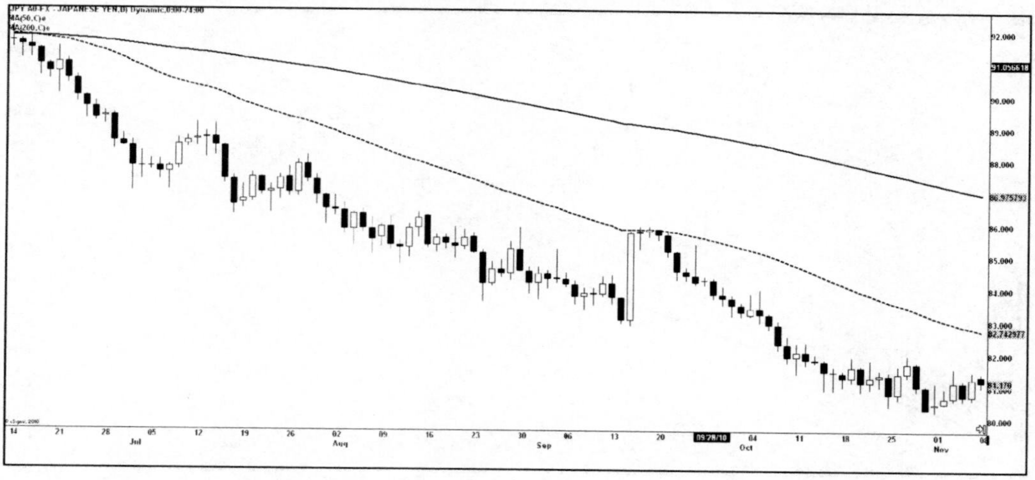

Moving averages are a valid tool for confirming the direction of a trend. Major and minor trend lines, however, are our main focus when determining the trend.

Trend line projection

One of the main criticisms of pure technical analysis is that it is nothing more than a review of historical data, providing no insight into the future. Although I disagree with such a view, I do appreciate why it is held. It is easy to look at a chart and analyze what has happened in the past - anyone can do that.

The skill of profitable trading, however, is the ability to differentiate between relevant and irrelevant information on the chart and then to project the relevant information into the future. This is why your trend lines must be drawn with the ray tool on your charting software, instead of the segment tool. The difference is that a ray extends out indefinitely, keeping the same angle and assists in predicting significant future turning points when the price action touches it. A segment stops at the current price action and provides no indication of future price movements.

In this section, we will look at the power of projected trend lines and will learn to analyze the zones that occur as a result of multiple trend lines.

The following example uses the GBP/USD daily chart. The first thing to notice is that the trend lines are extended to the future. As mentioned, this is essential for trend line projection. We will refer to the lower, single-sided trend line as trend line **A**, and the double-sided trend line above it as **B**.

Figure 1.19: example of projected trend lines

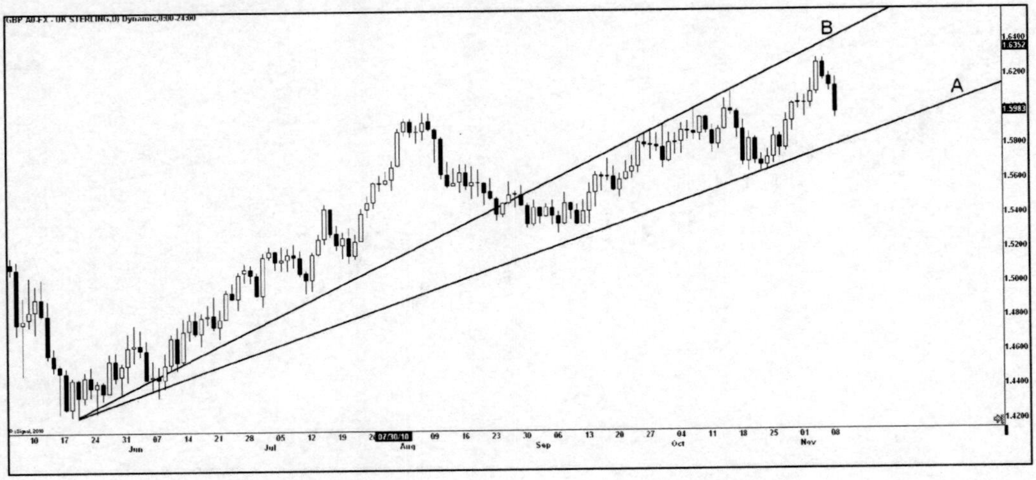

The projected trend lines create future turning points which can be anticipated. For instance, if the price action returns to trend line **A**, then we can expect it to bounce and begin an upward push towards trend line **B**. If the price reaches up to trend line **B**, then we can expect a bounce back down towards trend line **A**.

Trend line zones

Now let's talk about the zones that have been created by these two trend lines. If I were to ask you how many zones this chart has been divided into, what would your answer be? Figure 1.20 reveals the answer.

Figure 1.20: example of projected trend lines creating zones

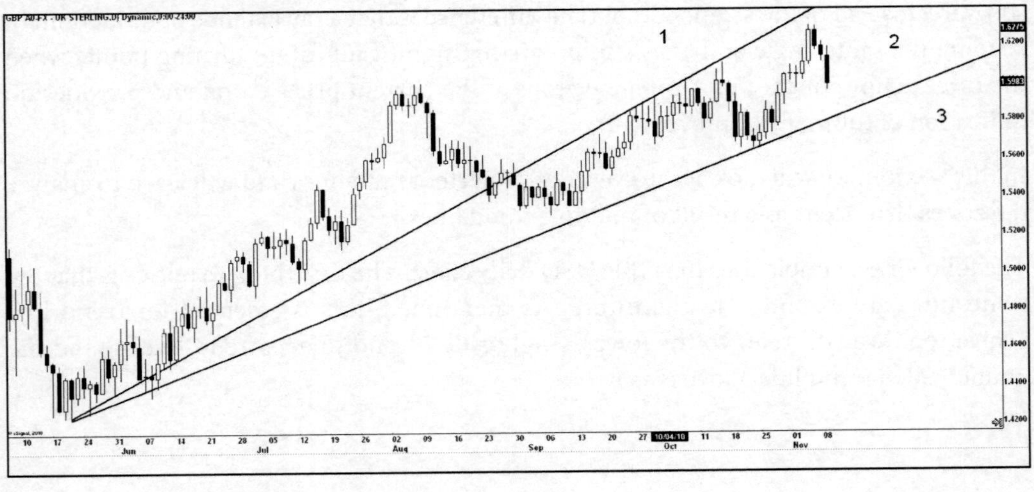

As you can see, the trend lines have divided the chart into three separate zones. To progress from here we need to understand not only what each zone represents, but also how to utilize each one to generate trading profits.

There are two types of zones which we will be addressing: *outer* and *inner* zones.

Let's look at the outer zones first.

In the above example, zones 1 and 3 are the outer zones, because they are located on the outside of the current price action and are only bordered by one trend line. The outer zones represent the more extreme extensions, both in line with the trend as in zone 1, and outside of the trend as in zone 3. For instance, if the price action were to cross up into zone 1, we would consider this move to be overextended and would expect a pullback in the near future. With this in mind, we would be very wary about placing buy orders deep into zone 1. The further the price action moves into zone 1, the more likely it is that a short pullback will take place. Zone 3, on the other hand, would be an overextension of price to the short side. The deeper that the price action falls into zone 3, the more likely that there will be a strong, long pullback, in line with the dominant trend.

Zone 2 is the inner zone, as it is located in between zones 1 and 3. This zone represents the current normal trending behaviour of the currency pair. This is the zone that we can expect the price action to continue trading within. The inner zone is where we will find the highest probability setups and is therefore the ideal zone to trade in. It is in line with the overall dominant trend and does not represent an overextension of the price action on either the up or the down side.

Let's look at another example of creating zones by drawing trend lines and labelling these zones. Labelling always begins with 1 and moves in a clockwise direction. Watch how the story of the chart develops as we add trend lines and create zones.

Figure 1.21 is of the AUD/USD daily chart. There are no trend lines or zones yet, just a picture of the price action.

Figure 1.21: example of price action without trend lines

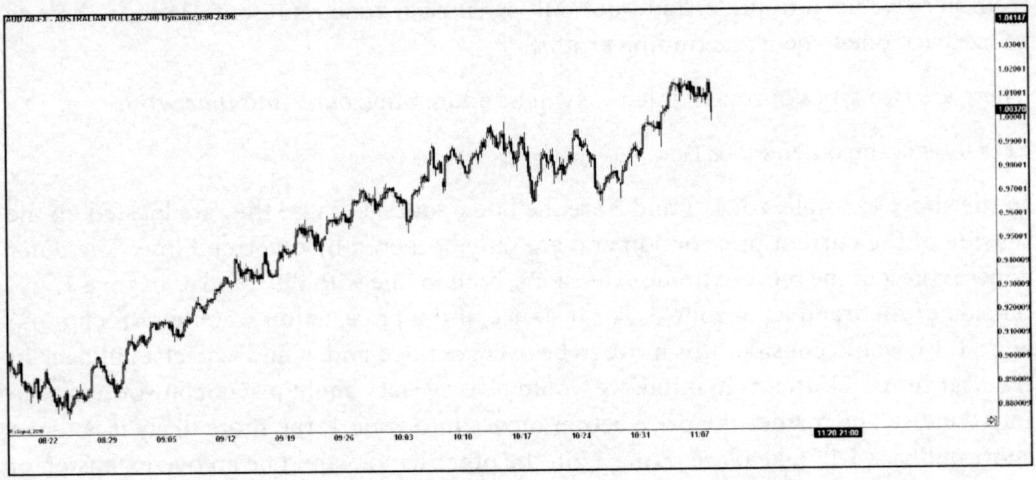

Now we'll add some trend lines.

Figure 1.22: example of projected trend lines

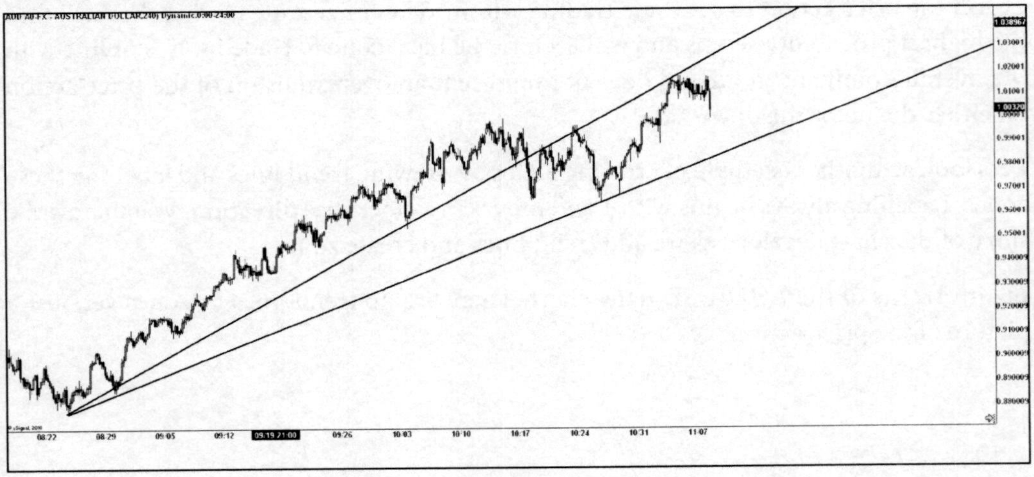

These are the two most obvious trend lines. The double-sided trend line is the major trend line, as it has more touches than the single-sided trend line beneath it.

Next, we'll identify and label the zones.

Figure 1.23: example of projected trend lines creating zones

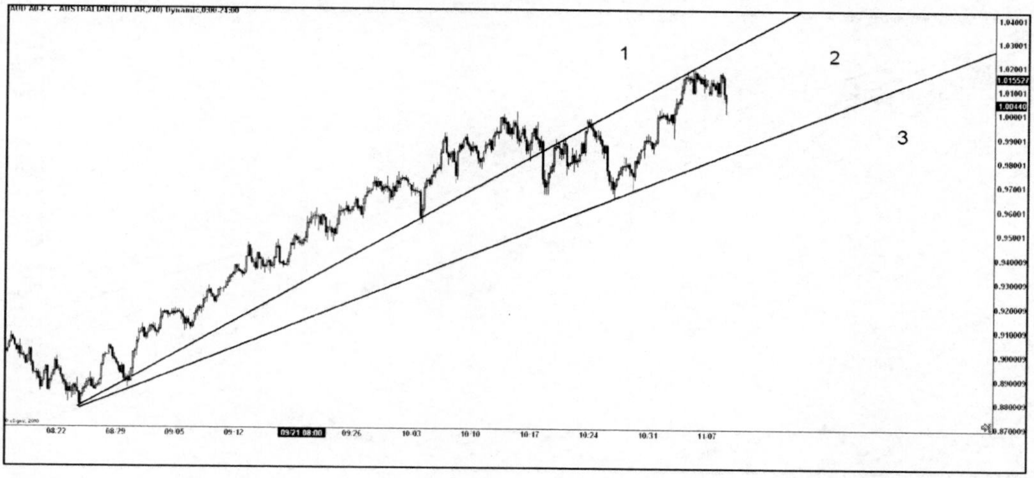

All three zones can now be seen clearly. We know that zones 1 and 3 are the outer zones, while zone 2 is the inner zone and the zone where will look for the majority of our setups.

Let's look at another example; this time the trend is moving down.

Figure 1.24 is the USD/SGD 4 hour chart. Again, watch how drawing trend lines and creating zones brings clarity.

Figure 1.24: example of price action without trend lines

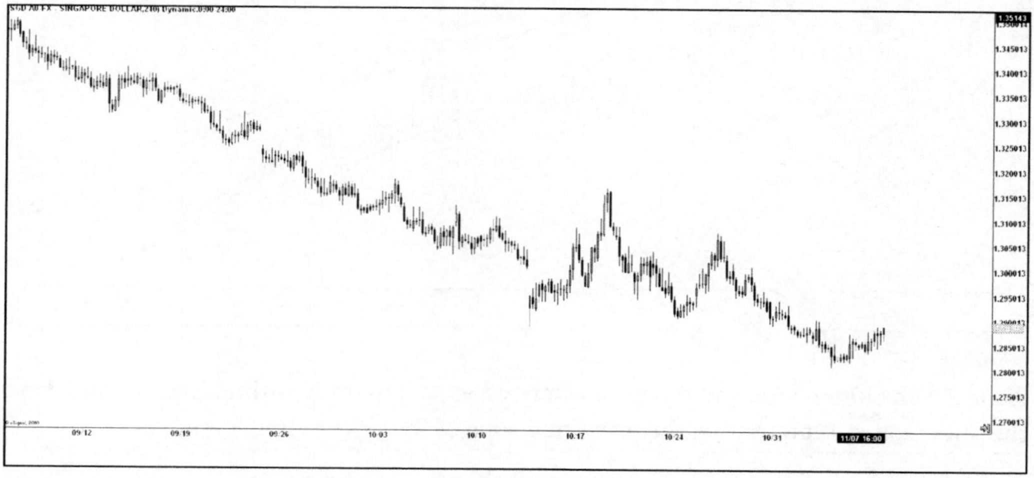

Let's add the trend lines.

Figure 1.25: example of projected trend lines

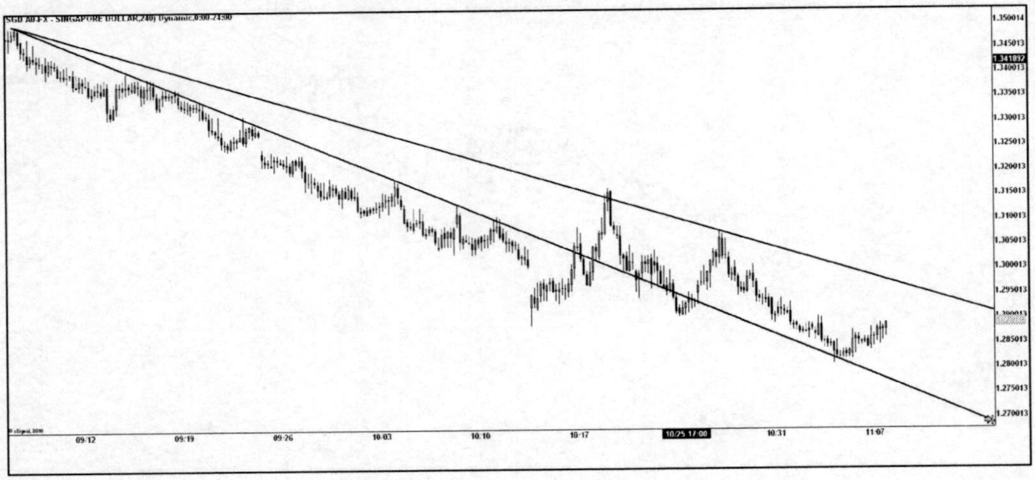

The addition of the major and a minor trend lines have created three zones again. Let's label them.

Figure 1.26: example of projected trend lines creating zones

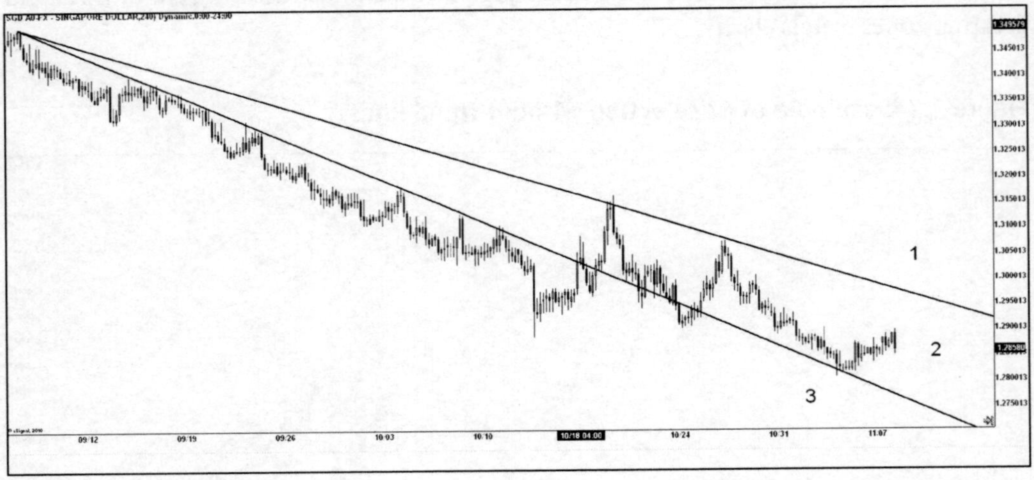

Zone 2 is the inner zone and the zone where we expect to trade within. Zones 1 and 3 are the outer zones, representing the overextensions of the price action.

A question now arises as to how many zones should be created.

To answer this, you must first remember that a busy chart causes confusion, frustration and poor trading results. To avoid busy charts, we will set the maximum number of zones at four; meaning not more than three trend lines should be drawn.

Remember that we are now talking about zone creation trend lines, which will be a combination of the major trend line and the minor trend lines but will not include the minor counter trend lines, as they run counter to the *visual flow* of the chart. Later on, we will explore the benefits of counter minor trend lines and the various patterns which they create on our charts.

Looking at Figure 1.26 again, you should be able to spot another trend line. Figure 1.27 reveals this third trend line.

Figure 1.27: example of an additional zone created by a further trend line

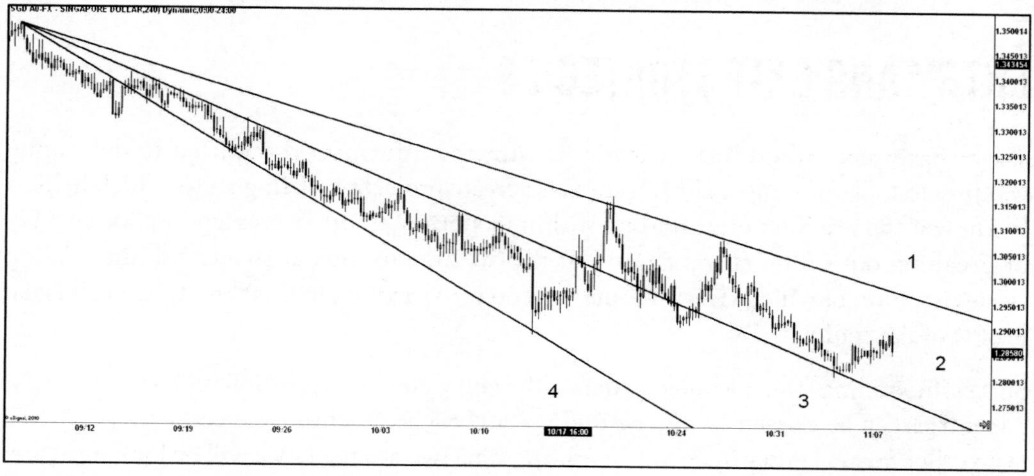

The addition of another trend line has created a fourth zone, meaning there are now two inner zones. We've already established that the inner zone is the place to expect most trading to be done, but now that we have two inner zones, we need to know whether one has greater value than the other.

To find out, we identify which inner zone the price action is currently trading in. In the example above, we can see that the price action is currently in zone 2. We can therefore consider zone 2 to have more value than zone 3 – even though both are inner zones. Before zone 4 was created, we considered zone 3 to represent an overextension of price, meaning we would expect potential sharp pullbacks and would be cautious about going short too deep into this zone. Zone 3, however, is now an inner zone, so trading within it becomes more appropriate.

It is worth noting that when we draw trend lines for the purpose of zone creation, they all start from the same peak if the general trend is down or from the same trough if the general trend is up. This is another reason why the minor counter trend lines are not used to determine trending trading zones – they cannot be drawn from the same peak or trough as the other trend lines.

Summary

In summary, drawing trend lines creates zones. It is best to keep the maximum number of zones at four, to guard against a busy chart. The outer zones represent the overextended areas of the chart and are therefore not ideal for trading. This is because when price gets too extended it becomes more difficult to predict turning points, which can be fast and furious. In the inner zones, safer, more stable price action is found. This is where we look for the majority of our setups. If there is more than one inner zone, greater value is placed on the zone where current price action is happening.

ENTRY AND EXIT STRATEGIES

As we have seen, trend lines provide us with the information required to determine whether to look for long or short trades and create projected trading zones which help us to know if the price action is trading within its normal trend, overextending too quickly or breaking out of the current trend. It is now time to look at two trend line trading strategies, both of which clearly define the entry, risk exit (stop loss) and target exit (take profit) of the trade.

Successful trading strategies always define the entry point of a position relatively precisely. All entries can be classed as either a bounce-off or a break-through a certain level. There is no other form of entry in technical trading. The two strategies we will be looking at are:

1. Trend line bounce strategy
2. Trend line break strategy

1. Trend line bounce strategy

The aim of the trend line bounce strategy is to catch the move of the price just as it bounces off the trend line and rejoins the flow of the trend.

This approach is relatively aggressive compared to more traditional styles of trading. By aggressive, I mean that we will be looking for buying opportunities while the price action is falling into an upward trend line and looking for selling opportunities while the price action is rising into a downward trend line.

More conservative traders wait for the price to action begin to change direction before entering a trade. But while this approach stops us from entering the occasional bad trade, it also reduces the amount of profit taken from winning trades. Over time, this will have a dramatic effect on the overall return.

Let's begin going through the trend line bounce strategy by clearly defining its entry. We will use the USD/CHF four hour chart in Figure 1.28 as our example chart.

Figure 1.28: price action without trend lines

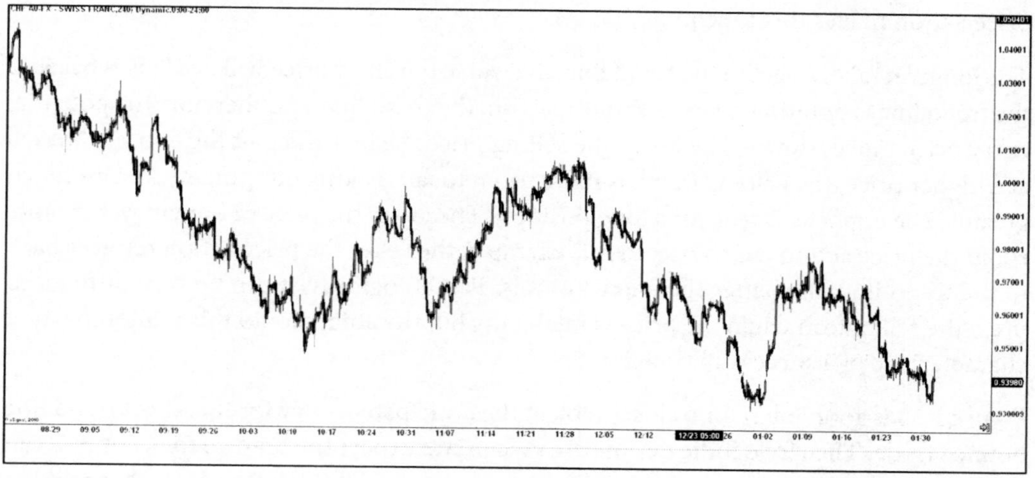

This image makes it clear that the price action is trending down, so we know that we only need to look for short positions. Let's draw some trend lines and see if we have any projected zones to work with.

Figure 1.29: projected trend lines creating zones

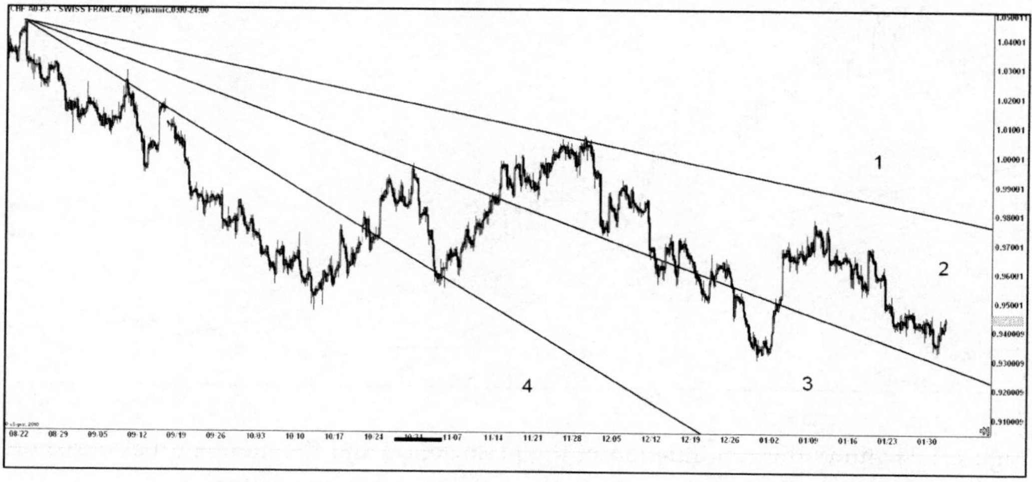

The addition of the three trends lines, as drawn in Figure 1.29, reveal four projected trading zones. Zone 2 is the primary trading zone because that is where the price action is currently located.

Entry

The entry for this trade should take place when the price action retraces back up to the trend line that divides zones 1 and 2 and touches it. While we can look at the chart to estimate when this touch is likely to occur, we can't define the exact entry price until the price action makes this touch.

The longer it takes to get to the trend line, the worse the entry price will be. This is because the trend line is pointing down. As time goes on, the trend line, and therefore the potential entry price moves down. The lower the selling price the less efficient the entry. If we sell at a higher price, the price action has more room to fall making our potential profit much greater. The opposite is true for a long position. The lower the price of our entry, the more room the price action has to rise. In this example, the faster the price action retraces back to the trend line, the better the entry point is. Psychologically, it can be very difficult to press the sell button when the price is racing up, but the ability to do this is an important characteristic of a successful trader.

Figure 1.30 is zoomed in for a closer look at the anticipated entry for this short trend line bounce trade. The circle indicates the area where we expect the bounce to occur. We can never know for sure where, or even if, the price action will hit the trend line, but making an estimate helps to build our intuition and confidence.

Figure 1.30: anticipated entry

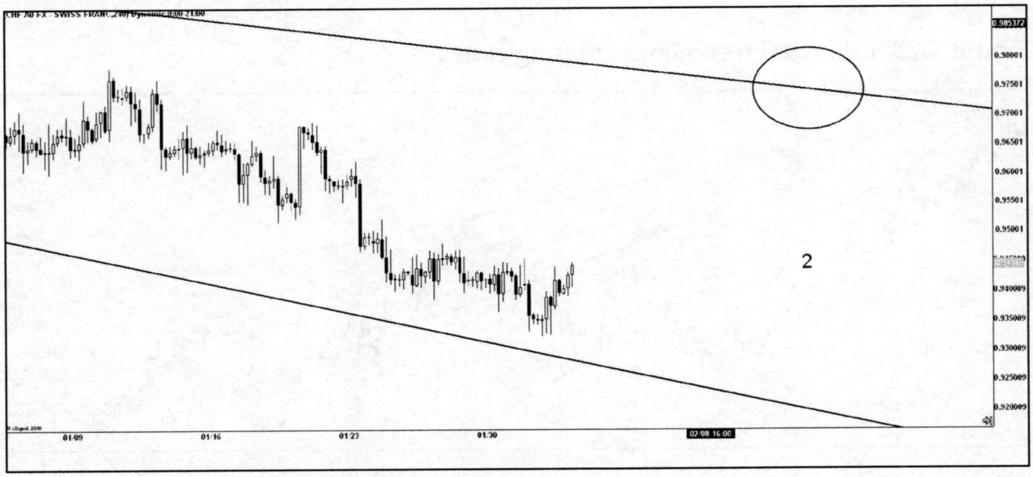

Figure 1.31 shows the continuation of the price action and the moment that our short entry should occur. The exact point of entry is indicated by the dotted line.

Figure 1.31: actual entry

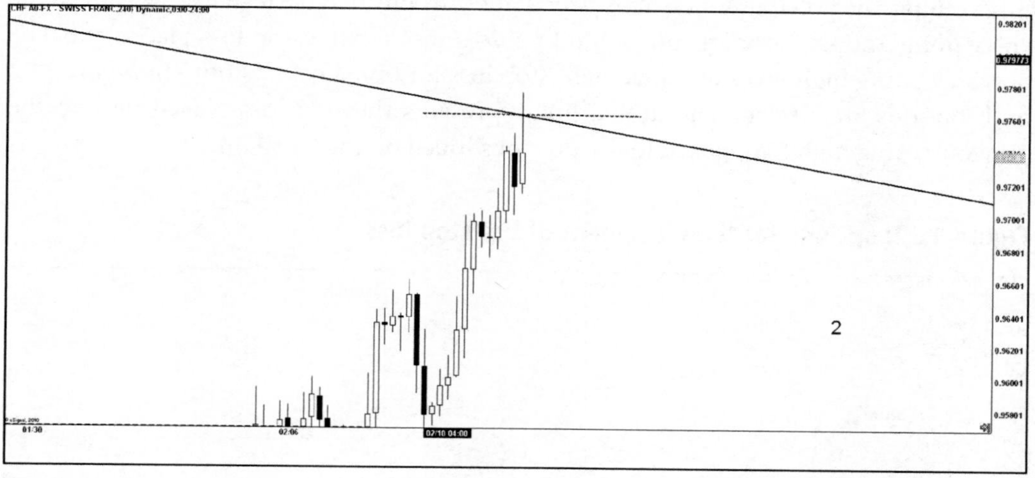

We enter at the exact moment that the price action touches the trend line.

Entry summary

The five steps of entering the trend line bounce trade are:

1. Determine the direction of the price action – up or down.
2. Identify and draw any trend lines.
3. Label the projected zones created by the trend lines.
4. Estimate a general area for the potential bounce to occur.
5. Wait for the price action to retrace (come back to) the trend line. Enter at the moment that the price action makes contact with the trend line.

Exit – Risk

Now that we know our entry we need to identify where our stop loss must be placed. Here you have two options:

1. Place the stop loss 5 pips above the previous swing high (if going long it would be 5 pips below the previous swing low). 5 pips allows for the broker's spread as well as a small amount of volatility.
2. Place the stop loss 5 pips above the previous touch of the trend line which was used to define the entry (if going long it would be 5 pips below the previous touch of this trend line).

The appropriate option to use is normally determined by the setup itself. For instance, in this example the previous touch of the trend line is a considerable distance away from the entry point and is, therefore, not a good guide to use for the stop loss placement. The previous swing high gives us a nice tight stop loss for our short position. In Figure 1.32 both options are circled. The dotted line represents the stop loss placed next to the previous swing high as opposed to the previous touch on the trend line.

Figure 1.32: options for the placement of the stop loss

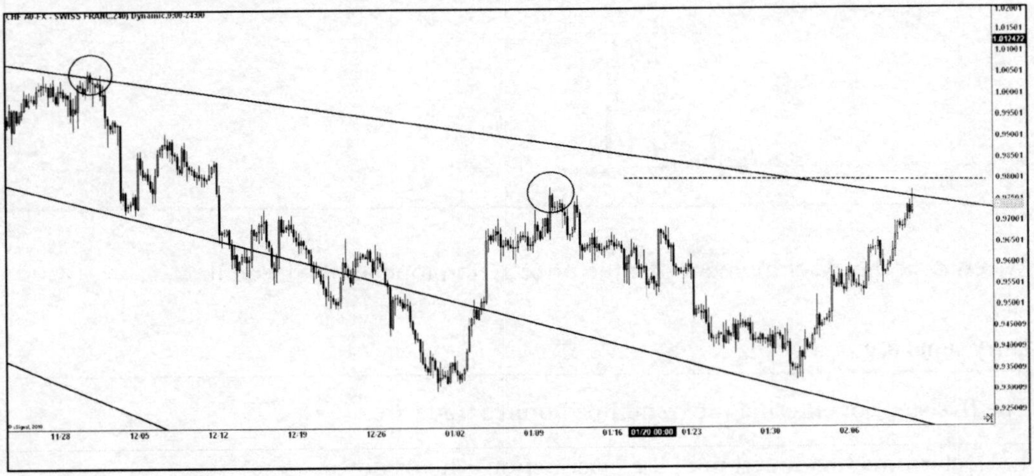

When seen on the chart, it is clear that the previous swing high is a better indicator for our stop loss placement in this specific trade.

Exit – Target

The target for this trade is determined by the previous dominant swing low of the price action. The exact target price is the price of the lowest point of that swing. The circle in Figure 1.33 highlights the dominant swing low and the dotted line represents the price level of the target.

Figure 1.33: target

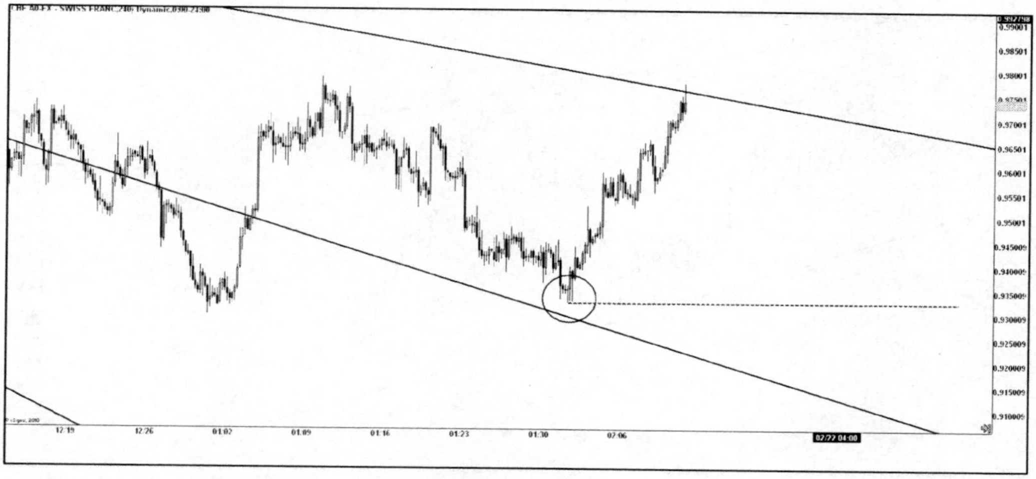

The chart also reveals that the target price is actually a support level which the price action has bounced off in the past. In Figure 1.34 shows this more clearly.

Figure 1.34: a support level that is consistent with the target

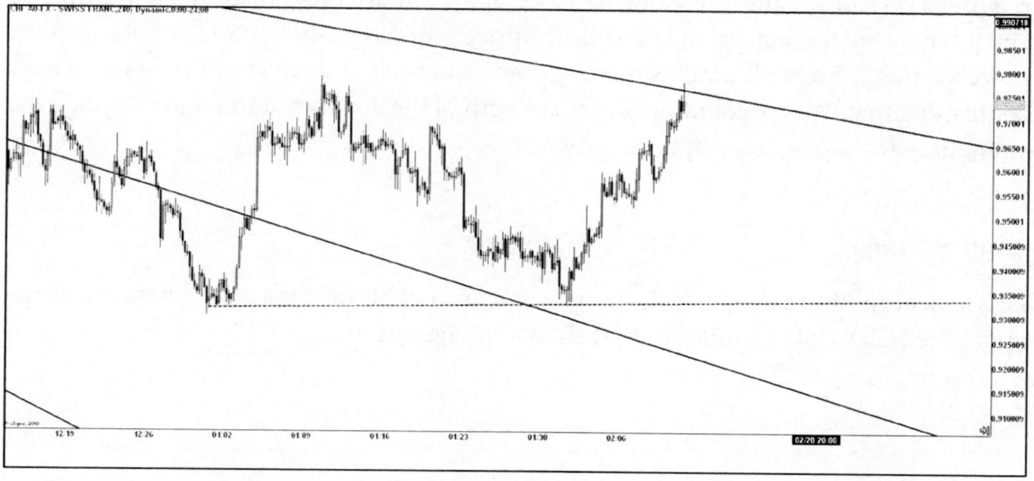

We have now defined our entry, stop loss and target price for this trend line bounce trade. Figure 1.35 shows the continuation of the price action as it reaches our target. Notice that the entry and both exit levels are all marked with dotted lines. From top to bottom these lines represent the stop loss, the entry, and the target.

Figure 1.35: entry, stop loss and target of the trade as well as the outcome

Summary

We see here that the trade runs smoothly down and hits its target. This type of trade requires a certain amount of confidence. Look at the upward move that led into the bounce entry. It may not feel natural to sell while the price action is pushing up so fast. Remember, however, that the overall trend was going down and we had three very strong trend lines confirming that. We are counting on the strength of the downward trend to outweigh the strength of the momentary upward move.

Another example

Let's look at another example of the trend line bounce. This time the price action is moving up on the NZD/USD 15 minute chart shown in Figure 1.36.

Figure 1.36: price action without trend lines

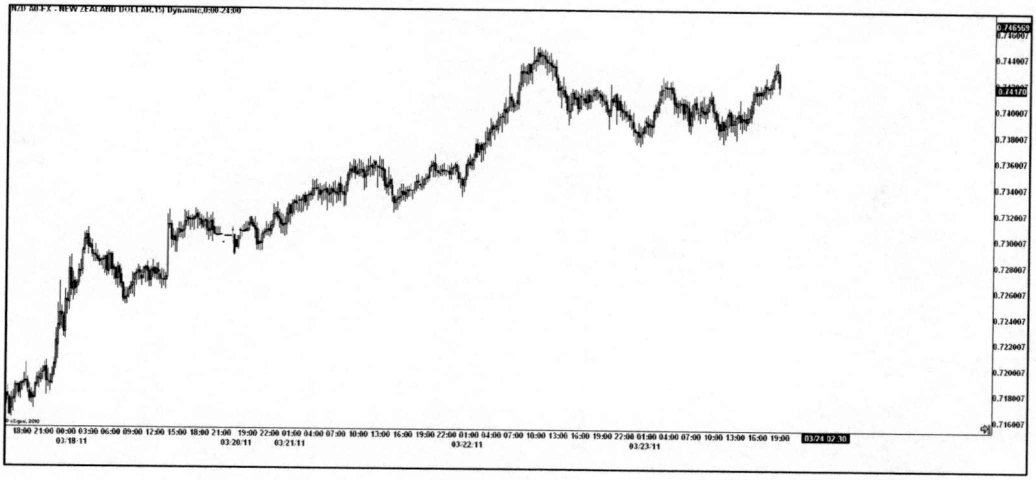

We know from this chart that we are only looking for long trades. Now we need to draw our trend lines and create our zones.

Figure 1.37: projected trend lines creating zones

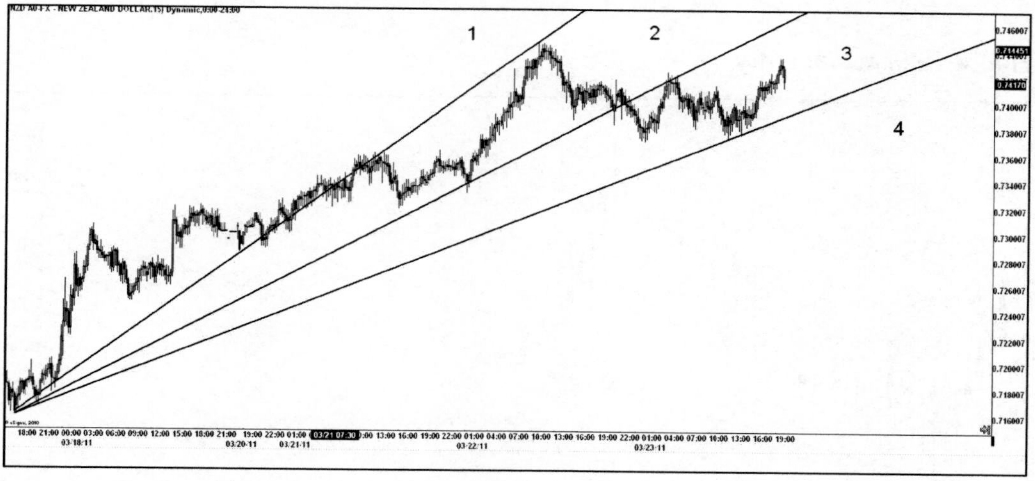

Having added our trend lines and zones as shown in Figure 1.37, we can see that the primary zone is zone 3 as this is where the price action is currently trading. We also know that we are looking for a bounce to occur on the trend line between zones 3 and 4. Figure 1.38 zooms in and highlights, with a circle, the area where we anticipate the bounce may take place.

Figure 1.38: anticipated entry

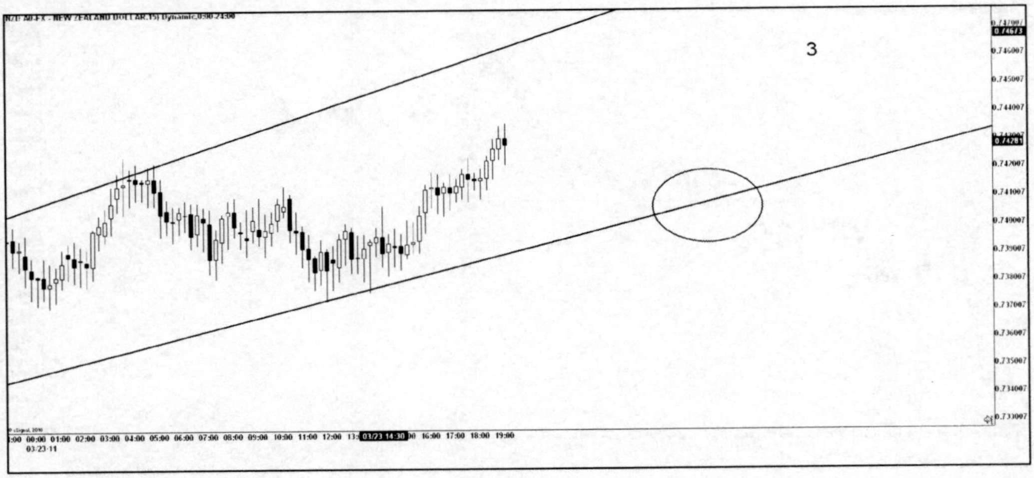

Remember, although it is impossible to predict the exact entry point, estimating the location of a potential bounce helps build a feel for trend trading and develops intuition.

Figure 1.39 zooms in even further to reveal the exact point of entry as the price action falls and touches the trend line. The dotted line marks this entry.

Figure 1.39: actual entry

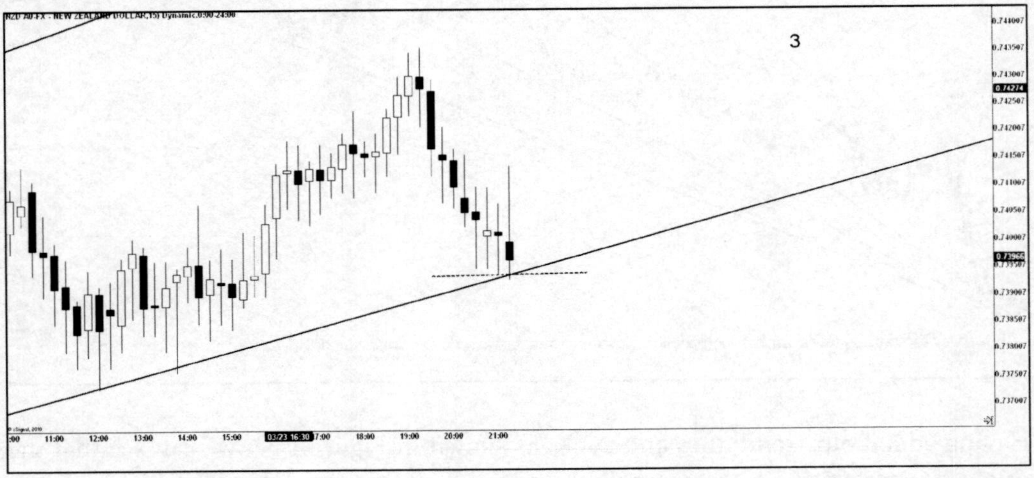

Once our entry has been determined, we can put our stop loss and targets in place for the long position. Again, we have two options for placing the stop loss. We could either use the previous swing low or the most recent touch on the same trend line which is being used to determine our entry. To do this, we would place the stop loss 5 pips below this last touch.

The target is decided by the previous dominant swing high. Figure 1.40 zooms back out to expose these two price levels with dotted lines. As we are going long, the stop loss is the lowest dotted line while the target is the highest dotted line. The entry is the dotted line in between the two.

Figure 1.40: entry, stop loss and target of the trade

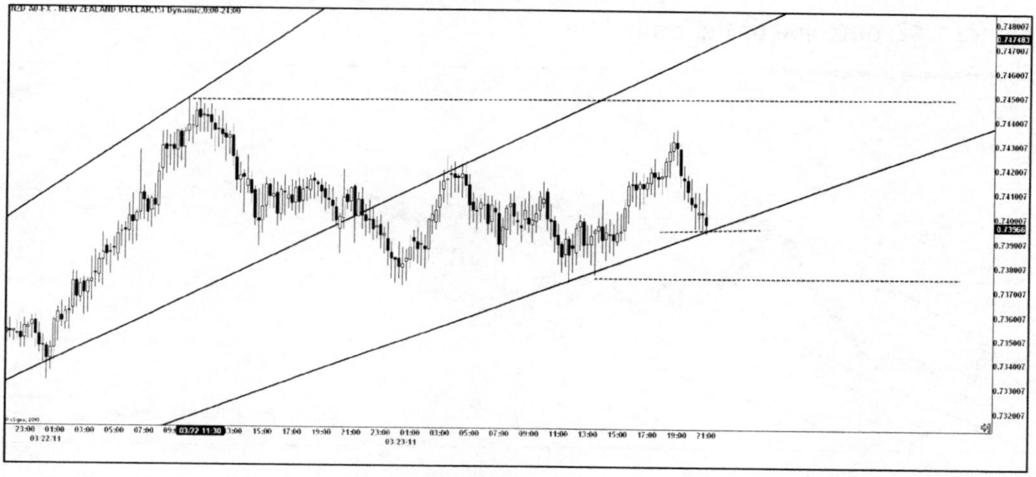

Figure 1.40 also reveals another interesting point. Notice how the stop loss level also happens to be a level of support. Figure 1.41 extends the dotted line further to the left to demonstrate this point.

Figure 1.41: support level that is consistent with the stop loss

The fact that we have had support at our stop loss level in the past is a good sign. From this, we know that to be stopped out of our position, the price action not only has to break down through its trend line, but also break a previous level of support.

Figure 1.42 zooms back out and shows the continuation of the price action as it reaches our target.

Figure 1.42: outcome of the trade

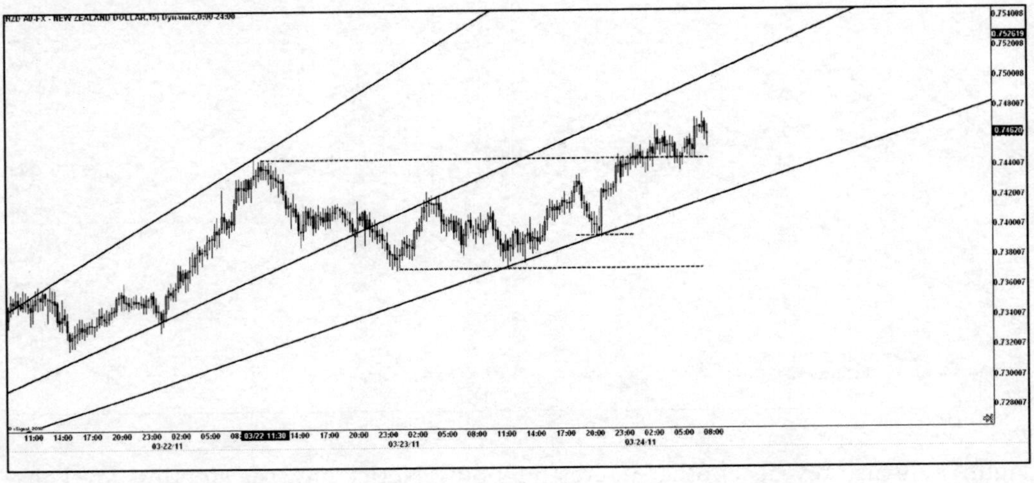

The NZD/USD 15 minute chart shows us a typical example of the trend line bounce strategy working effectively on a long trade.

Summary

Trading the trend line bounce strategy consistently on currency pairs that we are familiar with is a great way to generate considerable and sustainable trading profits.

2. Trend line break strategy

The purpose of the trend line break strategy is to profit from a move of the price as it travels from an outer zone back into an inner zone, rejoining the flow of the trend. On a four-zoned chart with three trend lines, this will mean that the price action breaks back into zone 2 from zone 1 when going short, or into zone 3 from zone 4 when going long. On a three-zoned chart with two trend lines, this will mean that the price action breaks back into zone 2 from zone 1 when going short, or into zone 2 from zone 3 when going long.

Let's begin exploring this strategy by looking at the entry.

Entry

Figure 1.43 is a USD/SGD four hour chart.

Figure 1.43: price action without trend lines

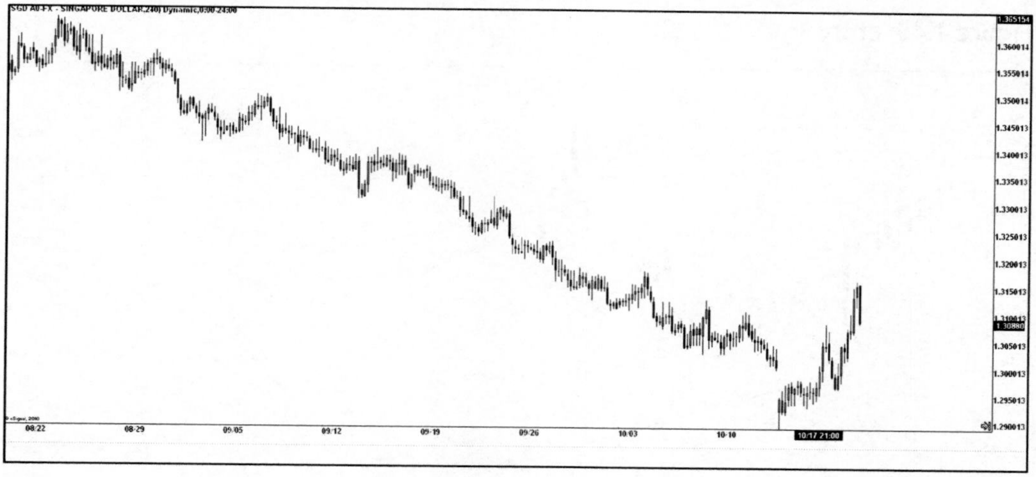

Clearly, the price action on this chart is trending down. This means we only need to look for short positions. Let's draw our trend lines.

Figure 1.44: projected trend lines creating zones

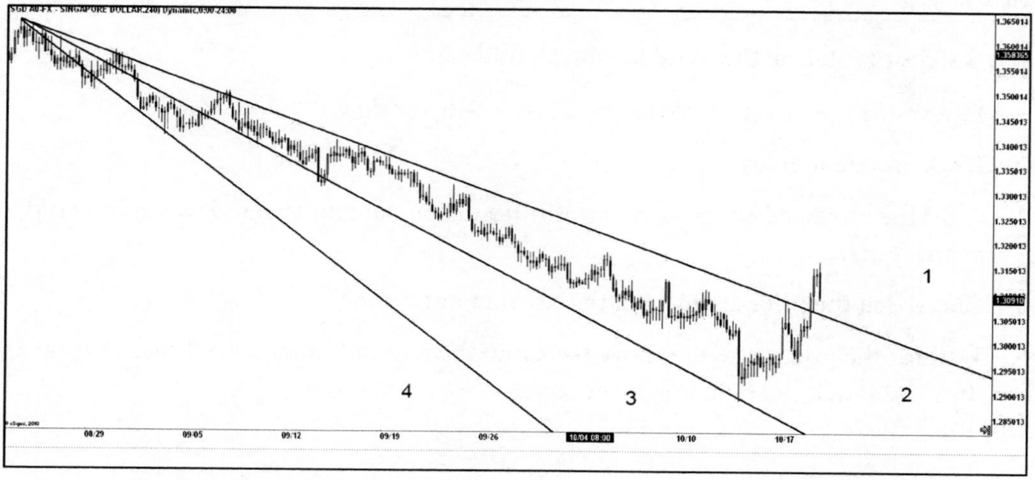

Figure 1.44 shows the trend lines and reveals four projected zones. We can see that the price action is currently trading in zone 1, which is an outer zone in a strong downward trend. At this point we wait patiently for the price action to enter back into zone 2. The quicker it drops, the better our entry will be.

Although we are expecting the price to drop back into zone 2, that in itself is not enough to warrant entering a trade. We first need to see the price come back into zone 2 and a candlestick to close in this zone. Figure 1.45 zooms in to show the moment this happened, highlighting the exact entry level with a dotted line.

Figure 1.45: entry

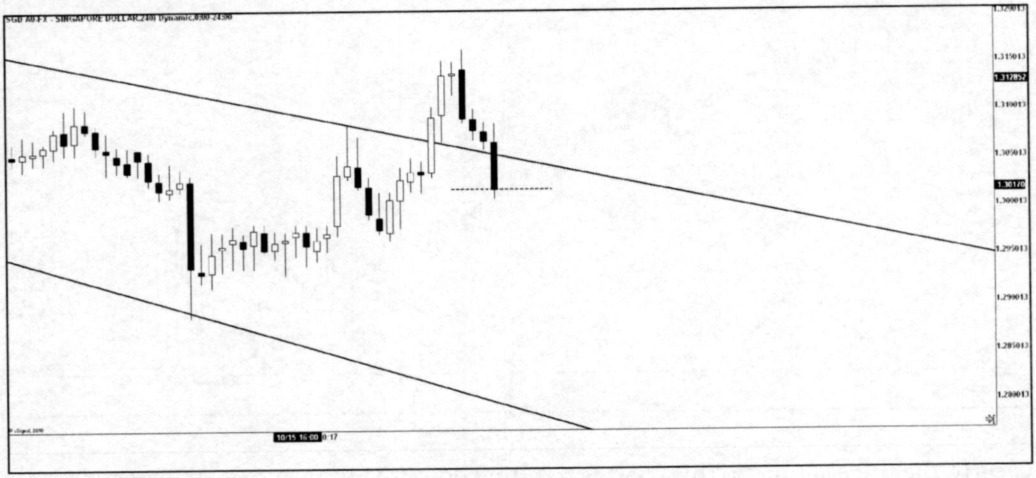

As you can see the short entry occurred as soon as the candlestick closed in zone 2.

Summary

The 5 steps to entering the trend line break trade are:

1. Determine the direction of the price action – up or down.
2. Draw any trend lines.
3. Label the projected zones created by the trend lines and understand which zone is the primary zone.
4. Check that the price action is in the relevant outer zone.
5. Wait for the price action to move back into the relevant inner zone. Enter as soon as the candlestick closes in this inner zone.

Exit – Risk

There are two options for the location of the stop loss in the trend line break strategy:

1. Place the stop loss 5 pips above the previous swing high when going short or 5 pips below the previous swing low when going long. Either of these swings will be located in the outer zone.

2. Place the stop loss at the level of the previous touch on the trend line which the price action is coming back to.

As with the trend line bounce strategy, the setup itself will be a strong indicator as to which option to use. For this example, we will place our stop loss 5 pips behind the previous touch of the trend line, a reasonably safe distance from our entry. Figure 1.46 zooms out to show each stop loss option which has been circled. The dotted line identifies the chosen option.

Figure 1.46: options for the placement of the stop loss

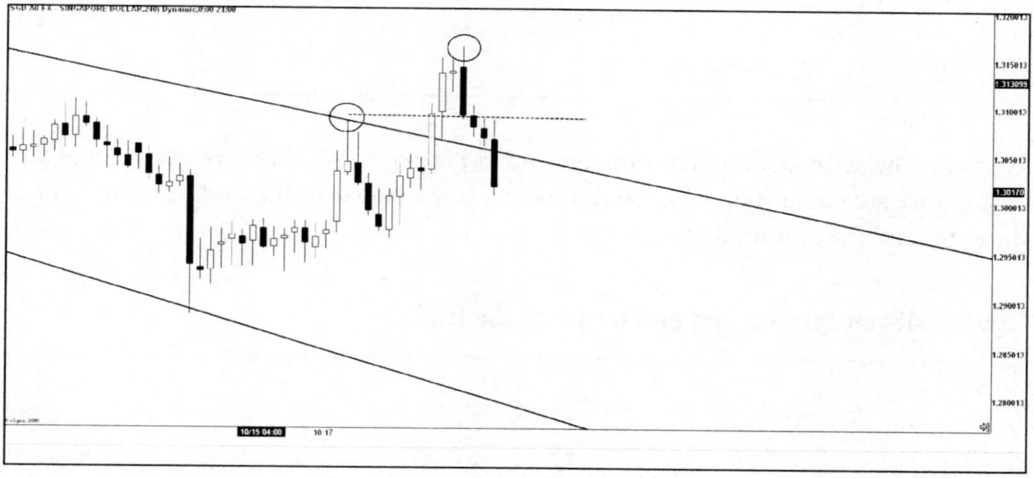

Exit – Target

The target for this trade is the previous dominant swing low, shown with a dotted line in Figure 1.47.

Figure 1.47: target

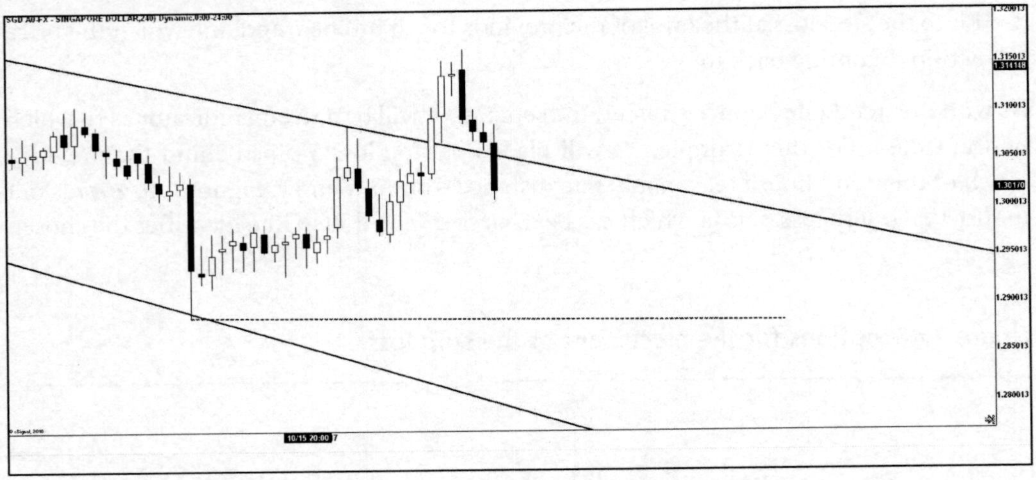

We have now defined our entry, stop loss and target prices. All three are shown in Figure 1.48. As we are going short, the top dotted line is the stop loss, the middle dotted line is the entry and the bottom dotted line is the target.

Figure 1.48: entry, stop loss and target of the trade

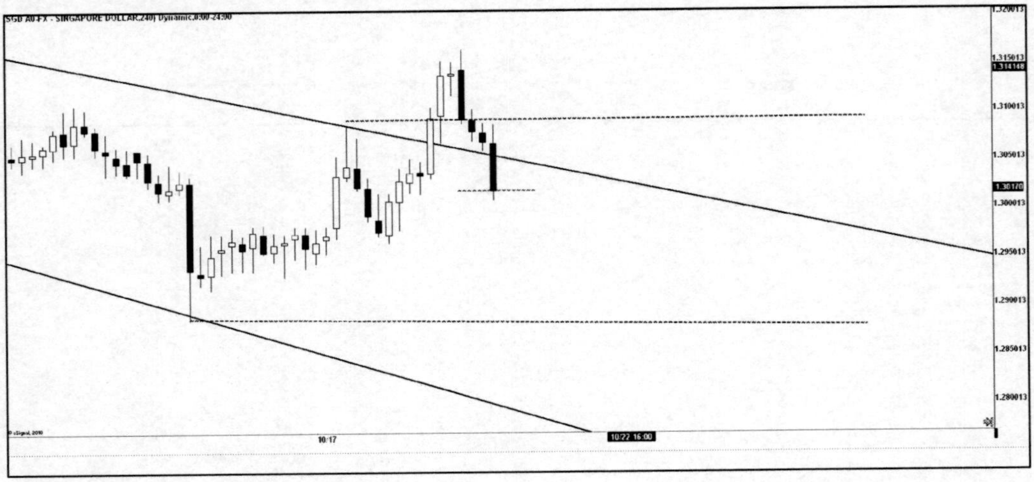

Figure 1.49 shows the continuation of the price action as the trade eventually reaches its target (which was just below 1.29003) – a successful execution of the trend line break strategy on a short trade.

Figure 1.49: outcome of the trade

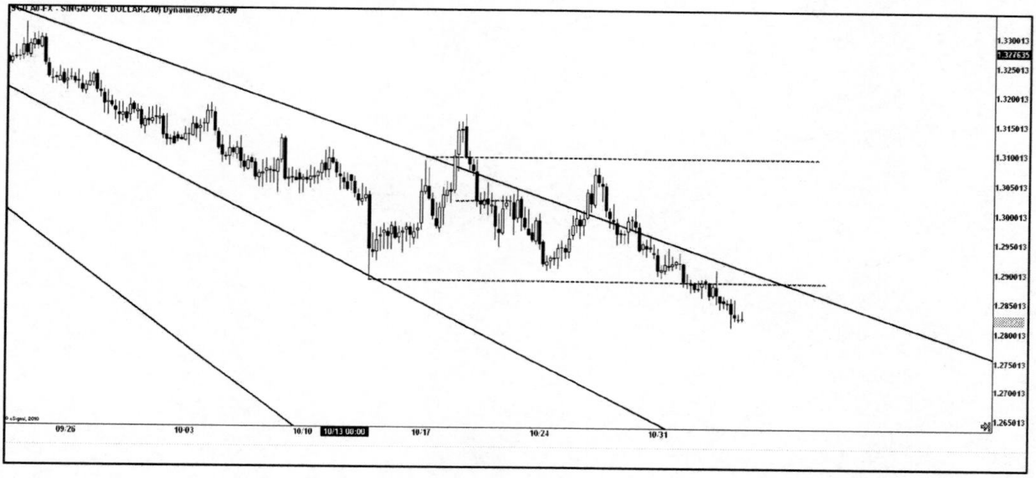

Summary

We see here that the trade runs smoothly down and hits its target. This type of trade demonstrates the power of the trend. For a relatively short period of time, the price moves upward against the trend. Once the pressure of the trend takes over, however, the price is pushed back underneath the trend line providing us with our opportunity to enter. In this setup, we are counting on the strength of the downward trend to outweigh the strength of the short-term upward move.

Key 1 Summary

Trend lines are one of the most powerful keys in forex trading. They add clarity to the charts and unlock the profit potential of trending currency pairs.

You should now be able to differentiate between major and minor trend lines and understand what makes them single or double-sided. You should also be able to break your chart into separate zones without allowing it to become too busy. Most importantly, you should be able to spot profitable trades using nothing more than the price action and a few, simple trend lines.

KEY 2
CHANNELS

Channel trading is a highly profitable way to trade the foreign exchange market. Unfortunately, like trend line trading, the concept of channel trading has been rather lost in recent times as the popularity of more complex indicators has grown. In this chapter, you will learn how to highlight major and minor channels. You will also learn the difference between the inner and outer channels and the projected zones which they create. Using this knowledge, you will then be able to identify exact entry and exit points and to discover how to generate consistent profits by trading with nothing more than a single channel.

THE THEORY

Primary strength: creates a trending range

A basic channel is made up of two parallel, single-sided trend lines. Such lines will therefore create a trending range. A trending range is useful for three main reasons:

1. It shows the market sentiment of a currency pair.
2. It highlights specific areas where we expect the price to bounce and change directions.
3. It highlights significant breakouts that will affect future trading decisions.

These three points allow us to effectively analyze the price action and identify potential trading setups.

Channel characteristics

Figure 2.1 is a basic example of a channel on the GBP/USD one hour chart.

Figure 2.1: basic channel

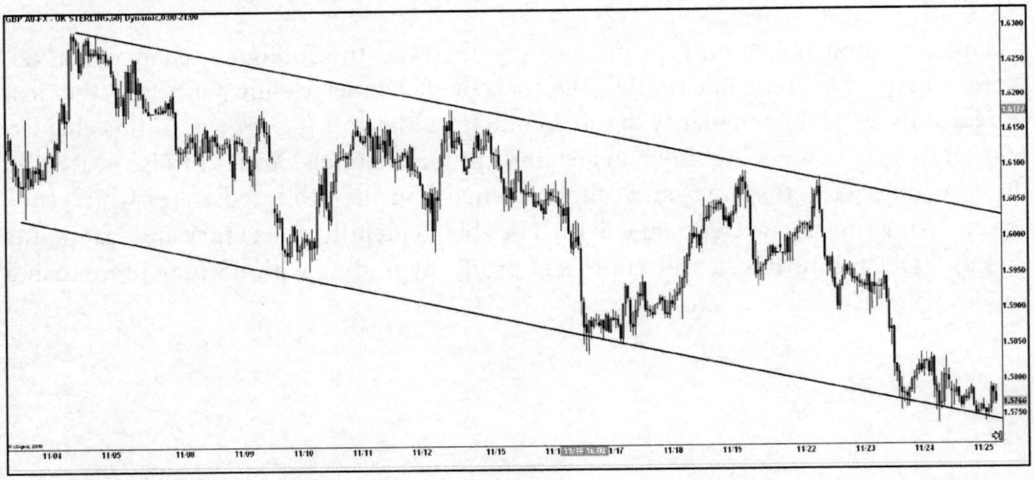

Using the example from figure 2.1, let's start from the beginning and look at the best possible way to identify and draw the channel. We will start by looking at the price action on its own.

Figure 2.2: example of price action without the channel lines

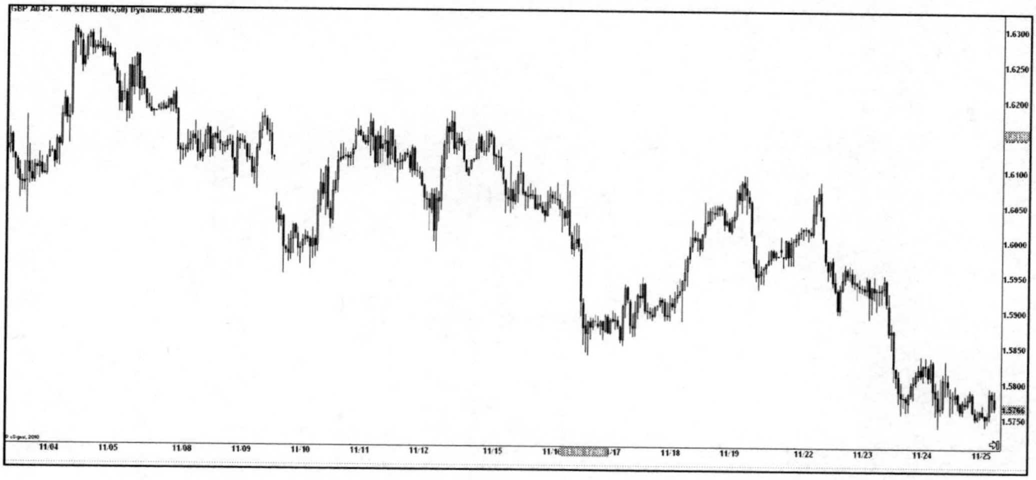

First we notice that the *visual flow* of the chart is going down. Knowing this, we look for a single-sided downward trend line. Figure 2.3 illustrates this.

Figure 2.3 example of single-sided trend line forming the top of the channel

As the *visual flow* of the chart is going down, the first trend line to draw when identifying the channel is on the peaks of the price action. Once the first trend line has been drawn, we need to see if it is possible to draw another trend line with the same angle which connects at least three troughs on the price action. The best way to do this is to "copy" the first trend line using your charting software and then simply try to "paste" it just below the troughs of the price action. By copying the first trend line and using it to determine the bottom of the channel, you are ensuring that the channel is made up of two perfectly parallel lines. Remember, both trend lines are single-sided. Refer to Figure 2.4.

Figure 2.4: the channel revealed through parallel trend lines

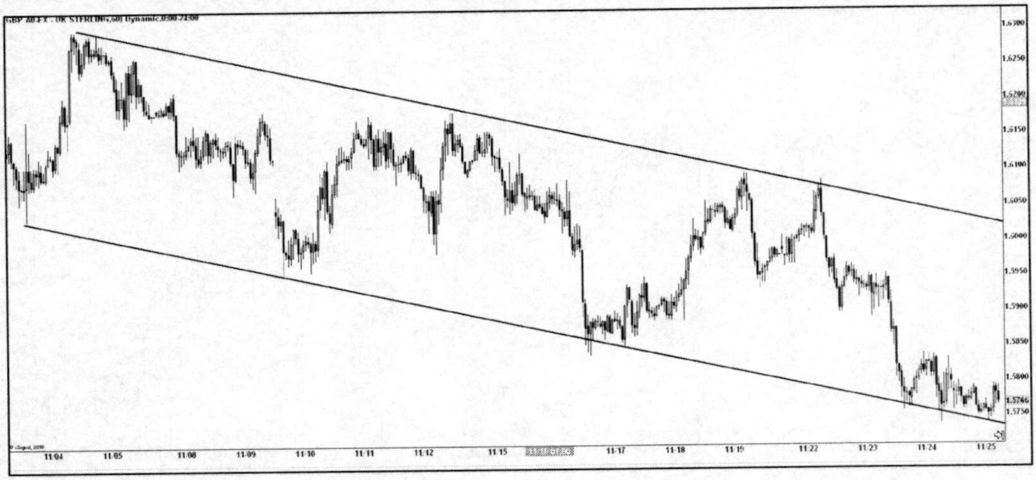

By combining the parallel trend lines and the price action, we have identified a channel. This has given us a trending range and has highlighted key turning points of the price action.

A helpful channel will show which direction to trade by its angle. A channel which is made up of two horizontal levels is of no use to the trend trader. Figure 2.5 is a horizontal channel which shows the price going sideways. If you see a chart like this, walk away and look for potential trades elsewhere.

Figure 2.5: horizontal non-trending chart

Let's look at a chart that fits the criteria for the basic channel. This time we are looking at the price action of the AUD/CHF four hour chart in Figure 2.6.

Figure 2.6: price action action

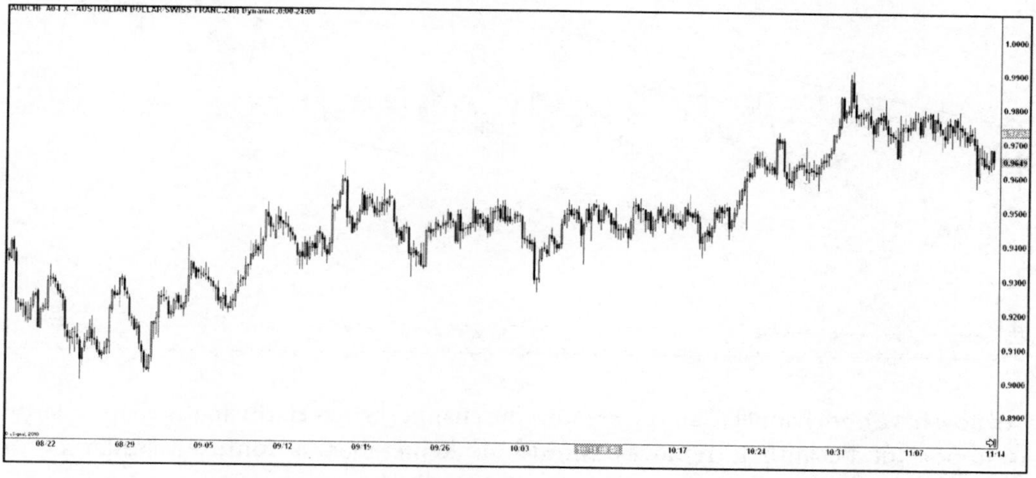

The *visual flow* of the price action is going up, so we look for a single-sided upward trend line and place it on the chart. Refer to Figure 2.7.

Figure 2.7: price action with a single sided upward trend line

Once we have identified the upward trend line, we can copy it and try to place it across the peaks to form a channel. Look at Figure 2.8.

Figure 2.8: channel revealed by two parallel trend lines

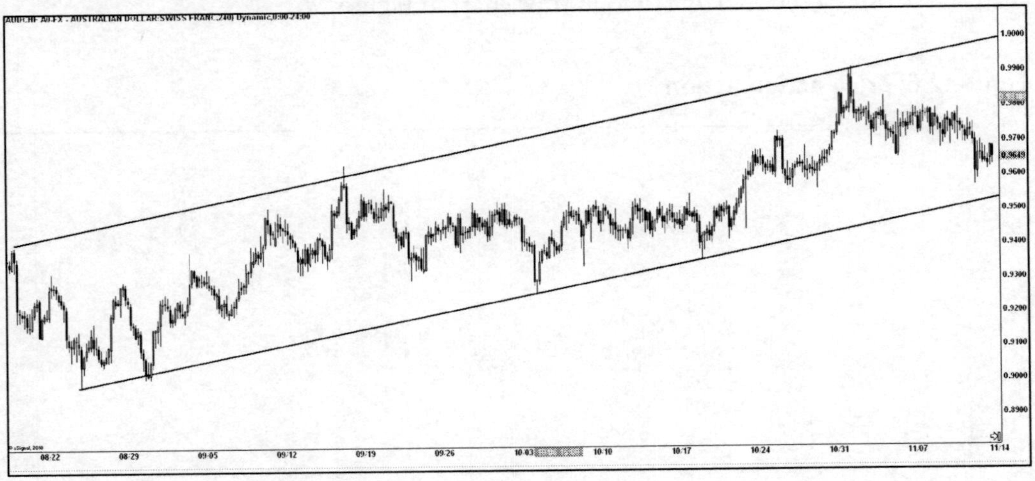

We now have our channel. Can you see how the channel brings clarity to the chart? Clarity is important because it removes confusion. Remember, a confused trader is an unprofitable trader. A trader who is clear about what he is doing on the other hand is much more likely to be successful.

Channel types

Now that you understand how to identify and draw basic channels, it's time to have a closer look at these channels. In the upcoming sections, we are going to study different types of channels, the purposes that they serve and how they can be used to identify relevant entry and exit positions in the market.

Major channel

The major channel is the big picture channel and is drawn in agreement with the long term *visual flow* of the chart. The direction of the channel tells us whether to look for buy or sell trades. As with trend lines, if the major channel is pointing up, then we look for potential buying opportunities; if the major channel is pointing down then we look for potential selling opportunities. That is trading with the trend. Entering short positions on upward pointing channels or entering long positions on downward pointing channels is trading against the trend.

In Figure 2.9 we see the EUR/CAD one hour chart.

Figure 2.9: example of downward pointing channel

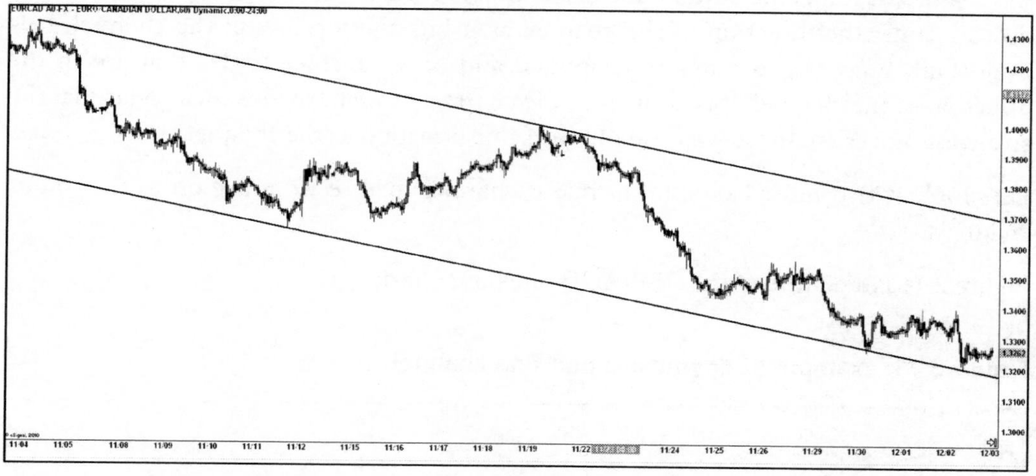

The long term *visual flow* of the price action is going down which means the major channel is pointing down. As the major channel is pointing down, we are looking for potential short positions.

If the *visual flow* of the chart is up, as it is in Figure 2.10 of the AUD/USD one hour chart, then the major channel will also be pointing up.

Figure 2.10: example of upward pointing channel

An incredible feature of a channel is that it will highlight turning points in the price action, both in the direction of the channel and also in the opposite direction. This is clear from Figure 2.10. You can see where the price action is likely to bounce up in the direction of the channel as it hits the bottom line of the channel and also where it is likely to bounce down against the direction of the channel as it hits the top line of the channel. It is important, however, to remain disciplined and only consider trades that are in the direction of the channel. It is clear from the charts that we have looked at so far that the strongest moves are those which are in the same direction as the channel.

Let's look at two more examples of major channels before we move on to the minor channels.

Figure 2.11 is a picture of the GBP/AUD one hour chart.

Figure 2.11: example of downward pointing channel

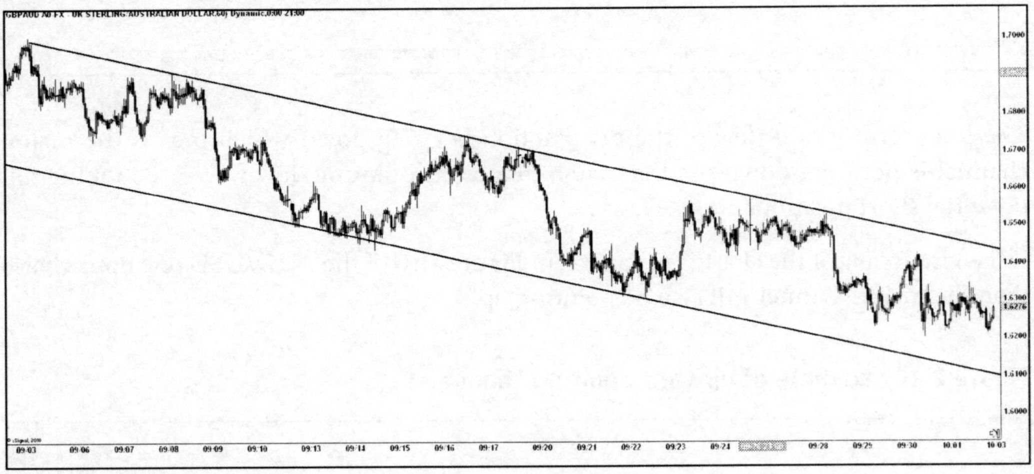

The *visual flow* of the chart is going down and so the major channel is also pointing down. This indicates that we would only be considering potential sell positions. This chart is also a great example of why we only trade in the direction of the channel, even though a channel highlights potential price action turning points in both directions. Notice how the downward movements of the price action as it bounces off the top of the channel are much sharper and faster than the upward movements off the bottom of the channel.

Figure 2.12 also demonstrates the power of trading in agreement with the direction of the major channel. Again, notice how the price movements which are in line with the direction of the channel are generally much more decisive than the movements which are against it.

Figure 2.12: example of upward pointing channel

The major channel is normally the most obvious channel on the chart and is always consistent with the *visual flow* of the price action. It is this channel that you use to determine whether you should be considering a buy or a sell position. Remember that when drawing these major channels: you first assess the general direction of the price action and then identify a single-sided trend line. Next, you copy the trend line and place it on the opposite side of the price action to form the channel. This ensures that your channel is made up of two parallel lines.

Minor channels

Minor channels are channels which are located inside a major channel. Minor channels can either be in agreement with the direction of the major channel or counter to the direction of the major channel. A minor channel which is in agreement with the major channel I call an *agreeing minor channel* and a minor channel which runs counter to the direction of a major channel I call a *disagreeing minor channel.*

Agreeing minor channels

As minor channels are found inside major channels, the first step in identifying a minor channel is to find a major channel. Figure 2.13 is of the AUD/CAD thirty minute chart. Let's start drawing the major channel. To do this, we must first draw a downward trend line across the peaks of the price action, as the *visual flow* of the chart is going down. We then copy the trend line and paste it below the troughs of the corresponding price action, giving us our major channel. Refer to Figure 2.13.

Figure 2.13: example of major downward pointing channel

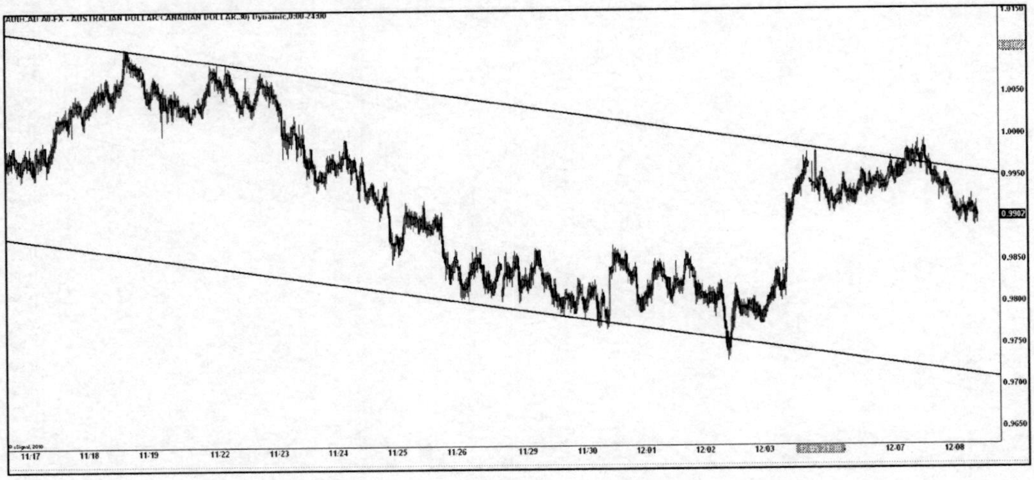

Now that we have our major channel, we can begin to look for agreeing minor channels within the major channel. To identify a minor agreeing channel, look for downward trend lines within the channel. Figure 2.14 shows a downward trend line within the channel.

Figure 2.14: major downward channel with minor agreeing channel

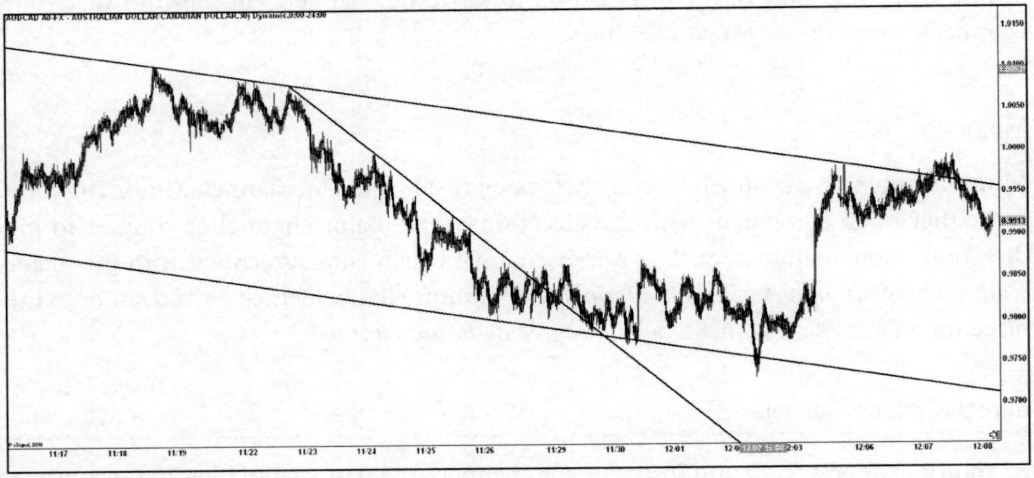

Once the downward trend line is drawn, we copy it and paste it to the corresponding troughs to see if an agreeing minor channel can be formed. Refer to Figure 2.15.

Figure 2.15: minor agreeing channel within major channel

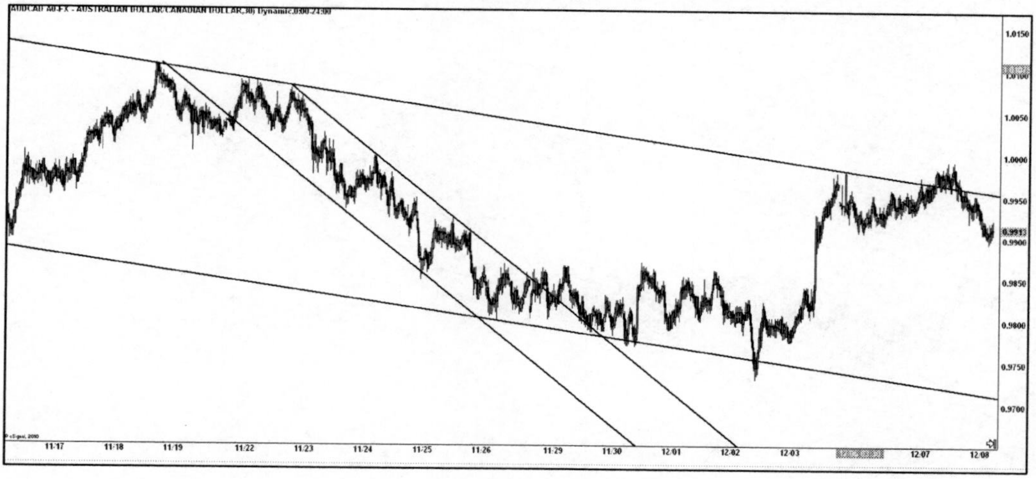

Notice that both the major and minor channels are pointing down, so we can conclude that the minor channel is an agreeing minor channel.

Let's look at another example of agreeing minor channels, this time on the GBP/USD thirty minute chart. Remember, we first identify the major channel. Refer to Figure 2.16.

Figure 2.16: example of major upward channel

As you can see, the major channel is pointing up. Once it has been drawn, we can look for an agreeing minor channel. Figure 2.17 shows the minor agreeing channel.

Figure 2.17: minor agreeing channel within major upward channel

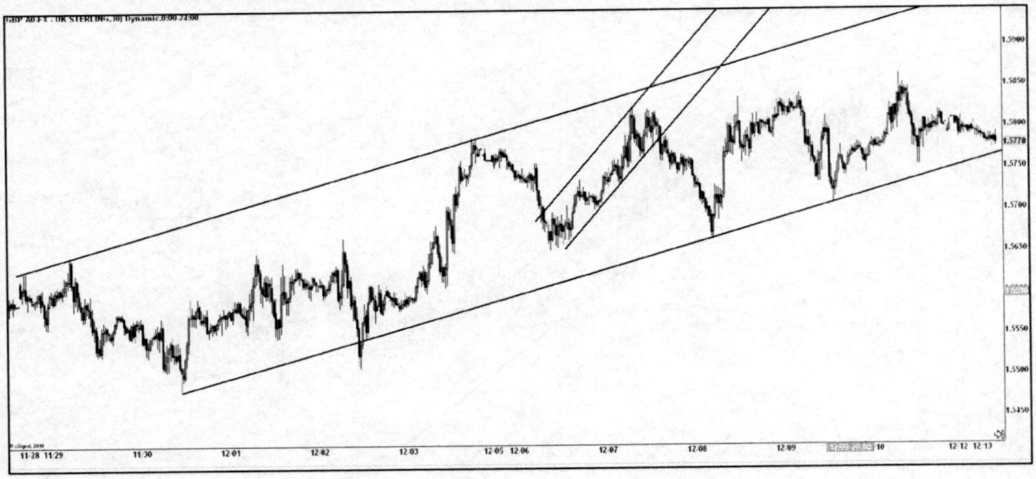

Both channels are pointing up, which makes the minor channel an agreeing minor channel. You may have noticed from the last two examples that the agreeing minor channels are always at a steeper angle than the major channel. This is also true of the disagreeing minor channels.

Once an agreeing minor channel has been identified, we can use it to understand how to make trading decisions.

Generally speaking, we do not use the agreeing minor channels to determine an entry into the market, but rather to address an exit from an already open position. To demonstrate this point, we will refer to the AUD/CAD 30 minute chart that we looked at earlier in the chapter. Let's assume that we are in a short position and that we are currently about halfway through the agreeing minor channel. In other words, imagine everything to the right of the dotted line on the following chart is in the future and has not happened yet. This type of exercise will help build the skill of anticipating future market movements.

Figure 2.18: major channel with minor agreeing channel

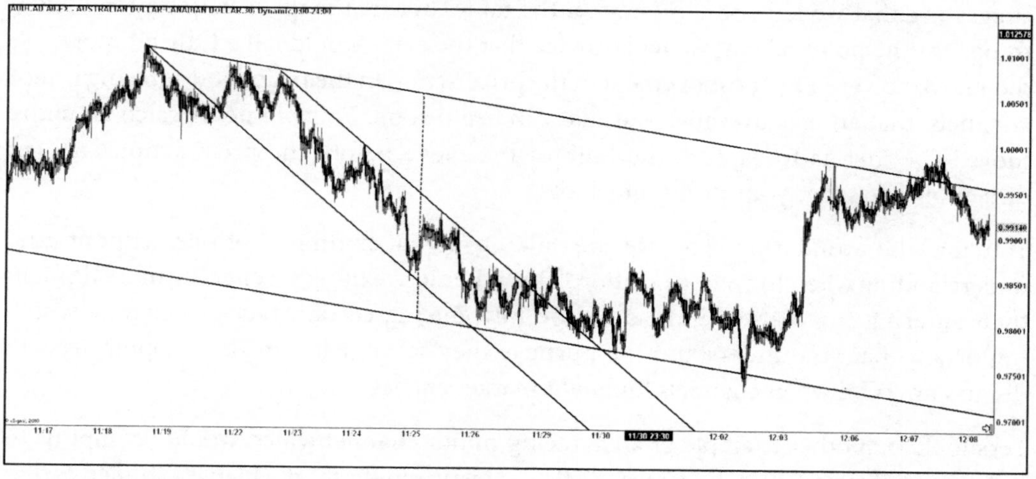

At this point, our position is running in profit and we are looking for the most efficient time to exit the trade and bank the profit. While the price action is still within the agreeing minor channel, we can feel safe that the current downward movement is likely to continue. While this is the case, it would not be unreasonable or greedy to hold the position in the hope of collecting more profit. However, once the price action breaks through the upper line of the agreeing minor channel, we need to consider exiting the trade immediately. Especially, as in the case above, if the break out of the agreeing minor channel occurs as the price reaches the lower part of the major channel. The circle in Figure 2.19 shows an efficient exit of the trade based on the breakout of the agreeing minor channel.

Figure 2.19: example of exiting based on the price action relationship with the major and minor agreeing channels

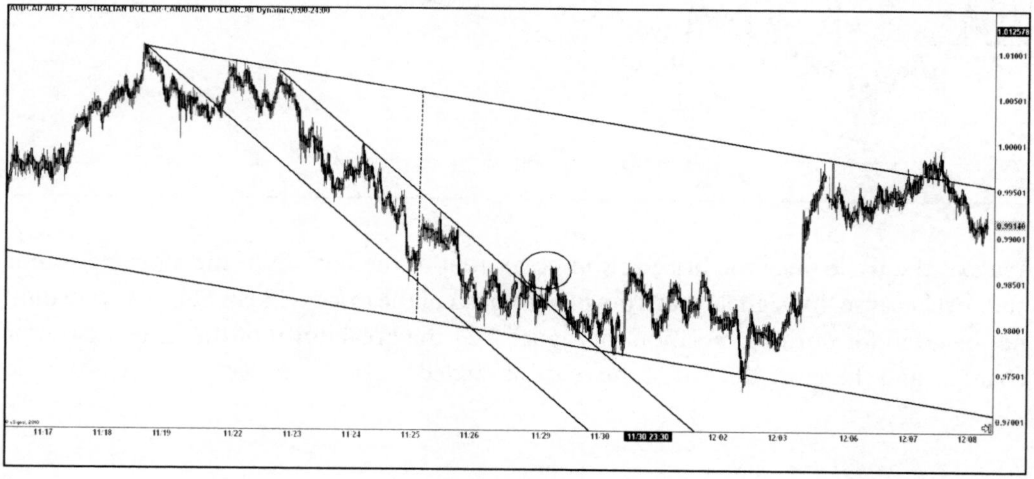

You may have noticed that the price action continued to fall after our chosen exit point, suggesting that we left some money on the table. But that is the wrong way to look at things. At the point of exit, we had no idea that the price would fall a little bit more. We did know, however, by the movement of the price action in the major and agreeing minor channels, that an upward move was likely to begin soon. You will never catch an entire move. The idea is to capture the bulk of the move before the price action changes directions and turns your profit into a loss.

You may be wondering why we are talking about exiting positions without first understanding when to enter a position. This is because exiting is generally more difficult than entering the market and, as we are introducing certain types of channels, it is important that you understand the purpose they serve. Later in this chapter, we will discuss how and when channels highlight market entries.

Let's look at another example of an agreeing minor channel which would prompt us to exit a trade. Figure 2.20 is the same GBP/USD thirty minute chart which we studied earlier in this chapter. This time we are in a long position. Once again, we'll say that the dotted line represents the present time and will consider everything to the right of this line as still in future.

Figure 2.20: upward major channel with minor agreeing channel

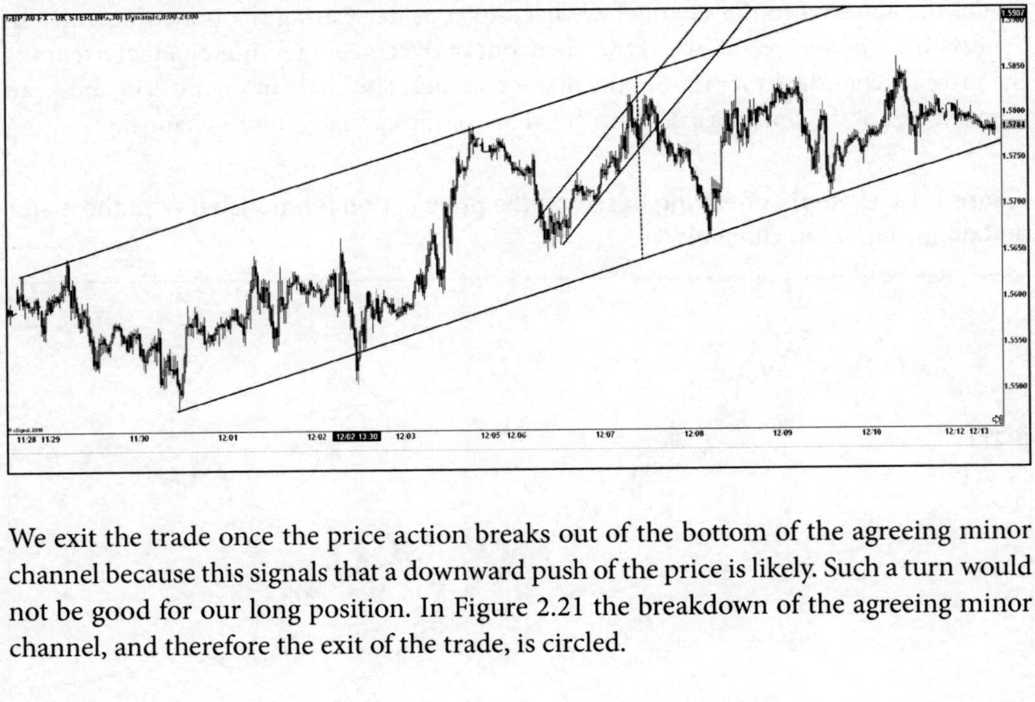

We exit the trade once the price action breaks out of the bottom of the agreeing minor channel because this signals that a downward push of the price is likely. Such a turn would not be good for our long position. In Figure 2.21 the breakdown of the agreeing minor channel, and therefore the exit of the trade, is circled.

Figure 2.21: example of exiting based on the price action relationship with the major and minor agreeing channels

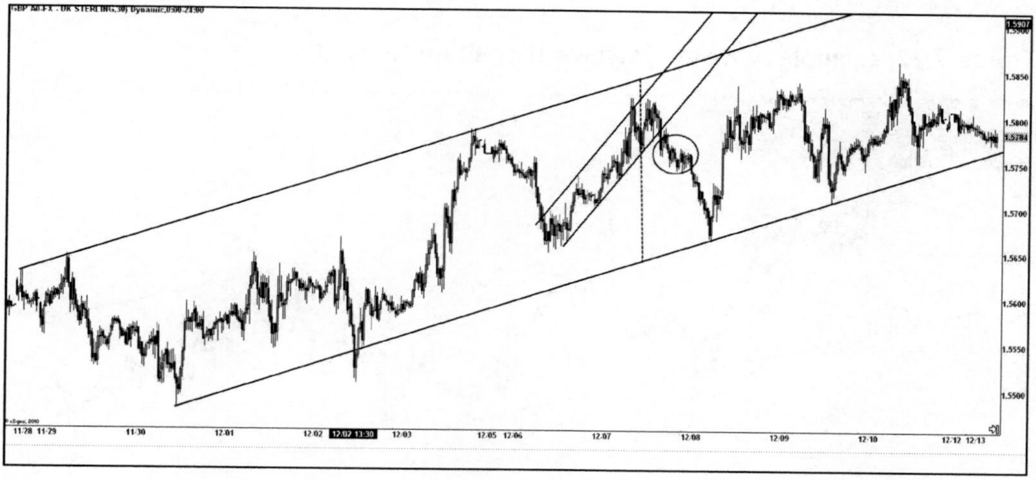

This example shows just how efficient this type of exit can be. Once the price action broke out of the agreeing minor channel, it went on to drop right down to the bottom of the major channel.

In summary, agreeing minor channels can only be drawn once we have an established major channel. It is impossible to draw a minor channel that is in agreement with a major channel which does not yet exist. Agreeing minor channels bring a further element of clarity to our trading charts and assist us in knowing when we should exit existing positions in the market.

Disagreeing minor channels

A disagreeing minor channel is a channel found inside a major channel and pointing in the opposite direction of the major channel. It is referred to as *disagreeing* because it is not in agreement with the major channel. As disagreeing minor channels are found inside major channels, it is essential that we determine our major channel before identifying any possible disagreeing minor channels.

Figure 2.22 is the AUD/NZD 15 minute chart that has formed a major channel pointing down.

Figure 2.22: example of major downward pointing channel

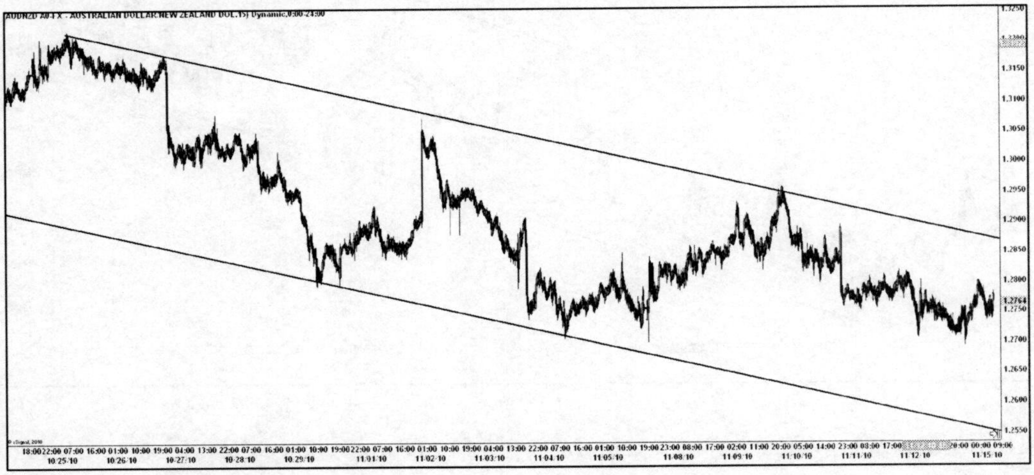

As the major channel is pointing down, the disagreeing minor channel is pointing up. Figure 2.23 highlights the disagreeing minor channel.

Figure 2.23: example of major downward channel with disagreeing minor channel

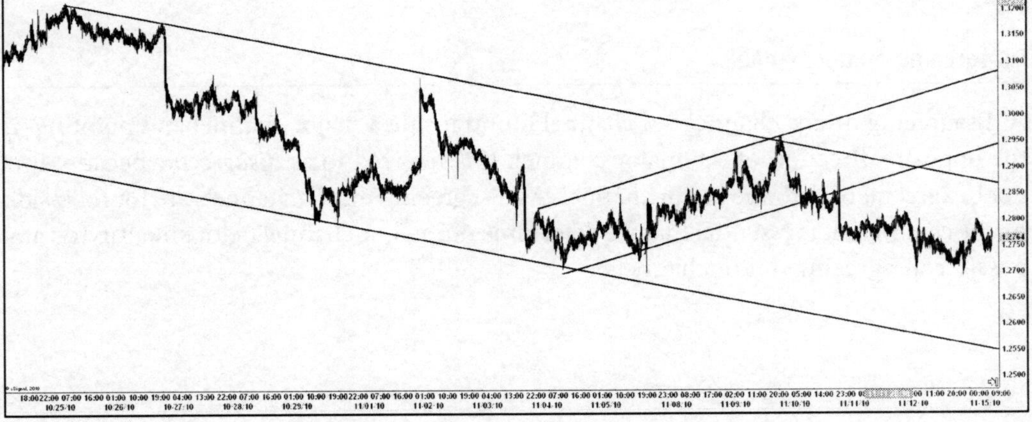

Once the disagreeing minor channel is highlighted you can see clearly why it is referred to as disagreeing. It is moving against the *visual flow* of the chart and counter to the major channel.

Before we discuss the role of the disagreeing minor channel, let's look at another example. In Figure 2.24 we are looking at the GBP/SGD 30 minute chart. The price action has formed a major channel pointing up.

Figure 2.24: major upward pointing channel

As the major channel is pointing up, the disagreeing minor channel will be pointing down. Before we move on to the next chart, see if you can spot this disagreeing minor channel in Figure 2.24. To trend trade successfully, you must train your eyes to identify these patterns in the price action.

Refer to Figure 2.25 to see if you were correct.

Figure 2.25: major channel with minor disagreeing channel

The major channel is up and the disagreeing minor channel is down.

Earlier in this chapter, we discussed how the agreeing minor channel could be used to help determine when to exit a profitable position. With that in mind, we can do just the opposite with a disagreeing minor channel, using it to identify an entry into the market. When the price action breaks out of a disagreeing minor channel and begins to move in the direction of the major channel, this is an indication that the strength of the major channel is taking over again. This is a good time to enter a trade.

Let's refer back to the two charts in this section and see how we can use the breakout of a disagreeing minor channel as an entry signal. The chart in Figure 2.26 is the AUD/NZD 15 minute chart. The dotted line indicates the current time and everything to the right of it is in the future.

Figure 2.26: major channel with minor disagreeing channel

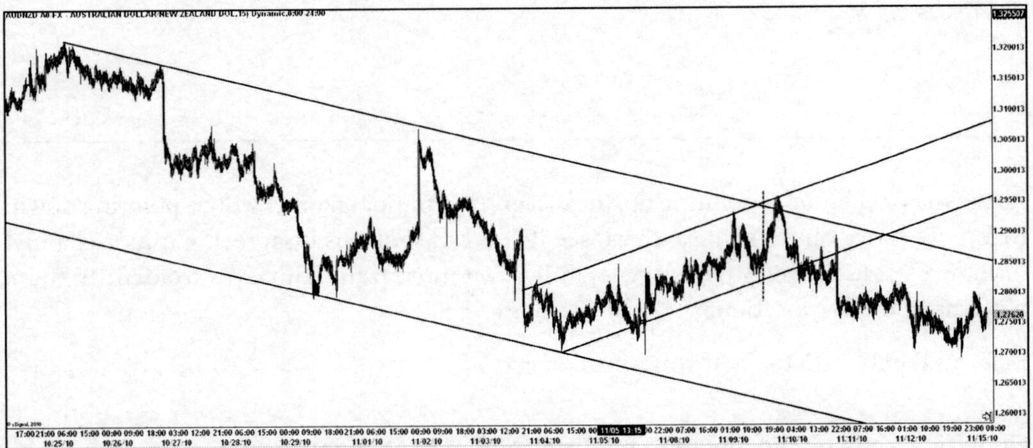

We enter the trade once the price action breaks out of the bottom of the disagreeing minor channel because this signals a likely downward push by the price action, putting it back in line with the direction of the major channel. In Figure 2.27, the breakdown of the disagreeing minor channel, and therefore the entry into the trade, is circled.

Figure 2.27: example of entering based on the price action relationship with the major and minor disagreeing channels

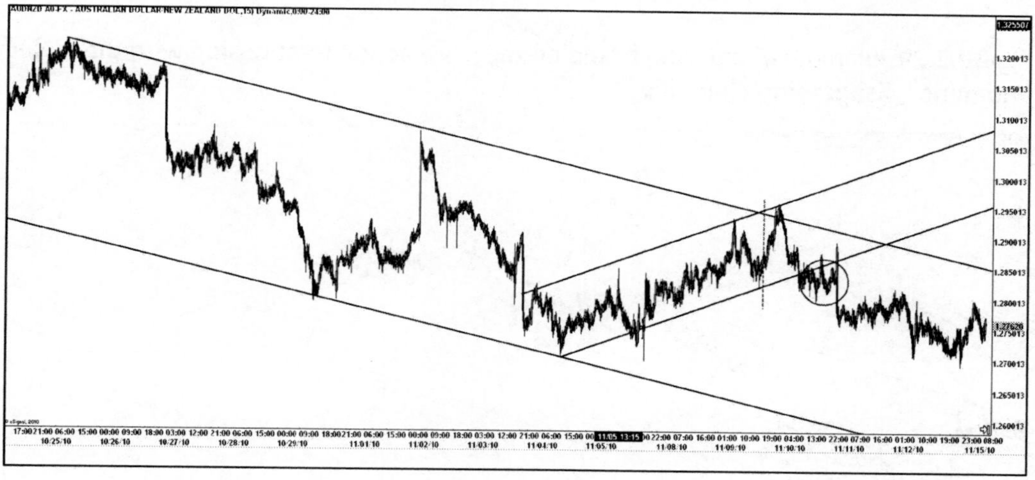

You can see that once the price action breaks down through the disagreeing minor channel, it begins to flow in line with the major channel and make decisive downward moves.

The following GBP/SGD thirty minute chart provides us with another illustration of how to enter on the breakout of a disagreeing minor channel. Again, we will use the dotted line to mark our current position.

Figure 2.28: major channel with minor disagreeing channel

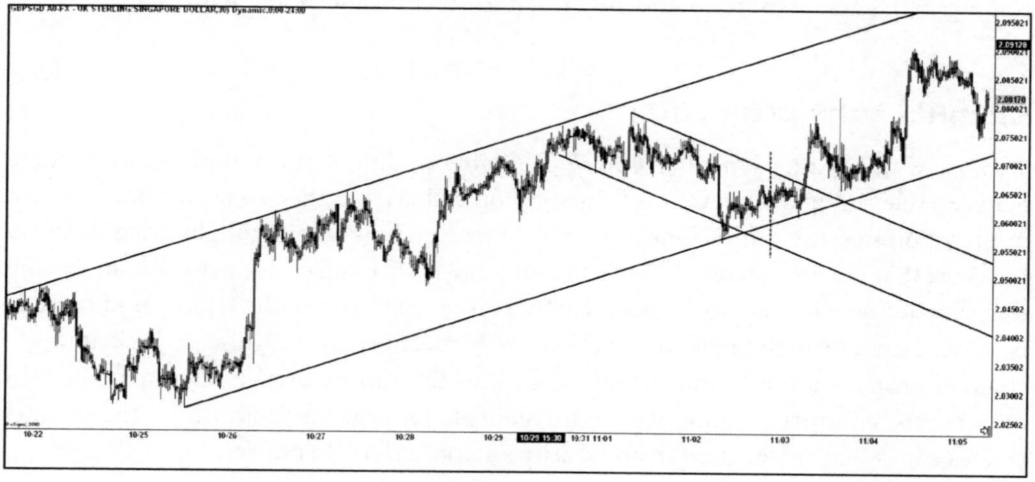

We enter the trade once the price action breaks out of the top of the disagreeing minor channel, because this signals a likely upward push of the price action in the direction of the major channel. In Figure 2.29 the breakdown of the disagreeing minor channel, and therefore the entry into the trade, is circled.

Figure 2.29: example of entering based on the price action relationship with the major and minor disagreeing channels

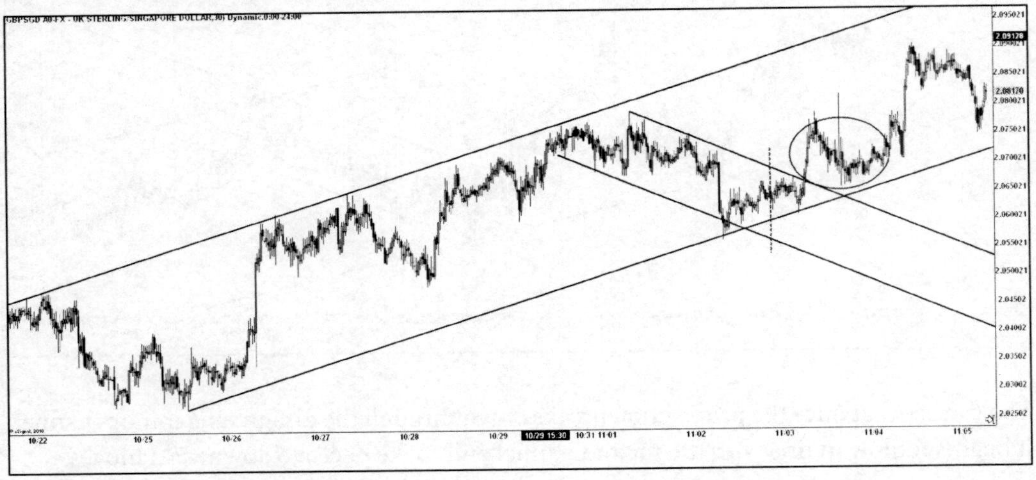

Once again, we can see the significance of the price action breaking up through the disagreeing minor channel and coming back into agreement with the major channel.

In summary, disagreeing minor channels can only be drawn once you have an established major channel. Disagreeing minor channels bring a further element of clarity to our trading charts and assist us in knowing when to enter positions in the market.

Channel zone projection

As we saw in Chapter One, the skill of profitable trading is the ability to differentiate between relevant and irrelevant information on a chart and then to project the relevant information into the future. One aim of technical analysis is to highlight price levels on the chart that the price action is likely to either break through or bounce off – something the price action will react to. This statement is true regardless of the type of trading style or system used to analyse the price action. In this section, we are going to look at how a channel projects information into the future which can be used to anticipate certain movements of the price action. We are also going to see how the projection of the channel creates zones that can be used to add clarity and objectivity to our trading.

Whenever we draw a channel in accordance with the method defined earlier in this chapter, a channel projection naturally occurs. A channel projection is the continuation of a channel into the future, beyond where the price action is currently trading. In Figure 2.30, everything to the right of the dotted line is a projection of the channel.

Figure 2.30: example of channel projection

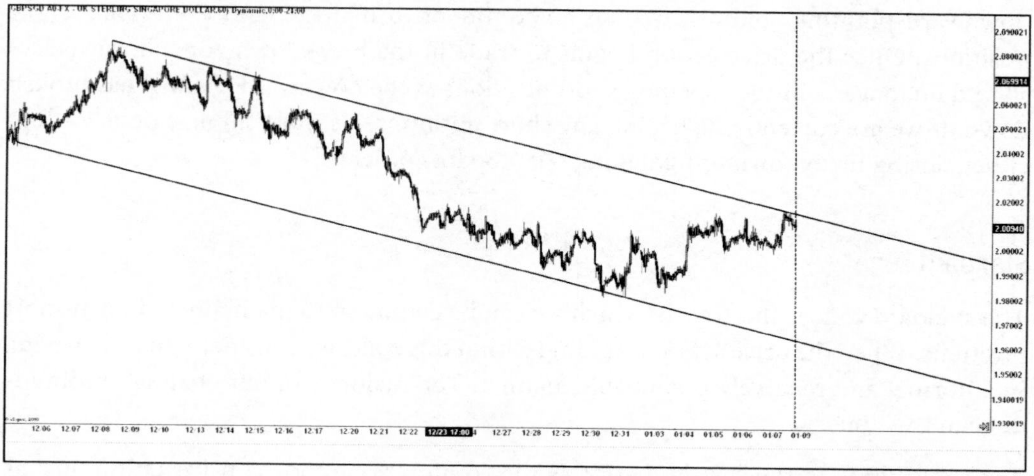

A channel projection creates three zones. The names of these zones are the *breakdown zone*, the *standard zone* and the *overextended zone*. In Figure 2.31 these zones are labelled.

Figure 2.31: example of zones created by extended channel lines

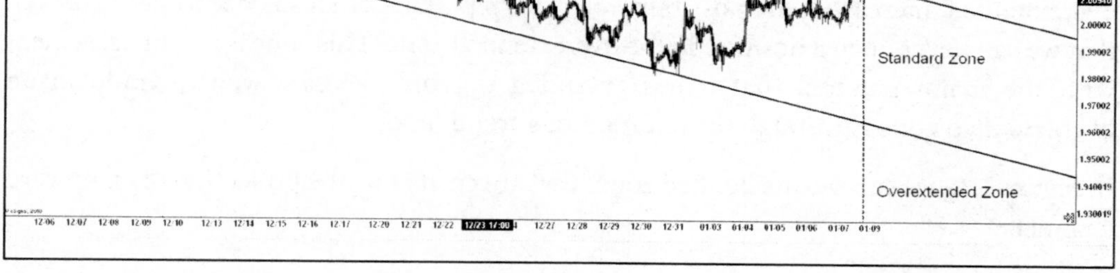

Each zone gives a different message about what to expect from the price action. Each message is very important to future trading decisions. Referring to Figure 2.31 again, we will go through each zone individually.

Breakdown zone

The breakdown zone represents the breaking down of the current channel. In this example the channel is pointing down, meaning the price action is being held down by the trend line which has formed at the top of the channel. While the price action remains in this downward pointing channel, we can be confident to manage, and even open, short positions. Once the price action begins to trade in the breakdown zone, however, we should no longer consider opening short positions as the downward channel has broken down. If we are currently managing any short positions, we must think seriously about either closing them down or tightening our stop loss orders.

Standard zone

The standard zone is the zone in which we can be confident to maintain and open short positions. When the price action is trading within this zone, we consider it to be behaving in a normal and relatively predictable manner. The majority of our channel trading is done in this zone.

You could think of the standard zone as the comfort zone for the price action. Just as people generally become more predictable when they are feeling comfortable, so does the price action.

Overextended zone

An overextended zone occurs when the price action extends out of the channel, but does so in line with the direction of the channel. In our example, the channel is pointing down so the overextended zone is below the channel. Once the price action extends into this zone, it is best to be cautious about placing any trades. We would certainly not want to place any new long orders, as this would be trading against the direction of the channel, and we should be wary of placing any sell orders because the price action has become overextended, increasing the possibility of a sharp pull back. This is not to say, however, that we can never open a position in the overextended zone. This zone is still in agreement with the major channel that it has extended out of. The safe way to trade in an overextended zone is through the addition of a trend line.

In Figure 2.32 we can see the defined zones that are created by the projection of an upward channel.

Figure 2.32: example of zones created by extended channel lines

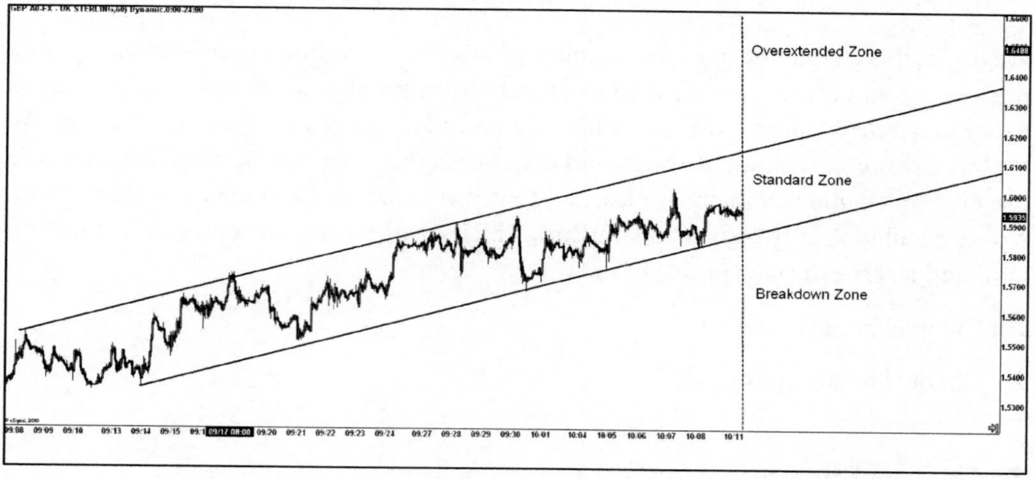

Notice that unlike the channel in Figure 2.31, the breakdown zone is now at the bottom of the three zones while the overextended zone is at the top. This is because the zones are not defined by their order from top to bottom, but rather by their relationship to the direction of the channel which they are associated with.

The movement of the price action out of the upward channel into the breakdown zone indicates a breakdown of the channel and signals that we should not enter any buy positions. If we have a long position, it is time to tighten up the stop loss or close the position down. If the price action moves up into the overextend zone, we proceed with caution, knowing that the price action is overextending to the upwards and that a downward pullback is becoming more and more likely. If we happen to be in a long position when the price action breaks into the overextended zone, it is time to consider exiting the trade with a profit. While the price action is in the standard zone, however, we can feel comfortable to execute long positions in the confidence that the price is trading in a stable, relatively predictable zone.

Defining the *standard, breakdown* and *overextend zones* brings further clarity and objectivity. Objective trading is a characteristic of most, if not all, successful technical traders. Objective trading removes the temptation to over-analyze the market. This is important, as over-analysis often leads to confusion. Objective trading also helps to stop a trader from seeing what he wants to see and creating scenarios that don't actually exist.

ENTRY AND EXIT STRATEGIES

We began this chapter by not only defining what a channel is but also by explaining what message a channel can give. We then went on to study the characteristics of a channel and to demonstrate the process of clearly identifying and drawing a channel on our chart. We explored major and minor channels and discovered the difference between agreeing and disagreeing channels. Finally, we learned to project channels and create trading zones. Now we will look at two channel strategies which clearly define the entry, risk exit (stop loss) and target exit (take profit) of the trade:

1. Channel bounce strategy
2. Channel break strategy

1. Channel bounce strategy

The aim of the channel bounce strategy is to profit from the movement of the price action from one side of the channel to the other. The angle of the channel determines whether we should trade long or short. If the channel is pointing up, then we are looking for long setups, if the channel is pointing down, then we are looking for short setups. Let's look specifically at the entry.

Entry

Figure 2.33 is the EUR/USD 60 minute chart. This will be our example chart.

Figure 2.33: example channel for the strategy

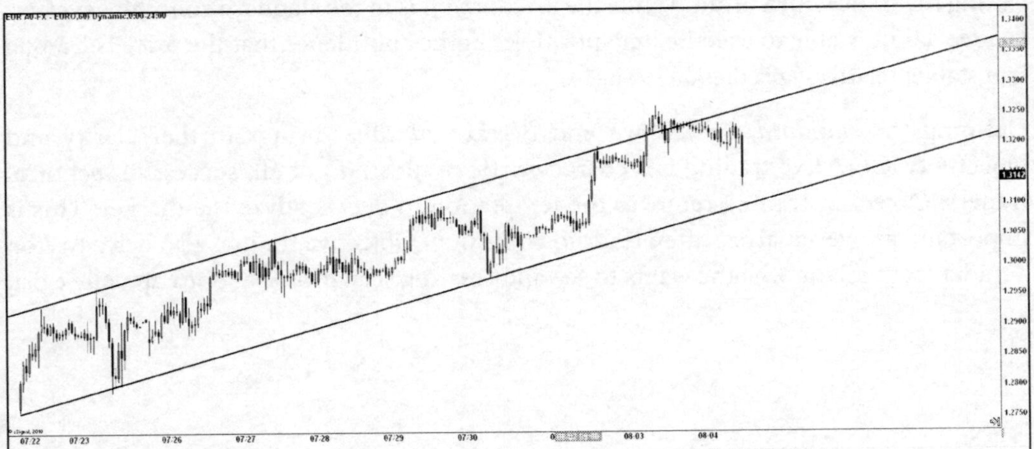

First, we need to determine the direction of the channel to confirm which direction to trade in – long or short. This chart shows an upward channel, so we are looking for long setups. Second, we need to define the projected zones of the channel. Figure 2.34 displays the zones.

Figure 2.34: zones created by channel lines

At this point, we are waiting for the price action to make its way down to the bottom line of the channel. It is this line that we are expecting the price action to bounce off. Figure 2.35 zooms in on the EUR/USD chart as the price action reaches the bottom line of the channel.

Figure 2.35: close up of the anticipated entry for the channel bounce strategy

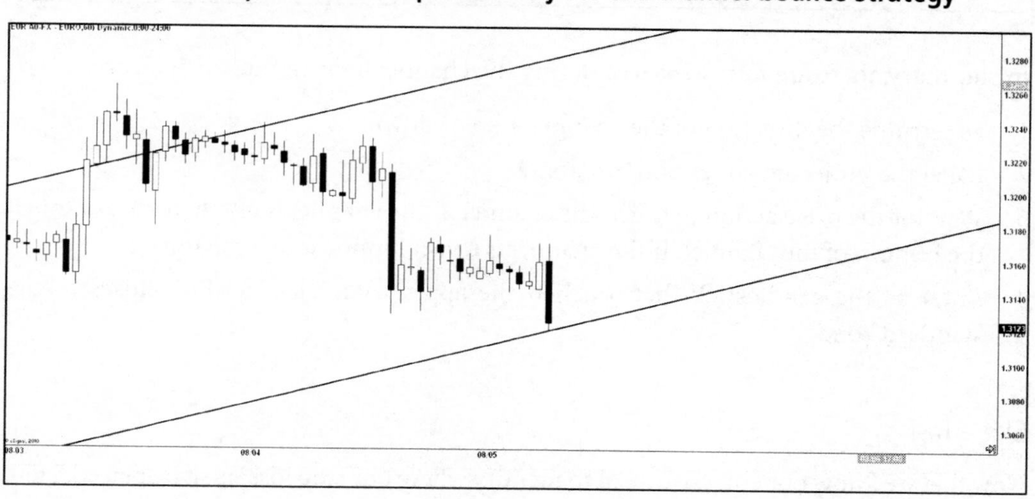

Once the price action touches the bottom channel line, we are ready to enter the trade. We enter the moment that the candlestick which touched the channel line closes above the channel line. If the candlestick that first touched the line goes on to close below it, then the trade is off. If it closes above the channel line, we enter immediately. We are not concerned if the price action dips below the channel line, during the formation of the candle as long as it closes above it. For instance, as this is a 60 minute chart, the candlestick does not lock into a closed position until the 60 minutes are up. During that time period, the price action may fall below the channel line, as long as it closes above it.

In Figure 2.36 the horizontal dotted line shows the close of the candlestick, just above the bottom wick of the candle and therefore the exact entry price for our long trade. (Please note that the image is still of the original chart, just zoomed in further for clarity.)

Figure 2.36: exact entry for the example

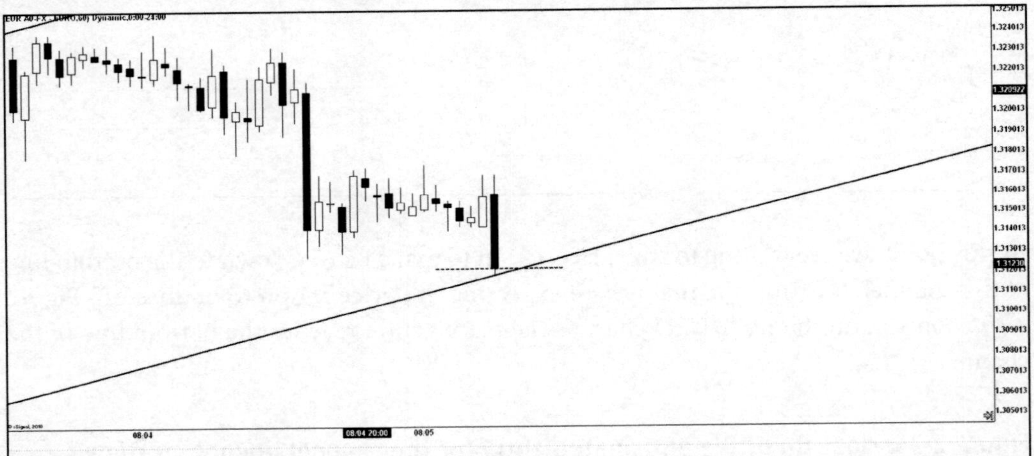

In summary, there are four steps to entering the channel bounce trade, which are:

1. Determine the direction of the channel – up or down.
2. Label the projected zones of the channel.
3. Wait for the price action to touch the channel. If the channel is up, then it must touch the bottom of the channel. If the channel is down it must touch the top.
4. Enter as the candlestick that touched the appropriate channel line closes in the standard zone.

Exit – Risk

Now that we know our entry, we need to identify where our stop loss most be placed. Here you have two options.

The first option is to place the stop loss 5 pips beneath either the previous swing low or level of support as shown in figure 2.37.

Figure 2.37: option one for stop loss placement

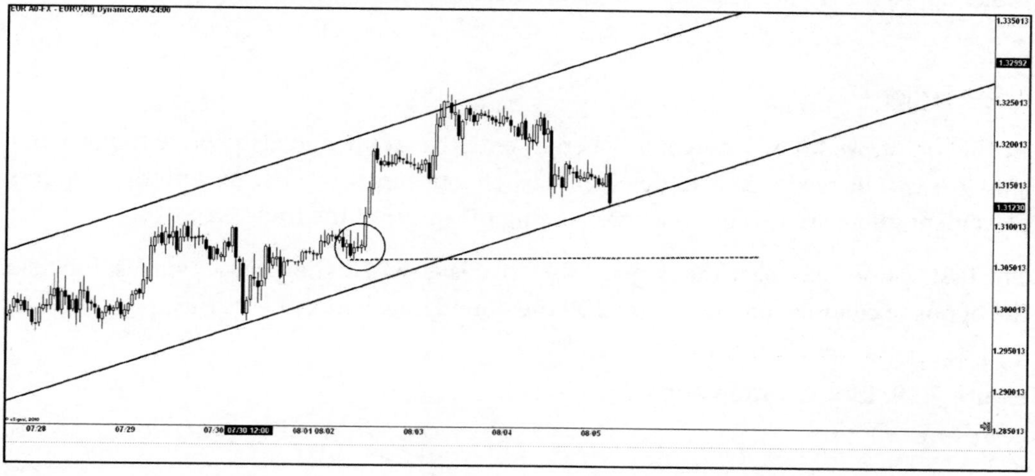

The second option is to place the stop loss 5 pips below the last touch of the price action on the channel line which we are anticipating it will bounce off of, as shown in Figure 2.38.

Figure 2.38: option two for stop loss placement

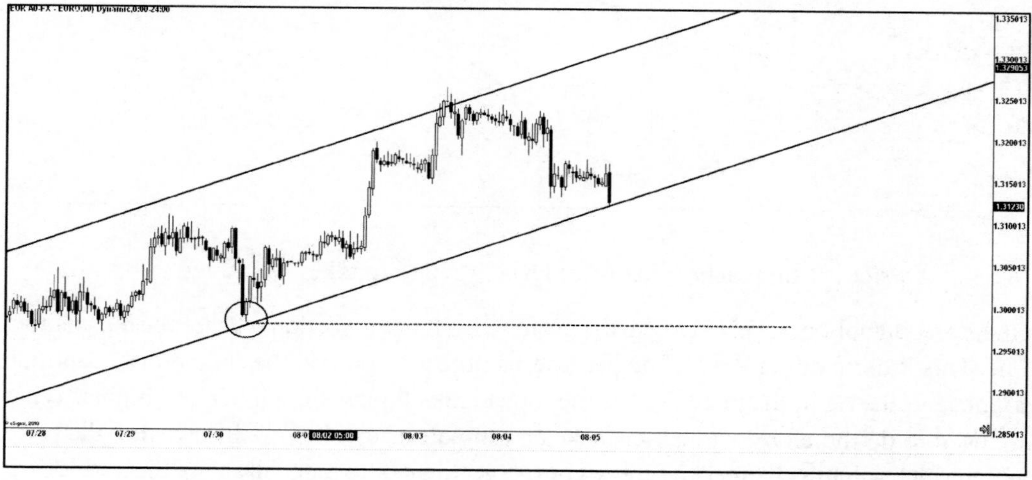

In this example, going with the second option puts the stop loss a considerable distance away from the entry making the reward to risk unfavourable. That doesn't mean that you couldn't use this option, it simply depends on your personal trading style. The further away your stop loss order, the less likely you will be stopped out. However, your reward will be smaller if you win. With the first option on the other hand, you are more likely to be stopped out, but your reward will be greater if you hit your profit target. Psychologically, some traders are more comfortable to win on more trades but make less money per winning trade. Others prefer to win on fewer trades but win more money when they do. Either approach is fine. The key is to be consistent in your approach.

Exit – Target

At this point, we know where and when to enter the trade and also where to place our stop loss is. The next step is to determine where our target will be. As with the stop loss placement, there are two options for deciding the target of the trade.

The first option is to place the target at the price level where the price action last touched the opposite channel line. In Figure 2.39 the dotted line demonstrates this.

Figure 2.39: target option one

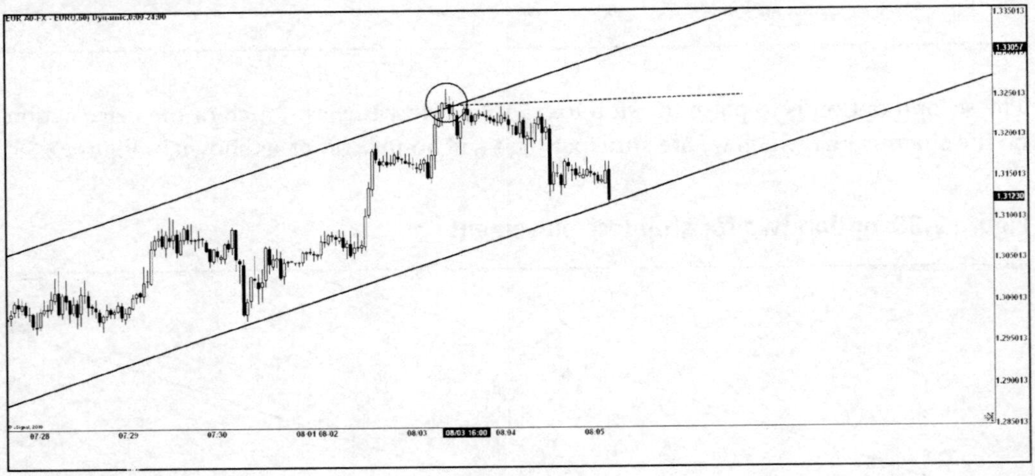

When the price action reaches that price level, it's time to take the money.

In the second option, we plan to take the profit when the price action reaches the top channel line. This is more difficult to define because, as time goes on and the candlesticks continue to move to the right, the price level of the top channel line moves higher and higher. What we need to do therefore, is to either make an estimate as to when we believe that the price action will reach this channel line and set our target there or to manually close the trade down once the price action hits the line. In Figure 2.40 the profit target is shown by the dotted line.

Estimating when the price action will hit the top channel line is not a science. Do not be discouraged if you rarely get it exactly right. The most important thing is that you estimate the general area where the touch will occur.

Figure 2.40: target option two

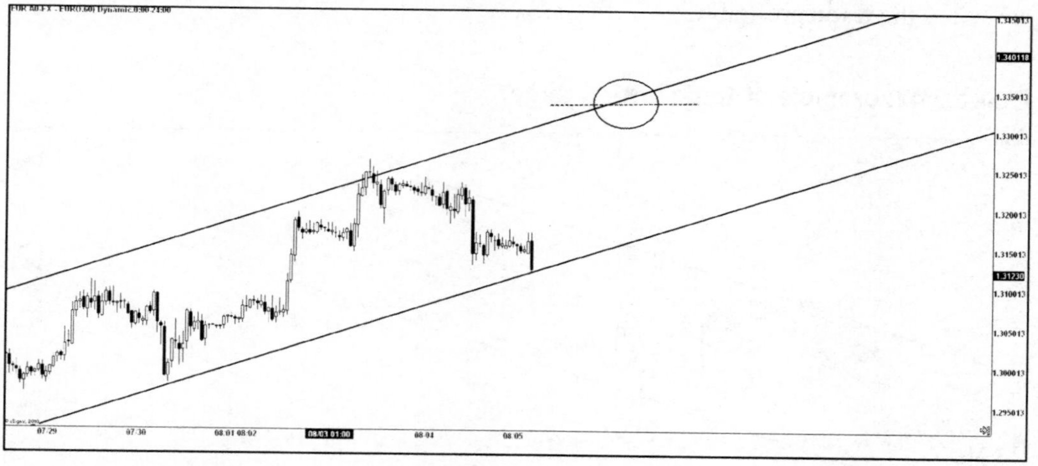

As you can see, while the first option of calculating the trade target is more exact and easier to implement, your target is lower. The second option requires more thought and time, but the potential reward is greater. Again, either option is fine provided that you choose a style and stick with it.

We now understand where our entry, stop loss and target prices should be located. Figure 2.41 highlights these price levels. Just to be clear, the top dotted line is the target, the middle dotted line is the entry and the bottom dotted line is the stop loss. We have gone with the first stop loss option, placing it just below the previous level of support as opposed to the previous touch on the channel line. We have also gone with the first option for taking profit, placing the target where the price action reaches the previous touch of the top channel line as opposed to waiting for it to reach the top channel line itself.

Figure 2.41: example of option one for both stop loss and target price

Figure 2.42 shows the completion of the trade. The dotted line is the target price where we exited the trade profitably.

Figure 2.42: example of trade hitting target

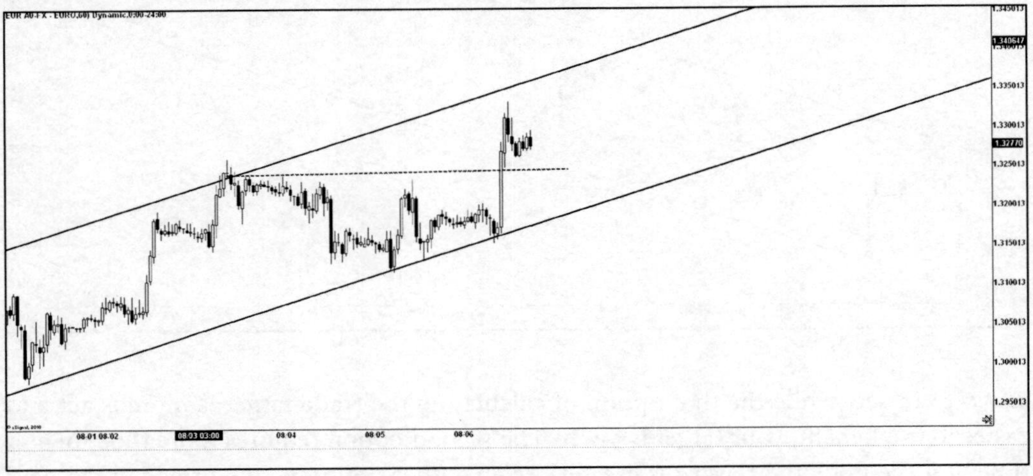

It is clear from Figure 2.42 that our trade was profitable. As you can see, the price action actually bounced all the way up to the top line of the channel.

The EUR/USD 60 minute channel was an example of trading a bounce within an upward pointing channel. Let's go through an example of trading a bounce in a downward pointing channel.

In this example we are looking at the USD/CHF 60 minute chart, as seen in Figure 2.43.

Figure 2.43: example of downward pointing channel

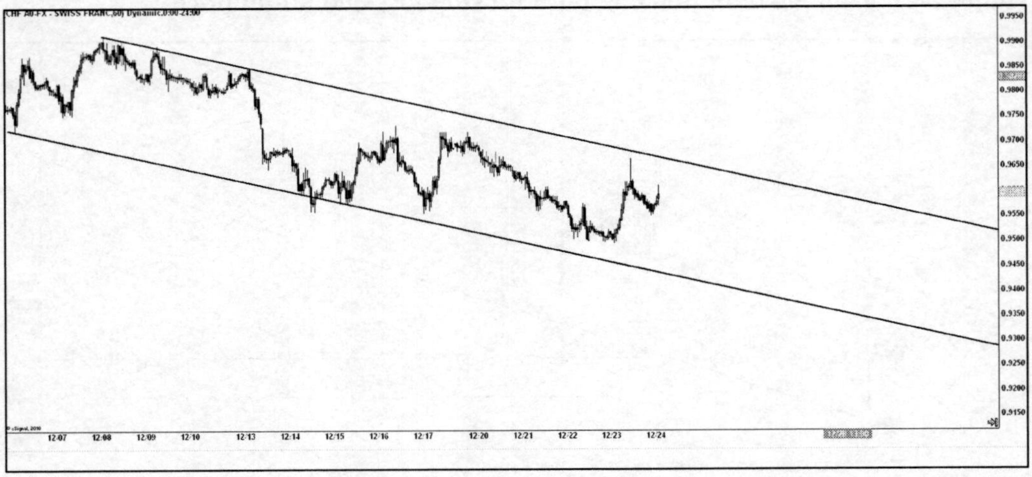

As the channel is pointing down we know that we are going to be looking for potential short setups. Figure 2.44 shows the projected zones of the channel. Remember that we want to trade in the standard zone.

Figure 2.44: projected zones created by channel lines

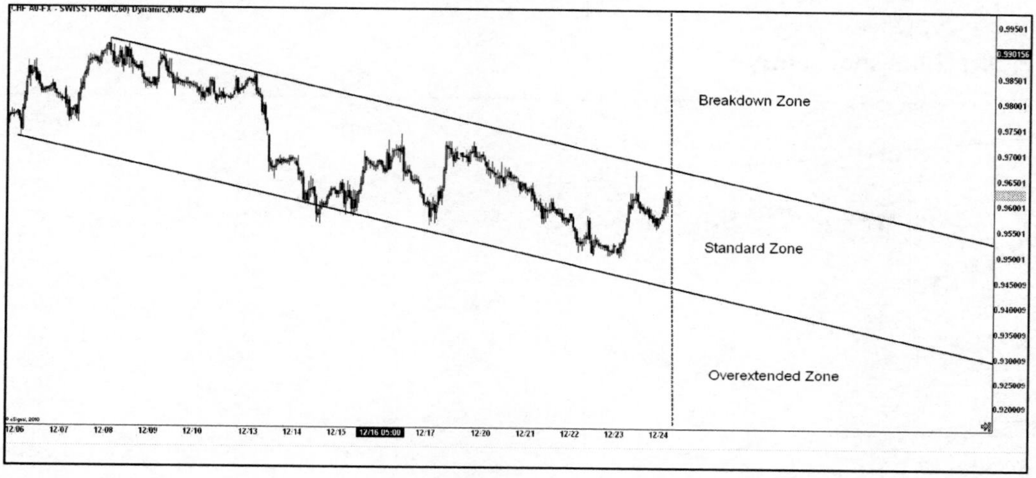

While we wait for a potential setup, when the price action touches the top channel line and closes beneath it, we can establish our stop loss and target prices. The dotted lines in Figure 2.45 highlight these prices. The higher dotted line is the stop loss while the lower dotted line is the target.

Figure 2.45: example of stop loss and target prices

At this point, we are completely ready for the trade. If we get our entry signal, we can calmly enter knowing that we have done our analysis and are in complete control.

Figure 2.46 magnifies the chart to show the entry price as the price action has moved up to the top channel line, touched it and then closed beneath it. We now have a short position on this currency pair.

Figure 2.46: short entry

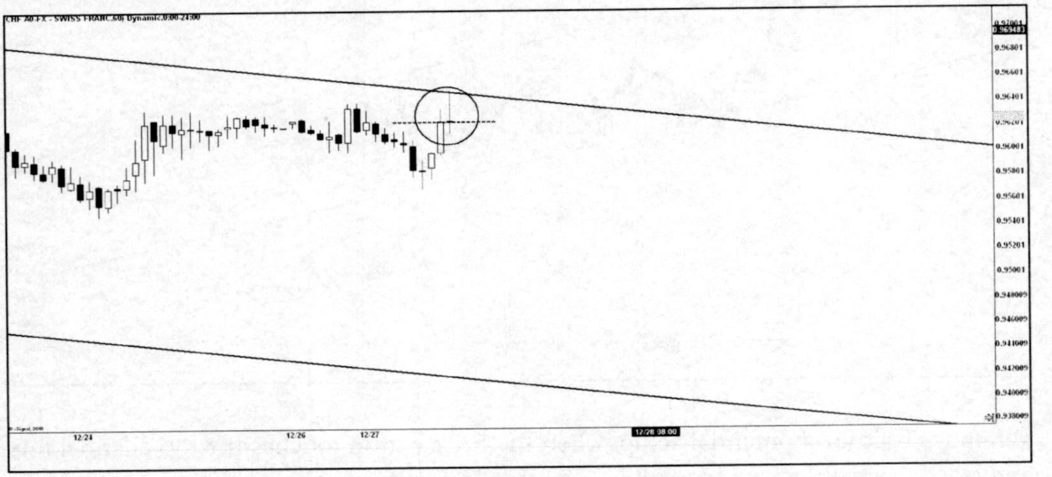

Figure 2.47 zooms back out and shows the completion of the trade. The dotted line is the original target price which was set before the trade triggered.

Figure 2.47: trade reaching target

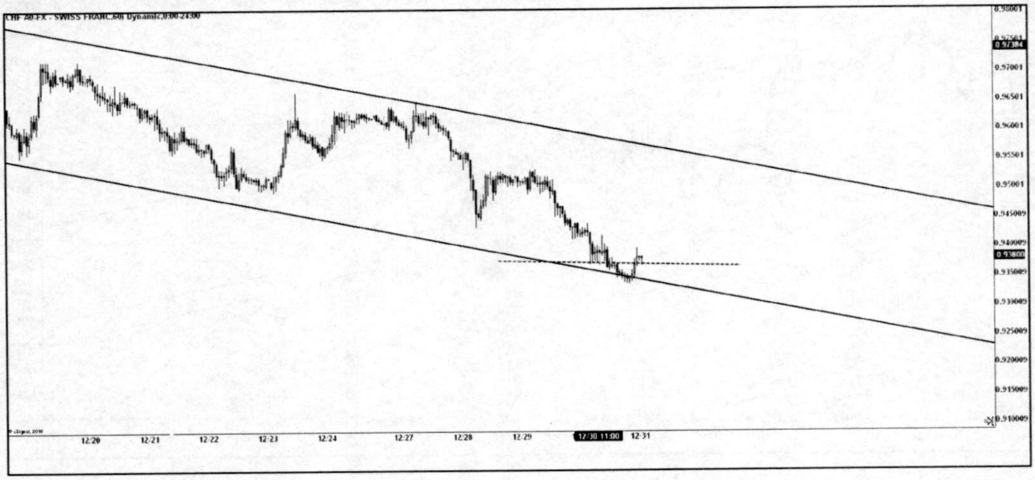

The image shows that we ended the trade and took a profit before the price actually hit the bottom of the channel. As I said earlier, there is nothing wrong with that. It is rare to estimate perfectly when the price will hit the channel. An alternative would have been to wait and manually take profit the moment that the price action hit the bottom channel line. The advantage of doing so would have been that we would have collected more pips and therefore more money. The disadvantage to taking profit manually, however, is the necessity of being present at the trading screen when the touch occurs. This means that an order can not be set to automatically exit the trade. Either way, this was a well planned and profitable channel trade.

Trading the channel bounce strategy consistently on currency pairs that we are familiar with is a very good way to generate considerable, long-term trading profit.

2. Channel break strategy

The purpose of the channel break strategy is similar to that of the channel bounce strategy but it goes about it in a slightly different way. Both strategies aim to capture profit on the price movement from one side of the channel to the other. As we go through the entries and exits of the channel break strategy, you will see that this strategy is more aggressive than the channel bounce strategy in some ways, yet more cautious in others. Let's start by looking at the entry.

Figure 2.48 is the GBP/CHF 60 minute chart, our first example chart for the channel break strategy.

Figure 2.48: example for the channel break strategy

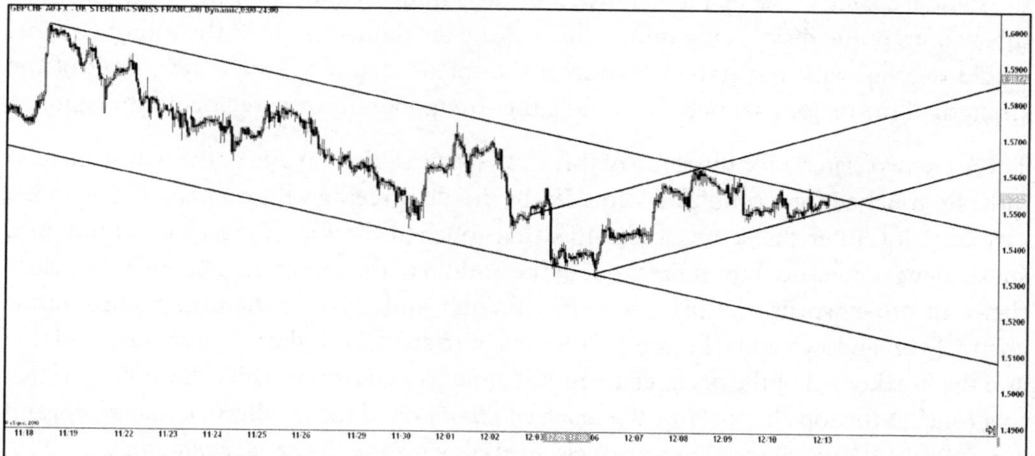

I've added the major channel trend lines and also a disagreeing minor channel.

Entry

The first step in trading the channel break strategy is to determine the direction of the major channel. This is important as it reveals the type of trade we are considering – long or short. And notice the presence of a disagreeing minor channel here - a required feature of the channel break strategy. Next, we must break the major channel down into its three projected zones. These should be fairly familiar by now, but just to be sure Figure 2.49 portrays the zones.

Figure 2.49: example of zones created by the extended channel lines

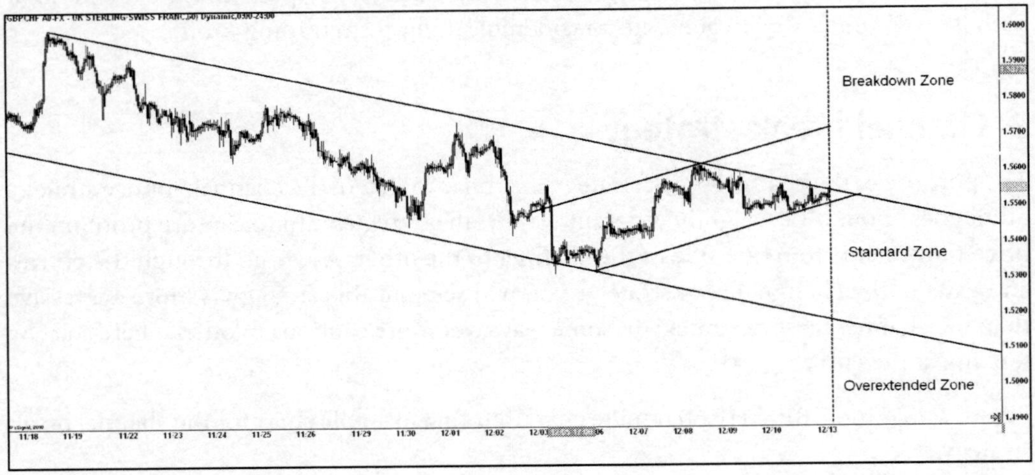

Just like the channel bounce strategy, the setup of the channel break strategy occurs in the standard zone of the major channel. It is interesting to note that if we broke down the three zones of the disagreeing minor channel the breakdown zone of the minor channel would overlap with the standard zone of the major channel. This is the result of the strength of the major channel overcoming the strength of the disagreeing minor channel.

There are two criteria for the setup of this strategy. First, the top line of the major channel must be touched by a candlestick located in the disagreeing minor channel. Second, a candlestick (either the same candlestick that touched the top of the channel line or a subsequent candlestick) must breakout of the bottom of the disagreeing channel and close there. In other words, the price action will enter and close in the disagreeing minor channel's breakdown zone. Figure 2.50 zooms in to show both the touch of the trend line and the breakdown of the disagreeing minor zone. For clarity, we will call the candlestick that touches the top channel line the *touch candlestick* and the candlestick that enters and closes in the disagreeing minor channels' breakdown zone the *break candlestick*.

Figure 2.50: entry

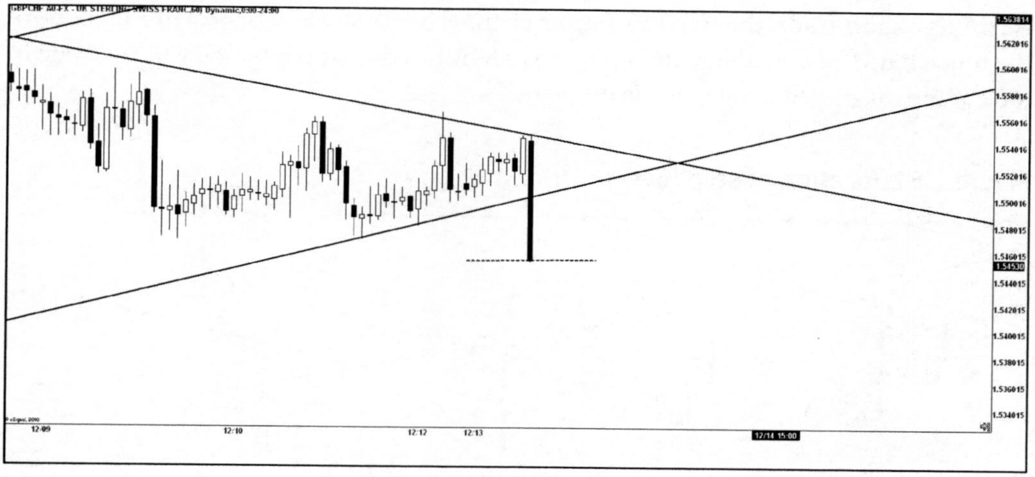

This image makes it clear that both the touch and break candlesticks are on this chart. The dotted line represents our short entry price as the break candlestick has closed in the breakdown zone of the disagreeing minor channel. This is also the standard zone of the major channel.

In summary, the six steps of entering a channel break trade are:

1. Determine the direction of the major channel – up or down.
2. Label the projected zones of the major channel.
3. Identify a disagreeing minor channel.
4. Wait for the price action within the disagreeing minor channel to touch the major channel. If the major channel is up, then it must touch the bottom of the channel. If the major channel is down, it must touch the top. This is the touch candlestick.
5. Wait for the price action to simultaneously enter the breakdown zone of the disagreeing minor channel and standard zone of the major channel. This is the break candlestick.
6. Enter as soon as the break candlestick closes.

The entry for the channel break strategy has two extra steps than the channel bounce strategy. This is because the entry is less aggressive than the channel bounce strategy. As a result, stop loss management in a channel break trade can be more aggressive.

Exit – Risk

As this is a short trade, the stop loss for the channel break strategy is located 5 pips above the touch bar. The dotted line in Figure 2.51 identifies this stop loss. We will continue to look at the magnified image for the moment.

Figure 2.51: location of stop loss

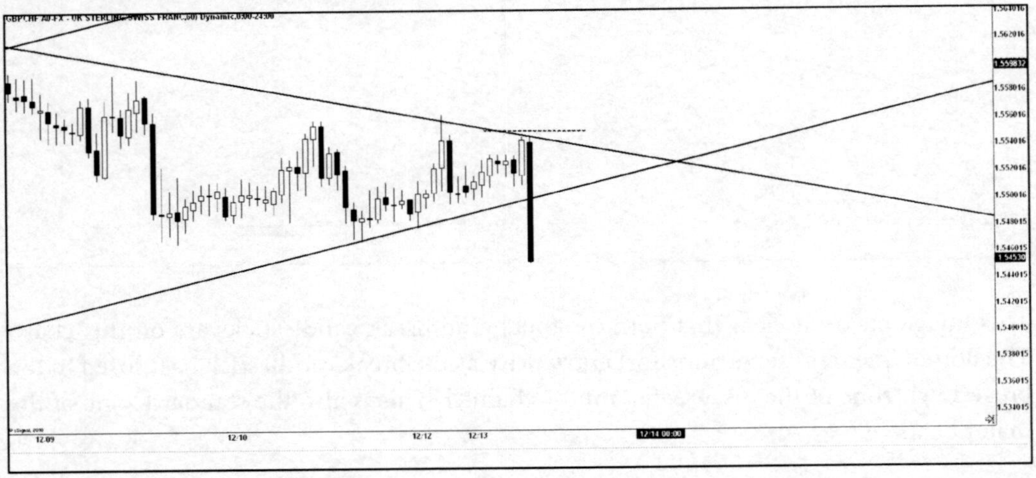

Generally this stop loss will be much more aggressive (closer to the entry point) than either stop loss locations in the channel bounce strategy. This is alright as the entry is much more conservative.

Exit – Target

The methods of targeting this trade are identical to those used in the channel bounce strategy. You can either target the price of the last touch on the opposite channel or take profit as the price action runs into the opposite channel line. The latter option requires us to make an initial estimate about where this will happen, meaning that we have to stay at the computer and exit the trade manually. Taking profit at the previous touch of the opposite channel line, however, allows us to place an order that will automatically close the trade down. Figure 2.52 shows both scenarios, as well as the continuation of the price action and the outcome of the trade.

Figure 2.52: two target options

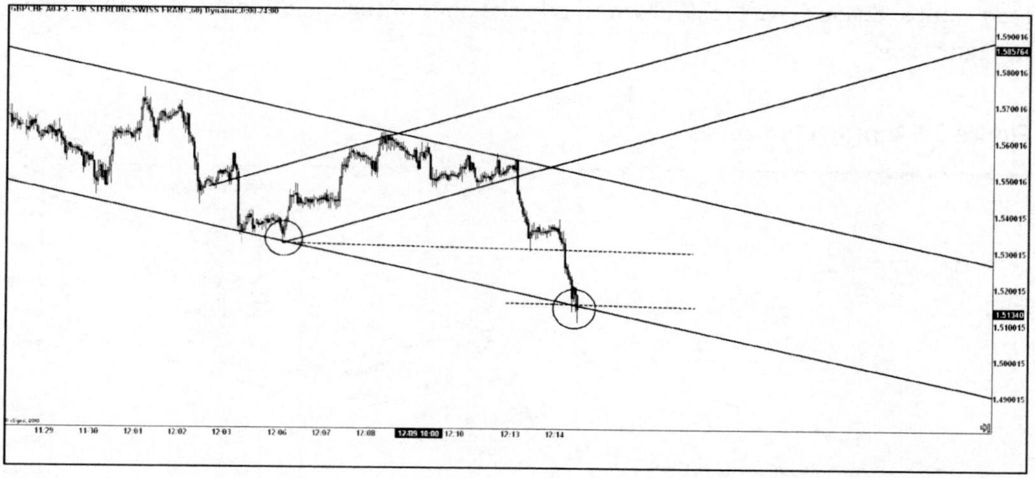

In this example, waiting for the price action to hit the trend line created almost twice as much profit. You must recognise, however, that the price action will not always make it to the next channel line. The most important point is that, regardless of the target option, the trade was profitable.

We have just gone through the use of the channel break strategy in a trade with a downward pointing channel. In the next example, we will look at a long trade in an upward pointing channel.

Figure 2.53 of the GBP/CHF 60 minute chart is our example.

Figure 2.53: example chart

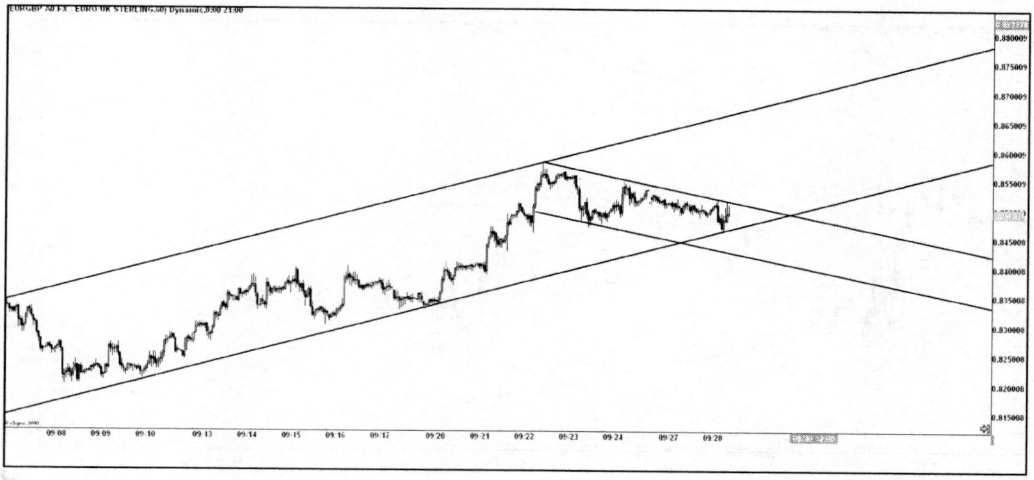

First, we recognise that the major channel is pointing up and we are looking for potential long setups. Second, we break down the three zones of the major channel, as illustrated in Figure 2.54.

Figure 2.54: projected zones

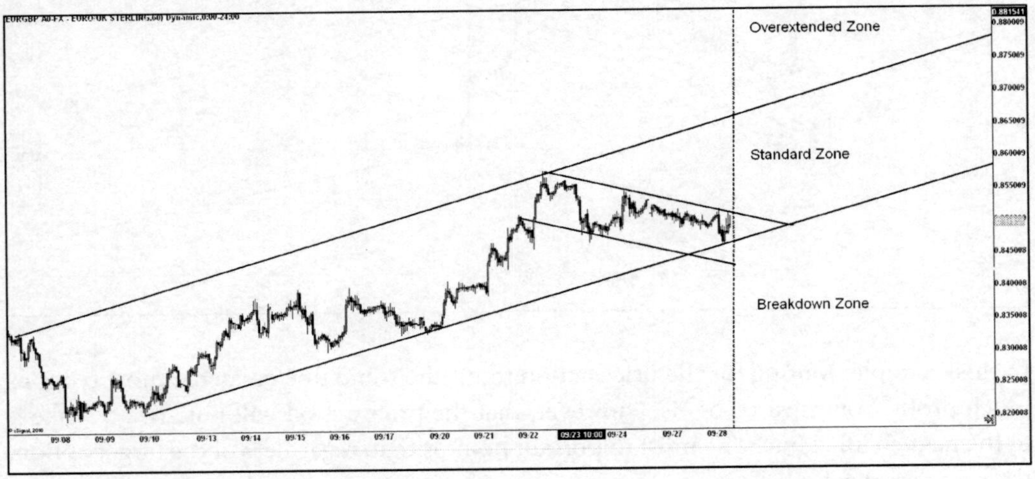

At this point, we have the zones of the major channel labelled. We have highlighted the disagreeing minor channel. The touch candlestick has formed in the disagreeing minor channel, indicating that a long trade is imminent. We now wait for the break candlestick to occur in the standard zone of the major channel. Image 2.55 zooms in and shows the break and the entry of the trade.

Figure 2.55: entry

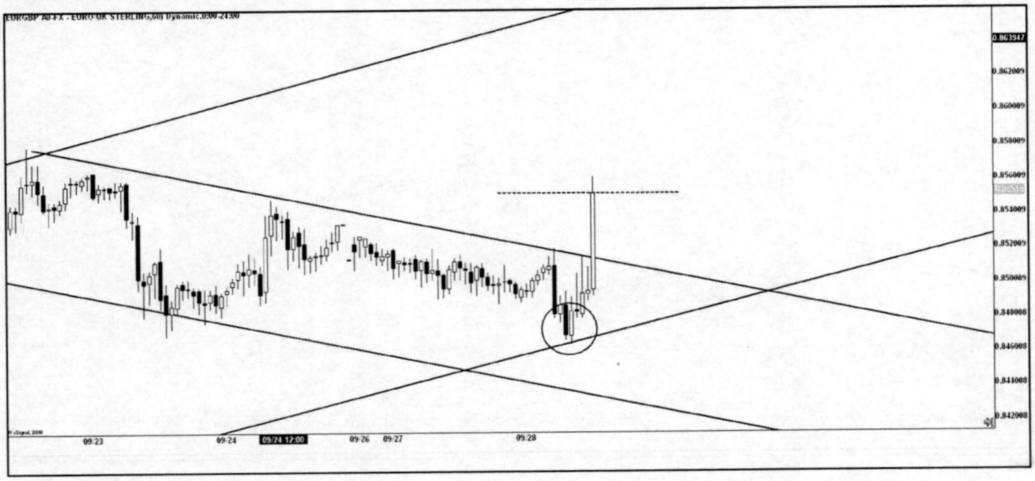

Now that we are in a long trade we can set our stop loss and target prices. Figure 2.56 illustrates these.

Figure 2.56: stop loss and target

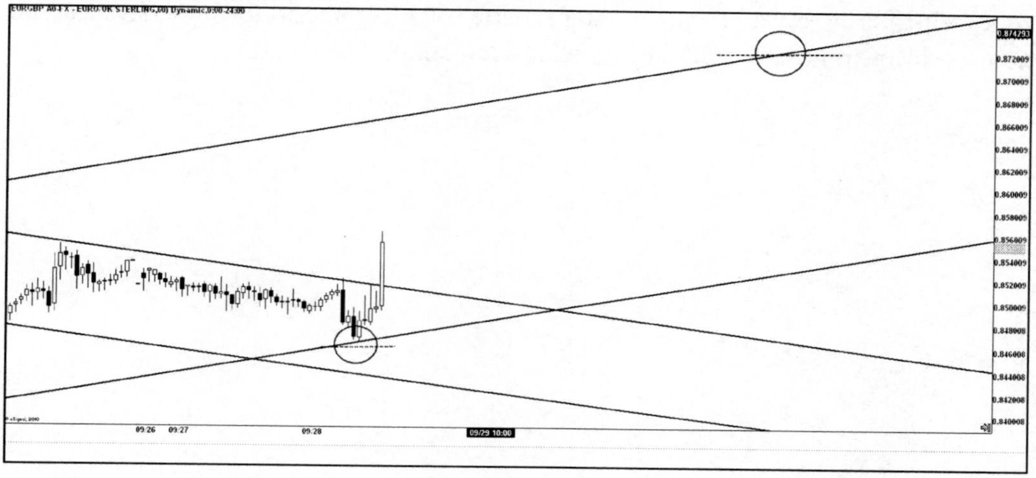

The stop loss is placed 5 pips beneath the touch candlestick and the target is set at the estimated point on the opposite channel line. Remember, it's fine to take profit on the previous touch of the opposite channel as well. You will collect less profit, but the price action is more likely to hit your target.

Figure 2.57 shows the continuation of the price action and the outcome of the trade.

Figure 2.57: trade reaching target

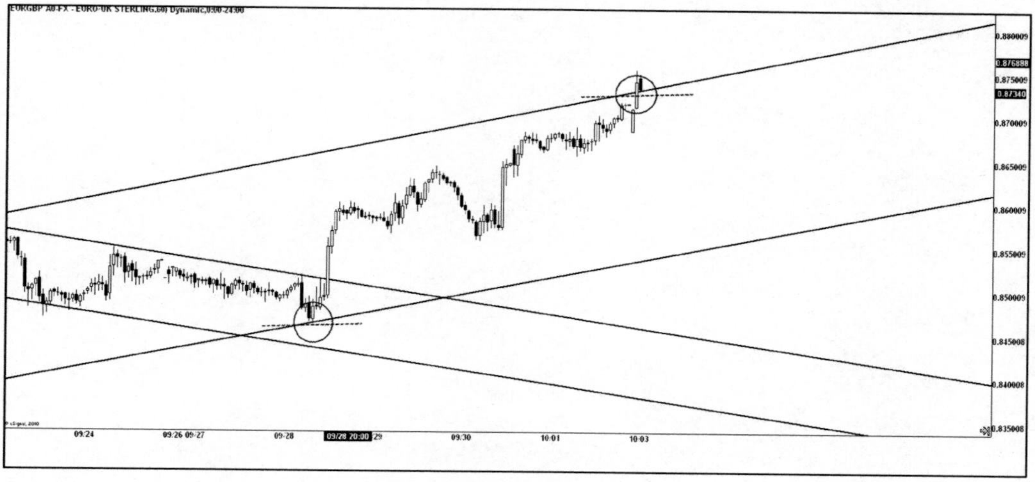

Key 2 Summary

In this chapter we have defined major, minor, agreeing and disagreeing channels and learned how to draw each of these using charting software. We have also explored the messages that each type of channel gives and how these channels naturally create useful zones which bring clarity to our trading experience. Most importantly, we have learned how to execute profitable trades by drawing a few simple channels.

KEY 3
FIBONACCI RETRACEMENT LEVELS

In this chapter, we are going to look at the Fibonacci number sequence and how we can apply it to our charts to identify key turning points in the price action. It would be very easy to get caught up in the interesting, but unnecessary, facts about the unique characteristics of the Fibonacci number sequence. We will avoid that. Instead, I will remark that, while the Fibonacci number sequence can be used in several ways, we are going to focus only on its retracement aspect.

THE THEORY

Primary strength: reveals hidden support/resistance levels

Fibonacci levels reveal hidden support and resistance levels by measuring the retracement of the price action after a definite upward or downward price swing. These retracement levels are significant because the price action responds to them and so we must make sure that these levels are marked on our charts. Without the knowledge of these levels certain movements of the price action will seem random and confusing. They explain why the price action has behaved in a specific way, bringing further certainty and clarity to the trading experience.

Fibonacci retracement level characteristics

The 5 main Fibonacci retracement levels are:

1. 38.2% level
2. 50% level
3. 61.8% level
4. 78.6% level
5. 100% level

These levels represent a percentage retracement of a distinct market move, or a swing, in the price action. For example, if the price action dropped 200 pips and than retraced itself back up 100 pips, it would be at the 50% Fibonacci retracement level. These levels create support and resistance levels which are otherwise hidden unless they are drawn on the chart.

The USD/JPY 30 minute chart in Figure 3.1 shows an example of a down swing from 85.90 to 83.65. From the swing high (85.90) we can place the five main Fibonacci retracement levels. For example, if the price subsequently moved up to 85.0405, we would say it had hit the 61.8% Fibonacci retracement level.

When the price swing is down, the 100% retracement level is equal to the high of the swing, as the price action has retraced 100% of its swing. You will notice that the 0% retracement is plotted on the chart. This level is there to allow us to see the low of the original down swing.

Figure 3.1: example of Fibonacci levels

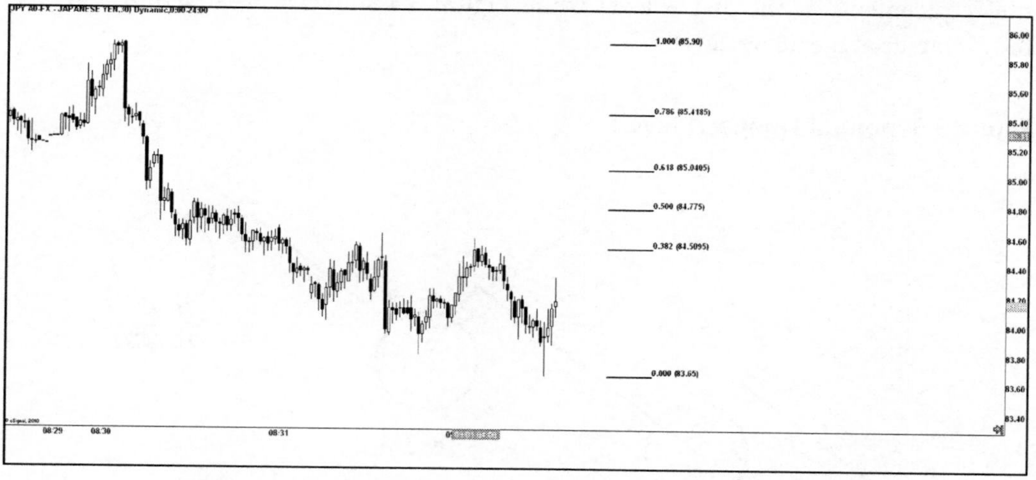

When dealing with an up swing like the AUD/USD 15 minute chart in Figure 3.2, the 100% retracement level is at the bottom and the 0% at the top.

Figure 3.2: example of Fibonacci levels

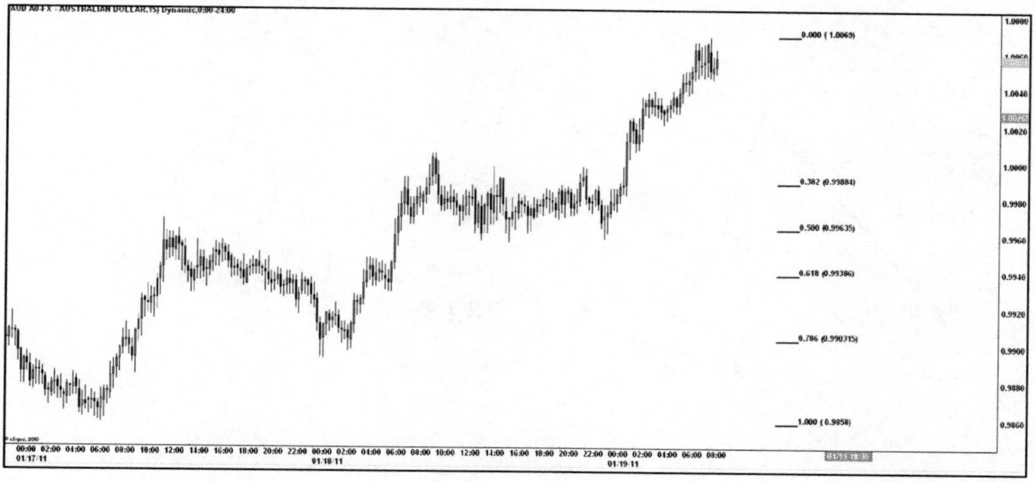

Key retracement levels

In trend trading the 38.2% and the 78.6% Fibonacci retracement levels are the most significant and both play a prominent role in the strategies explained at the end of this chapter. This is partly because these two levels look like standard trending levels. In other words, they are the levels most people would naturally use if asked to draw what a trend looks like.

Let's look at some examples. Figure 3.3 represents an upward moving price action with the retracements at the 38.2% level while Figure 3.4 shows a price action with the retracements at the 78.6% level.

Figure 3.3: natural Fibonacci levels

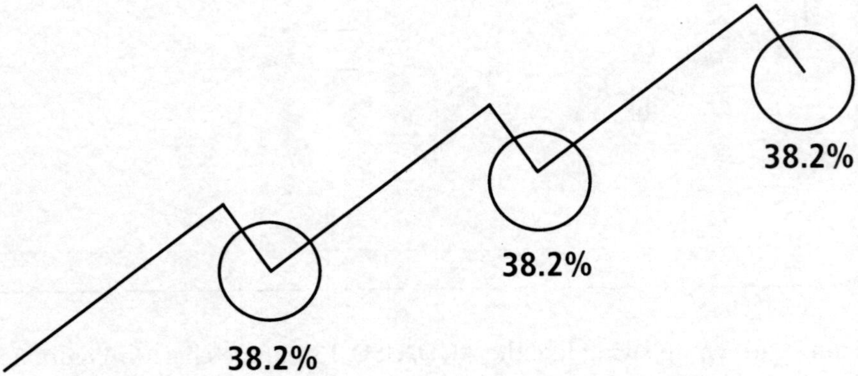

Figure 3.4: natural Fibonacci levels

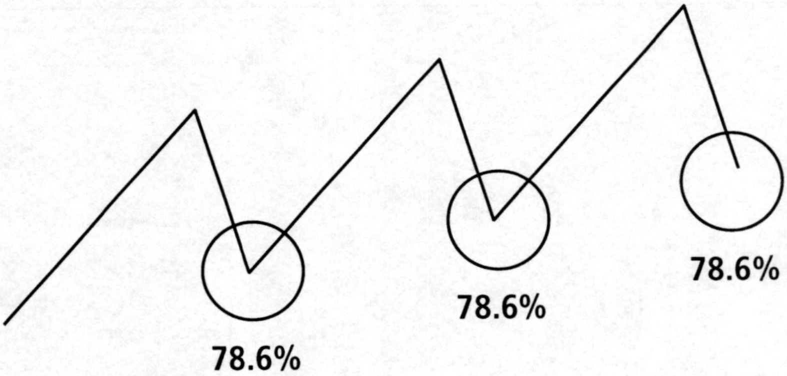

These percentage retracements levels look natural or right to the eyes of individual private traders and big time institutional traders alike.

We will revisit these retracement levels later in this chapter when we look at the Fibonacci bounce and break strategies. For now, you should just be aware that these levels regularly cause a reaction in the price action.

Fibonacci types

As far as the time frame aspect of Fibonacci retracement levels are concerned, they can be broken down into two types: major and minor Fibonacci. In this section we define these two types and discuss how to use them to get the full Fibonacci perspective on any currency pair.

Major Fibonacci

Major Fibonacci is referring to Fibonacci retracements that occur on either the daily or the 4 hour charts. A principle of Fibonacci retracement is that the larger the time frame the greater the significance. Therefore, the Fibonacci retracement levels found on a daily chart would take precedence over those on a 4 hour chart, a 4 hour chart would take precedence over those found on a 1 hour chart and so on. Larger time frames affect trading decisions on smaller time frames more than the smaller time frames affect trading decisions on larger time frames.

The reason for this is simple. Larger time frames are seen by more traders. For instance, a large percentage of foreign exchange traders look at the daily chart for each of the currency pairs that they trade. This is because the daily chart represents the broadest view of what the price action is doing and as traders, we want to trade using levels which the institutional traders, such as banks and hedge funds, are using, because they are the ones who move the market. Of course, one can regard Fibonacci levels as nothing more than self-fulfilling prophecies - traders expect the price action to react to the Fibonacci levels, and so make trading decisions based on the Fibonacci levels, which in turn causes the price to react to the Fibonacci levels.

It is common for traders to specialize in a specific currency pair. Let's assume that the currency pair that we specialize in is the GBP/USD currency pair. In determining our major Fibonacci levels, we would be interested in the Fibonacci retracement levels on both the daily and 4 hour charts, examples of which follow. It is important to look at the Fibonacci retracement levels on both of these charts. If you consider only one without the other, your major Fibonacci analysis will be incomplete.

The chart in Figure 3.5 shows the Fibonacci retracement levels on the daily chart. The upward swing measured in this example is from mid-January 2010 to mid-January 2011. The swing high is signified by the 0% retracement level at the top, while the swing low is signified by the 100% retracement level at the bottom. In this example, the upward swing is almost exactly one year, although the specific length of the swing is not a significant factor. Sometimes the swing we choose to measure on the daily chart will be longer than a year, sometimes it will be much shorter. Remember, you want to be looking at what the institutional traders are looking at - the more obvious the swing, the better.

Figure 3.5: price action with Fibonacci levels

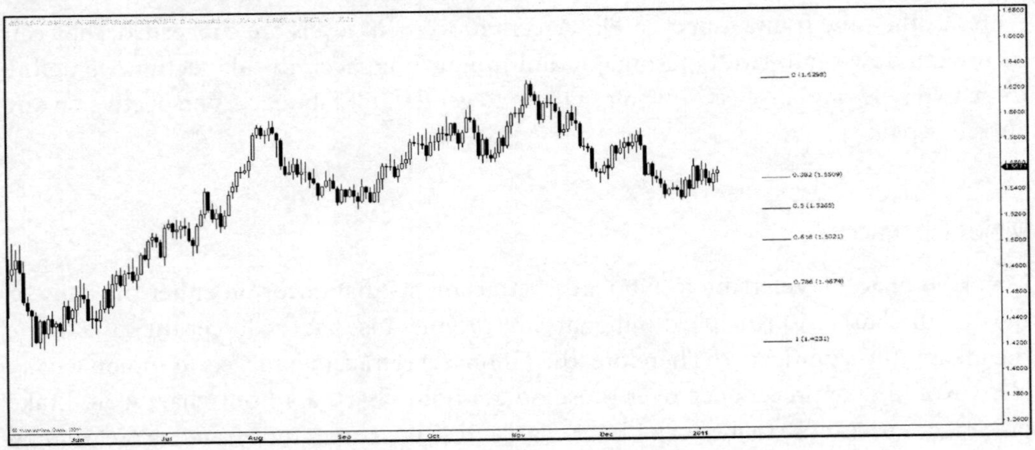

The chart shows not only the swing that we are measuring, but also the beginning of the retracement back down. You can see how the Fibonacci levels will be useful in the future to determine potential levels of support and resistance.

Figure 3.6 is also the GBP/USD, but is of the 4 hour chart as opposed to the daily chart. The swing here is between the end of October 2010 and the beginning of January 2011. You can see the resemblance of this period of time on the daily chart.

Figure 3.6: price action with Fibonacci levels

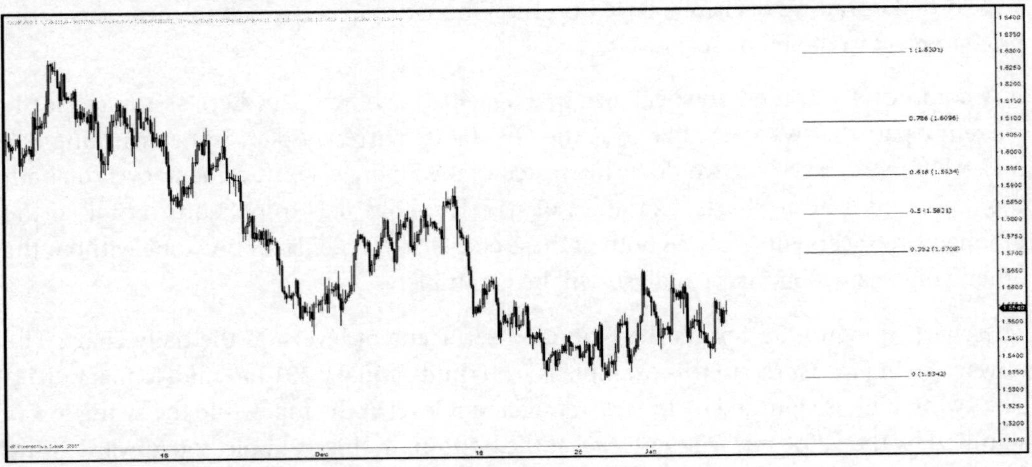

If the price action begins to retrace back upwards, the Fibonacci levels will highlight potential support and resistance levels during the retracement. Had we not drawn in these Fibonacci retracement levels, the support and resistance would have been hidden from us.

Figures 3.5 and 3.6 demonstrate the major Fibonacci retracement levels of the GBP/USD on the large time frame, or big picture, charts. Later in the chapter we will explore the significance of stacked Fibonacci levels occurring on different time frames. Before we do that, however, let's take at look at minor Fibonacci retracement levels.

Minor Fibonacci

Minor Fibonacci refers to Fibonacci retracement levels drawn on time frames of less than 4 hours. We call them minor because their influence over the daily and 4 hour charts, or the major Fibonacci charts, are very small. The usual time frames for minor Fibonacci levels are the 1 hour, 30 minute, 15 minute or 5 minute charts. It is not essential to consider all of these time frames. Choosing two of them to get comfortable with is sufficient for minor Fibonacci analysis.

Let's look at some examples of minor Fibonacci retracement.

We will keep with the GBP/USD currency pair from the previous section on major Fibonacci. Once we have looked at two charts of minor Fibonacci for the GBP/USD we will have a complete Fibonacci perspective for the GBP/USD.

Figure 3.7 shows the Fibonacci retracement levels on the 1 hour GBP/USD chart. The downward swing measured in this example is from the middle to the end of December 2010. There is no rule about which time period you should measure when it comes to Fibonacci retracement levels – major or minor. The important thing is to measure the most obvious swing. This increases the chance of plotting the retracement levels of a market movement which other traders are also studying. In this example, the swing low is at the 0% retracement level at the bottom of the chart, while the swing high is at the 100% retracement level at the top.

Figure 3.7: price action with Fibonacci levels

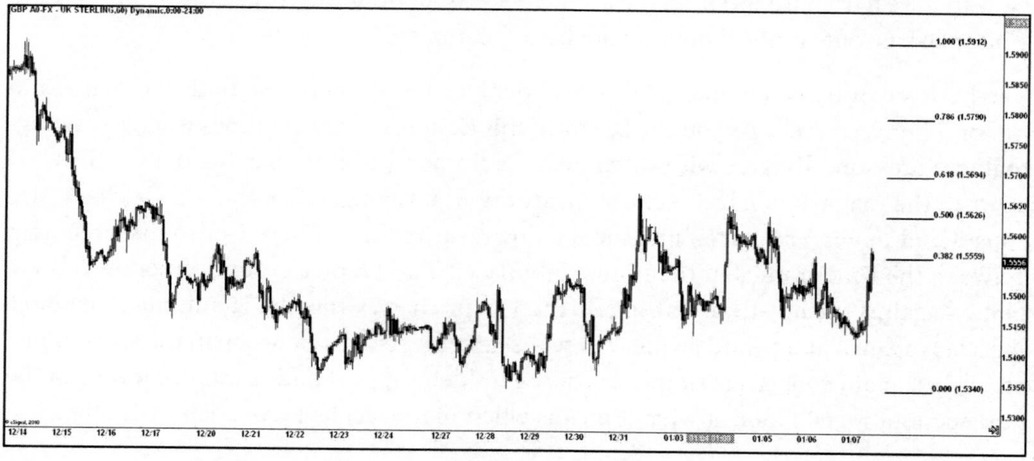

You can see from this example that the price action has begun to retrace itself back upwards. The Fibonacci levels provide us with key levels of support and resistance, when this happens, bringing clarity to our charts. You can see in Jan 2011, the price hit 1.5694 and retreated – effectively bouncing off the 61.8% Fib level.

Figure 3.8 shows the minor Fibonacci retracement levels on a 15 minute chart of the GBP/USD. As the price is swinging up, the 0% retracement level is at the top and the 100% retracement is at the bottom. The swing we will measure, as it is the most obvious on the chart, took place from the early morning of January 10th 2011 to late at night on January 12th 2011.

Figure 3.8: Fibonacci retracement levels stretched across price action

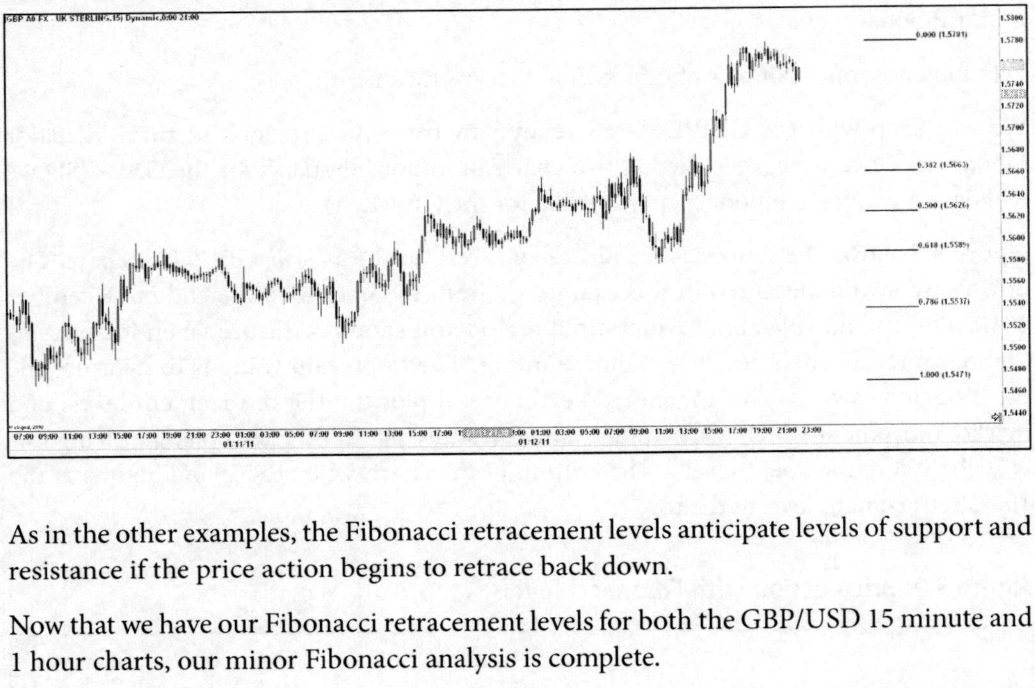

As in the other examples, the Fibonacci retracement levels anticipate levels of support and resistance if the price action begins to retrace back down.

Now that we have our Fibonacci retracement levels for both the GBP/USD 15 minute and 1 hour charts, our minor Fibonacci analysis is complete.

The best way to get a complete Fibonacci perspective is to analyse both the major and minor Fibonacci levels. As you can see from this example, there are times when the swings that you measure disagree with different time frames. For instance, the daily GBP/USD chart in the major Fibonacci section, measures an upswing, while the 4 hour chart, also considered major Fibonacci, measures a downward swing. There is also disagreement between the time frames in the minor Fibonacci. The Fibonacci retracement levels are plotted against the downward swing on the 1 hour chart, while the 15 minute chart plots the levels against an upward swing. These disagreements are not problematic and happen often. Our main concern is simply to expose hidden support and resistance levels. In the next section, we will look at what it means when Fibonacci levels overlap each other.

Overlapping Fibonacci levels

Overlapping Fibonacci levels are points on a chart where Fibonacci levels from different time frames, or from different swings in the same time frame, overlap each other. When Fibonacci levels overlap, we consider them to be more reliable than non-overlapping Fibonacci levels. Think of the principle that we have spoken about. Fibonacci is primarily a self-fulfilling prophecy. Therefore, the more traders who are trading off certain levels, the more that the price action will react to those levels. By looking at an overlapping level, you may be trading off a level which two separate groups of institutional traders are also using. Regardless of which specific Fibonacci setup either group of traders looks at, the level is likely to be important because of the number of traders who are using it to trade. These overlapping Fibonacci levels can, therefore, be used to identify key intraday and end of day support and resistance levels.

The best way to gain an understanding of overlapping Fibonacci levels is to see them on a chart. Let's start by looking at overlapping Fibonacci levels from different time frames. Figure 3.9 is the USD/JPY daily chart. The high and low of our chosen downward swing is circled and the relevant Fibonacci level, the 38.2% level, has a rectangle drawn around it. In practice, we wouldn't know that the 38.2% level was going to be overlapping without studying another chart, but for the sake of clarity this level has been marked now.

Figure 3.9: highlighted 38.2% Fibonacci retracement level

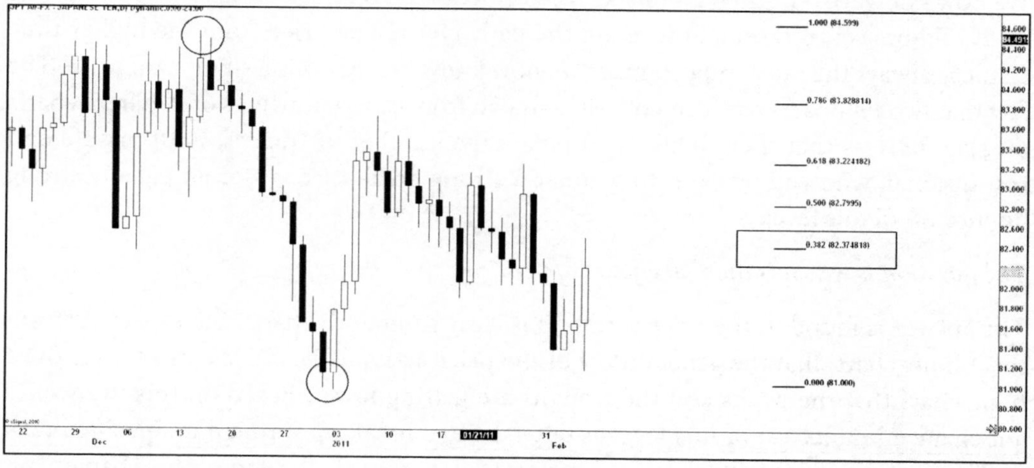

The 38.2% level is at the price level of 82.37. We now need to look at the USD/JPY 4 hour chart to find the overlapping Fibonacci level. As in the daily chart, the high and low of the chosen swing is circled and the relevant Fibonacci level has a rectangle drawn around it.

Figure 3.10: highlighted overlapping 50% Fibonacci level

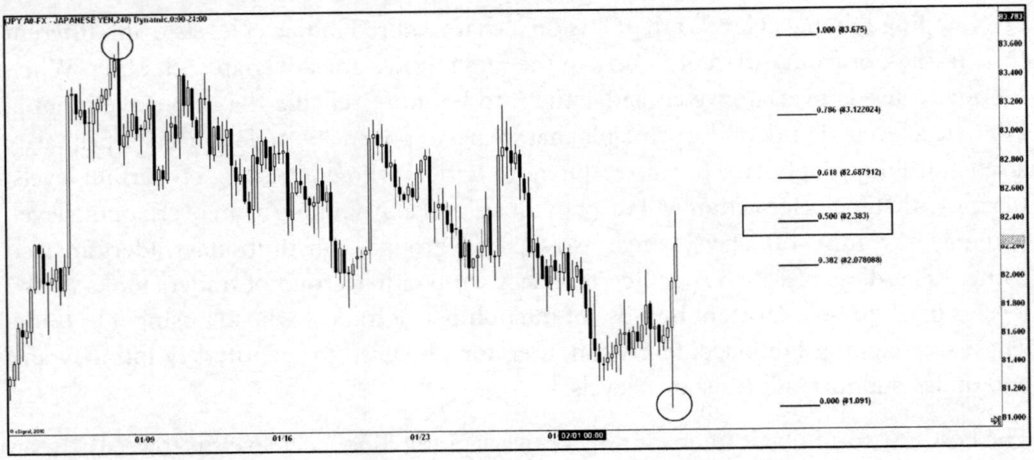

On the 4 hour USD/JPY chart, the 50% Fibonacci retracement level is at the price of 82.38. This is just 1 pip different than the 38.2% Fibonacci retracement level of the swing that was measured on the daily chart. While they are not exactly the same, it is acceptable to a difference of 10 or fewer pips to be overlapping. Having said that, the smaller the gap between overlapping Fibonacci levels the better, especially on larger time frames.

We now know that the 50% Fibonacci retracement level on the 4 hour chart overlaps the 38.2% Fibonacci retracement level on the daily chart. The price from the higher time frame is always the most important, so we now know that 82.37 is a significant price. The fact that two Fibonacci retracement levels, drawn from different swings on different charts overlap, tells us that there is likely to be a large number of traders, both private and institutional, who will be expecting either a strong break through or an equally strong bounce off of this level.

The question is which is more likely to happen?

The answer is found in the price action. It is clear from both charts, but especially from the 4 hour chart, that the general flow of the price action is down. We can see on the 4 hour chart that the peaks and the troughs are getting lower. Based on this, we would anticipate a bounce off of this level as opposed to a break up through it. Specific break and bounce strategies will be defined in great detail towards the end of this chapter, but there is a very simple trading opportunity I can mention here.

If you see an overlapping Fibonacci price level with both of the swings being measured as down, and the price action is making lower peaks and lower troughs as it is in this example, you can enter a sell trade at this overlapping Fibonacci level. You can use the first Fibonacci level above the overlapping level on the daily chart as your stop loss price and the first Fibonacci level below the overlapping level on the daily chart as your take profit price. Alternatively, you can use the levels above and below your entry level on the 4 hour chart as your stop loss and target prices. The chart you choose to use depends on how long you would like to be in the trade. If you are happy to trade on a longer term basis, you would use the daily chart. If you want to get results more quickly, you would use the levels on the 4 hour chart. Remember, we are going to go through specific bounce and break strategies later in the chapter. This is just a simple way to use overlapping Fibonacci levels to time your entry and exit into the market.

Figure 3.11: price responding to the overlapping Fibonacci retracement level

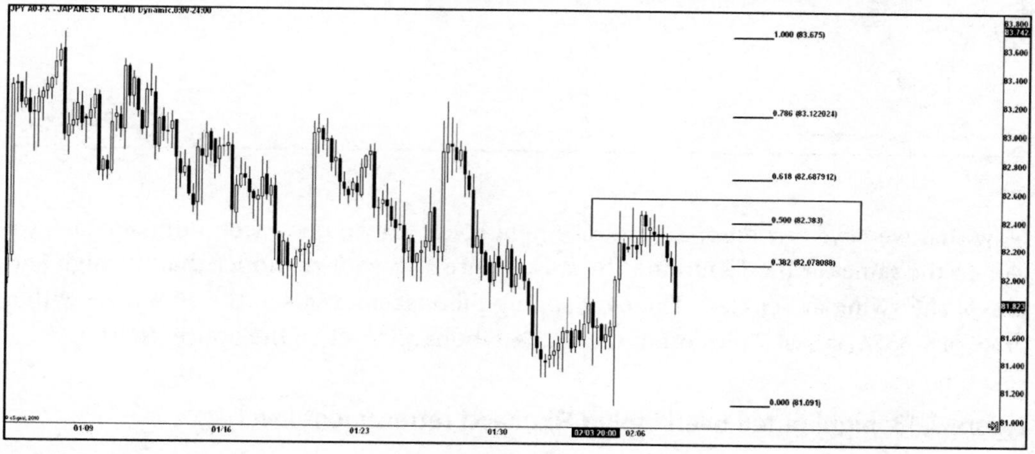

Figure 3.11 shows the result of the price action hitting the overlapping Fibonacci levels on the 4 hour chart. You can see from this image that the price action comes to a standstill at the overlapping Fibonacci level before bouncing back down several pips below the next Fibonacci level.

Let's look at another example of overlapping Fibonacci levels. This time we will be measuring upward swings on the GBP/USD 60 and 15 minute charts. Figure 3.12 is the GBP/USD 60 minute chart, measuring a 10 day swing from the 17th to the 27th of January 2010. As in the previous example, the low and high of the swing is circled. The 38.2% Fibonacci level, which will be the overlapping level, has a rectangle drawn around it. The price of that level is 1.3569.

Figure 3.12: highlighted 38.2% Fibonacci retracement level

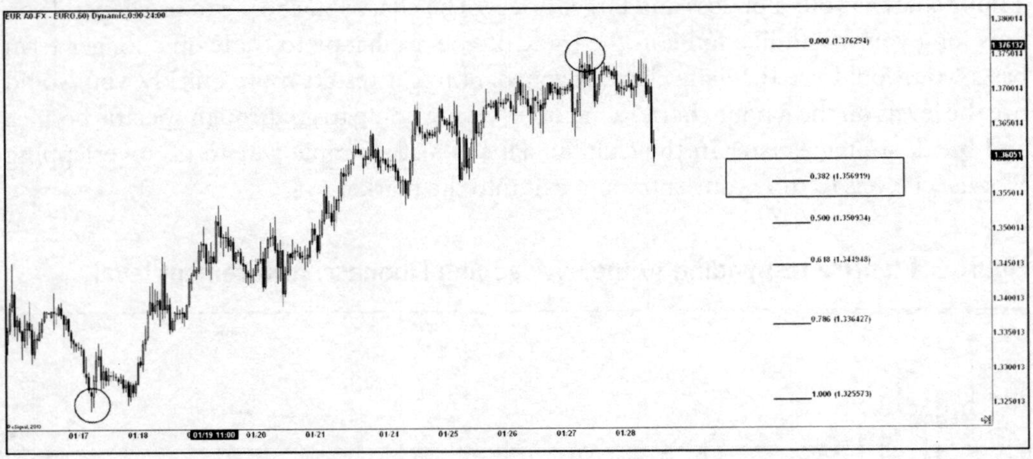

Now that we have our Fibonacci retracement levels drawn on our 60 minute chart, we can do the same for the 15 minute chart. In Figure 3.13 you will notice that the high and low of the swing are circled. The overlapping Fibonacci level is at the 50% level with a price of 1.3576, is just 7 pips off of the 38.2% Fibonacci level on the hourly chart.

Figure 3.13: highlighted overlapping Fibonacci retracement level

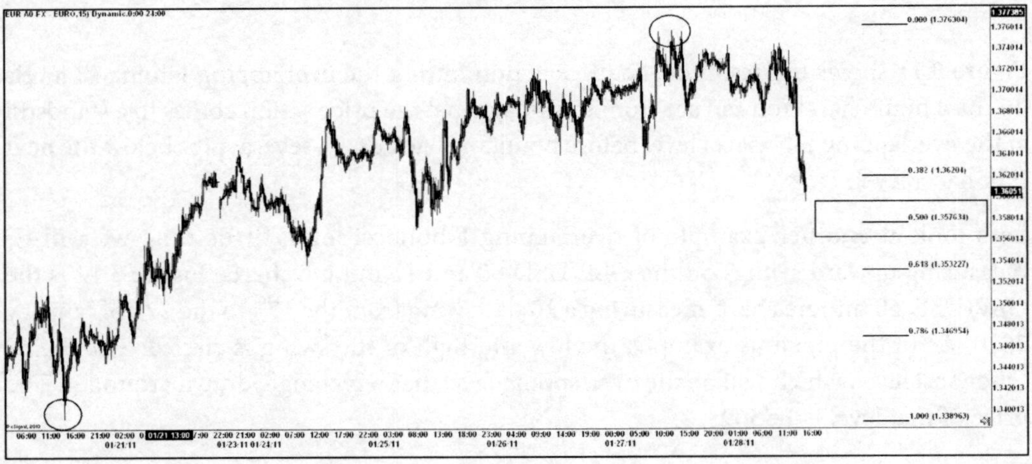

The overlapping Fibonacci levels tell us that this price of 1.3569, taken from the larger time frame, is significant. We therefore expect the price action to bounce strongly off of this level, or break through this level with equal strength. Considering that both the peaks and the troughs of the price action are getting higher and that both sets of Fibonacci levels are plotted against upward swings, we could conclude that a bounce off of this level is more likely than a break down through it. Figure 3.14 shows what happens next on the hourly chart.

Figure 3.14: price responding to the overlapping Fibonacci retracement level

As expected, the price action bounces off the overlapping Fibonacci level. As in the previous example of the USD/JPY, we could have bought at the overlapping Fibonacci level, using the first Fibonacci level beneath the entry as the stop loss and the first Fibonacci level above the entry as the target. This trade would have worked on both the 60 and 15 minute charts. The greater the time frame, the longer the position is open, as the levels are further away from the entry, so we decide which chart to use based on how long we want to be in the position.

The last two examples consisted of overlapping Fibonacci levels which had been plotted in different time frames. Next, we will look at overlapping Fibonacci levels that are found in the same time frame. It is generally easier to find these overlapping Fibonacci levels on intraday charts such as the 5, 15, or 60 minute charts, as the swings are over much shorter time spans.

Figure 3.15 is the USD/CAD 60 minute chart. The high and low of the swing are circled. There is a rectangle drawn around the 38.2% Fibonacci level, which will be our overlapping Fibonacci level. The price of the 38.2% Fibonacci level is .9971.

Figure 3.15: highlighted 38.2% Fibonacci retracement level

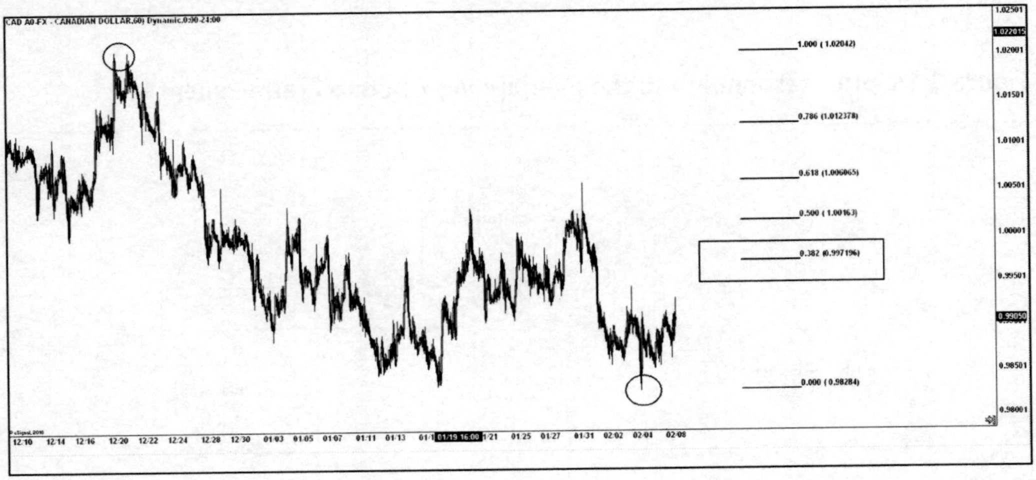

Now that our first set of Fibonacci levels are plotted, we look for another set on the same chart. This is a process of trial an error. There are quite a few peaks on the chart and we simply try each one until we discover an overlapping Fibonacci retracement level. Figure 3.16 shows the swing used to plot the next set of Fibonacci levels, ultimately exposing the overlapping levels. The high and low of this swing is circled. There is a rectangle around both the 38.2% Fibonacci level of the original swing, which is also the 61.8% Fibonacci retracement level of the new swing. The price of the 38.2% Fibonacci level from the first swing, and the 61.8% Fibonacci level from the second swing, is .9971. As stated earlier, two Fibonacci levels only need to be within 10 pips of each other to be considered overlapping, but the closer they are the better.

Figure 3.16: highlighted overlapping Fibonacci retracement levels

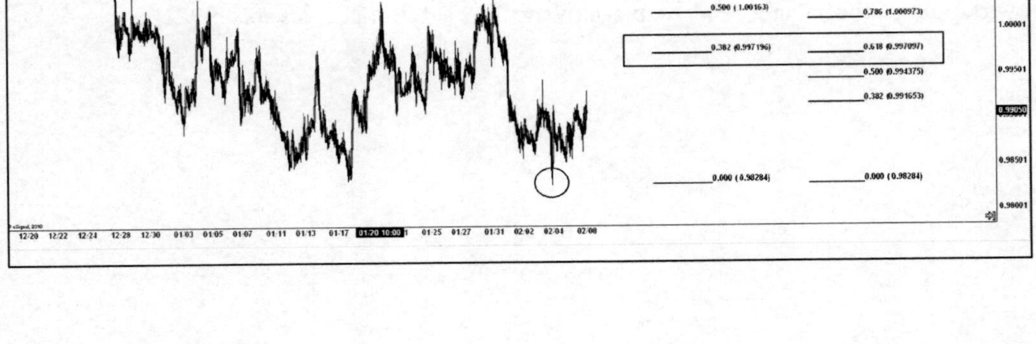

Based on our analysis, we have identified a clear level of resistance. If the price action begins to retrace back upwards, we will expect a bounce off the .9971 Fibonacci level.

Figure 3.17 shows what happens when the price action retraces upwards and runs into our overlapping Fibonacci levels.

Figure 3.17: price responding to the overlapping Fibonacci retracement levels

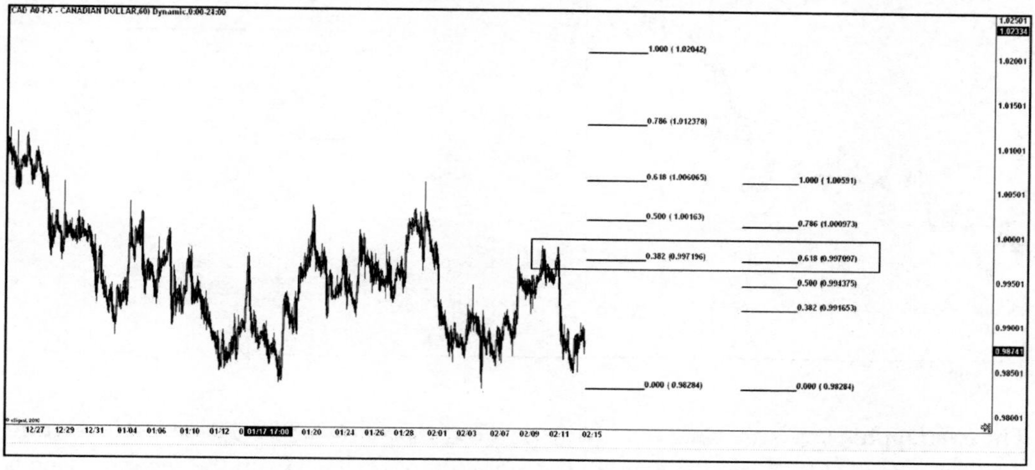

The price action reaches the overlapping Fibonacci levels and bounces off them very quickly. This bounce is consistent with the trend and the Fibonacci analysis.

Another example. In Figure 3.18 the Fibonacci levels are plotted on the upswing of the CHF/JPY 15 minute chart. The circles indicate the high and the low of the swing and the rectangle highlights the overlapping 38.2% Fibonacci level, which has a price of 86.77

Figure 3.18: highlighted 38.2% Fibonacci retracement level

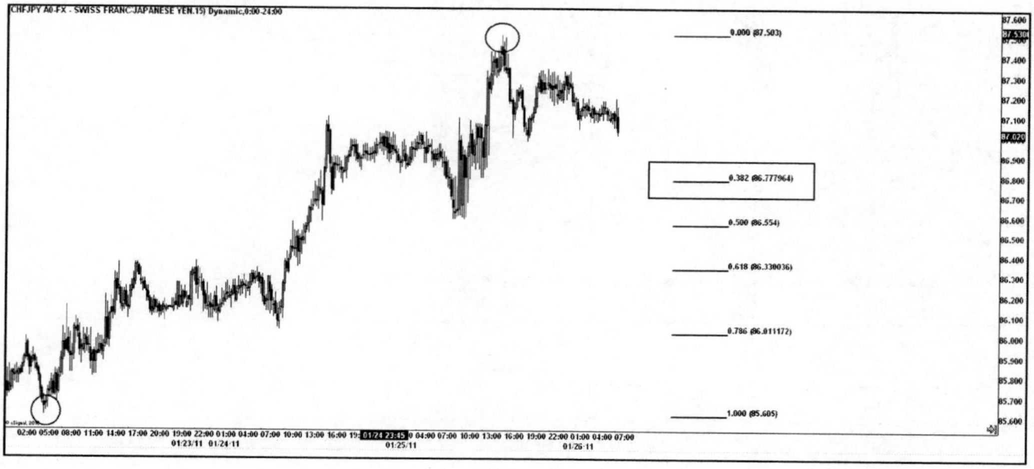

Figure 3.19 shows another set of Fibonacci levels taken from a different swing.

Figure 3.19: overlapping Fibonacci retracement levels

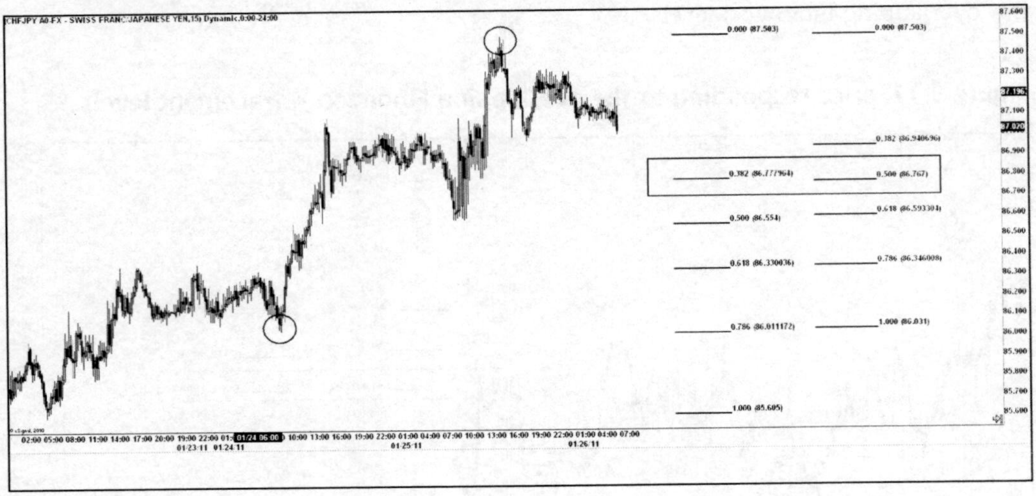

The overlapping levels are clear in this image. The price of the 38.2% Fibonacci level from the first swing is 86.77 and the price of the 50% Fibonacci level from the second swing is 86.76. As the price action is moving up, we expect the overlapping Fibonacci level to act as a support. Figure 3.20 shows how the price action retraces and bounces off this level.

Figure 3.20: price responding to overlapping Fibonacci retracement levels

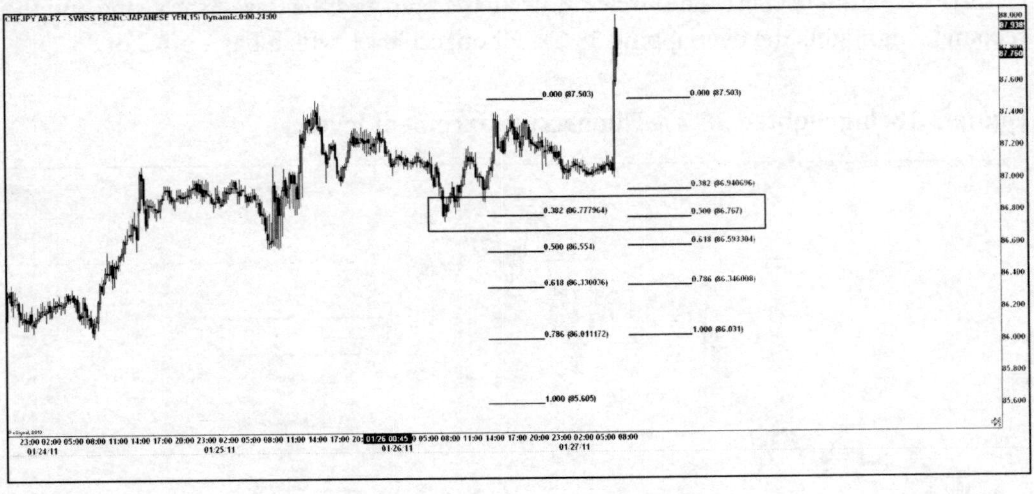

Overlapping Fibonacci levels can be found on different time frames or on the same time frame. They are useful for identifying strong Fibonacci retracement levels. In the following two sections, we are going to look specifically at some overlapping Fibonacci levels that determine key end of day and intraday Fibonacci retracement levels.

Important end of day Fibonacci levels

End of day traders enter positions that typically run between three and ten days. Because of this, they spend the majority of their time analysing larger time frames such as daily and 4 hour charts. It is on these charts that they look for overlapping Fibonacci retracement levels. Therefore, important end of day Fibonacci retracement levels are levels that overlap on the daily and 4 hour charts. Let's look at an example.

Figure 3.21 is an the USD/CHF daily chart. As shown by the circles, the high of the downward swing took place on 1 December 2010, while the low took place on 31 December 2010. The 61.8% Fibonacci level is the overlapping level and is marked with a rectangle. It has a price of .9785.

Figure 3.21: highlighted 61.8% Fibonacci retracement level

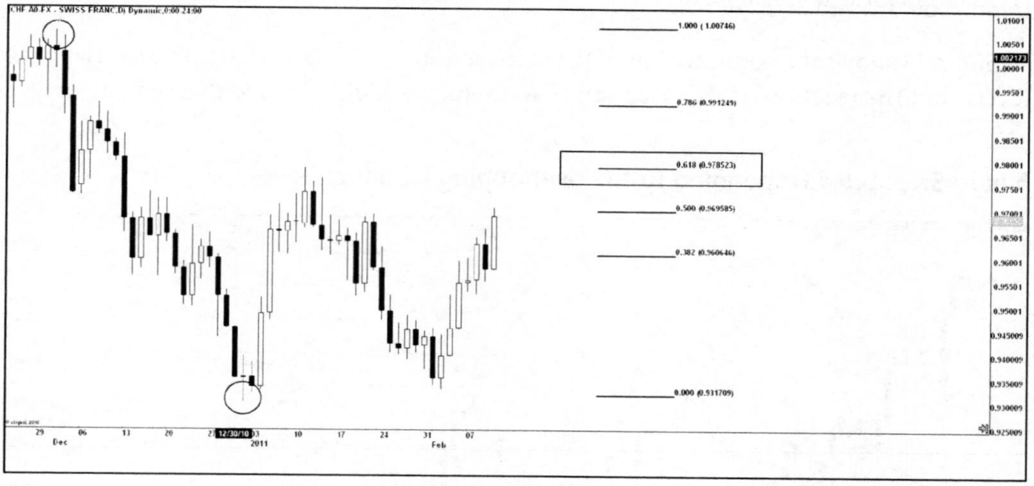

Now that we can see the Fibonacci retracement levels on the daily chart, it is time to look at the 4 hour chart.

Figure 3.22 is a USD/CHF 4 hour chart. The downward swing used here took place between 11 January and 2 February 2011. The 100% level is the overlapping level and is highlighted with a rectangle. The price of the 100% level is .9783.

Figure 3.22: the highlighted overlapping Fibonacci retracement level

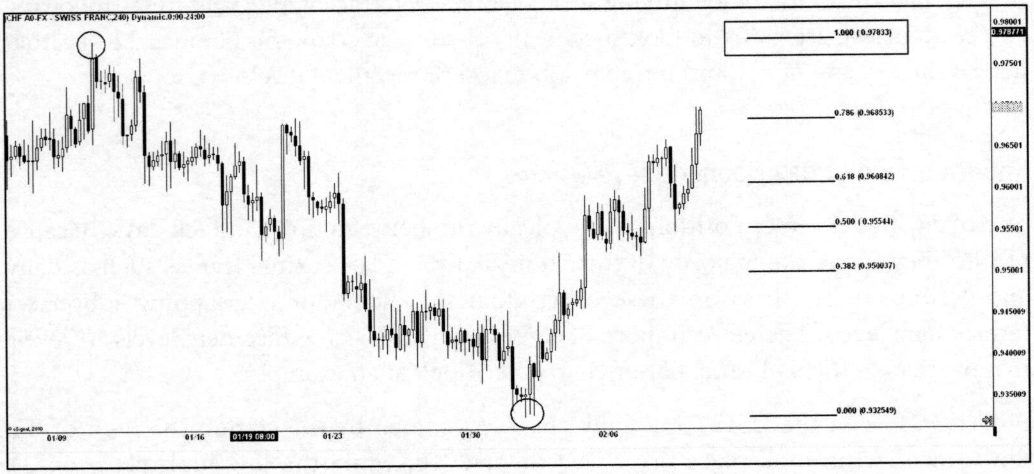

From the previous two images, we can see that the 100% Fibonacci retracement level on the 4 hour chart is just 2 pips different than the 61.8% Fibonacci retracement level on the daily chart. We therefore, could expect this level to be very significant. As the general flow of the price action is down on both charts, end of day traders would be anticipating a bounce off around .9783.

Figure 3.23 shows the continuation of the price action on the daily chart. The overlapping levels, and the reaction of the price action to them, are highlighted with a rectangle.

Figure 3.23: price responding to the overlapping Fibonacci level

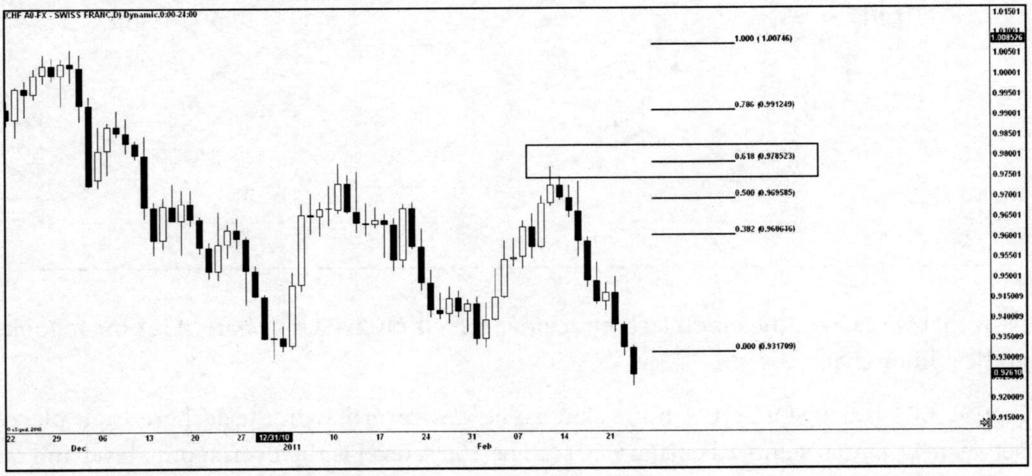

This image clearly demonstrates the significance of the overlapping levels. An end of day trader would have waited for this level to be hit, then entered a short position with the understanding that the trade would be active for about a week. Figure 3.24 shows two possible targets for a trade like this.

Figure 3.24: two possible targets

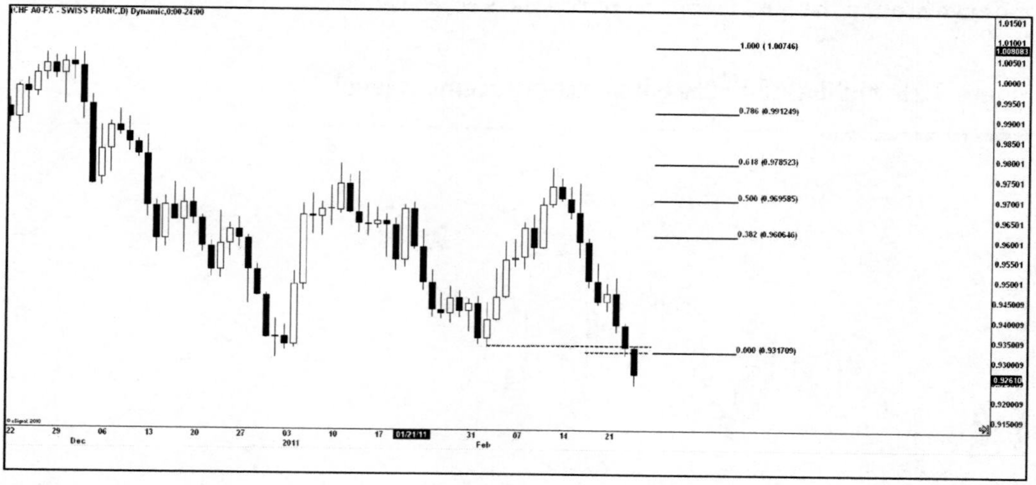

The two dotted lines represent the two most likely targets of the trade. The higher dotted line represents targeting the previous swing low, while the lower dotted line represents targeting the 0% Fibonacci level of the larger swing. Both possible targets are very close together, in which case it is common to use the more conservative target to exit the market.

Remember, later in the chapter we will to go through two Fibonacci strategies thoroughly. The purpose of discussing the trade target now is to begin to train our minds to think methodically about Fibonacci retracement levels.

The example of the USD/CHF daily and 4 hour charts, showed how end of day traders would have identified a key Fibonacci level and used it to enter a profitable trade.

Important intraday Fibonacci levels

The process of identifying key intraday Fibonacci levels is the same as that of identifying key end of day Fibonacci levels, except the 1 hour and 15 minute charts are used instead of the daily and 4 hour charts.

Intraday trading involves entering and exiting the market in the same day. This is not to say that some intraday trades do not run into the following day. In foreign exchange there are several days in a day! By that I mean that a person living and trading in the Australia time frame will have a different day than someone living and trading in the UK time zone. The UK time zone is considered to be the standard time zone because London is known as the foreign exchange capital of the world. More currency is traded during London's trading session than any other session in the world.

In this section, we will look at identifying key intraday Fibonacci retracement levels by finding levels that overlap on the 1 hour and 15 minute charts. Figure 3.25 is the NZD/USD

1 hour chart. The circles highlight the high and low of the upward swing and the rectangle is drawn around the 50% Fibonacci retracement level, which has a price of .7361.

Figure 3.25: highlighted 50% Fibonacci retracement level

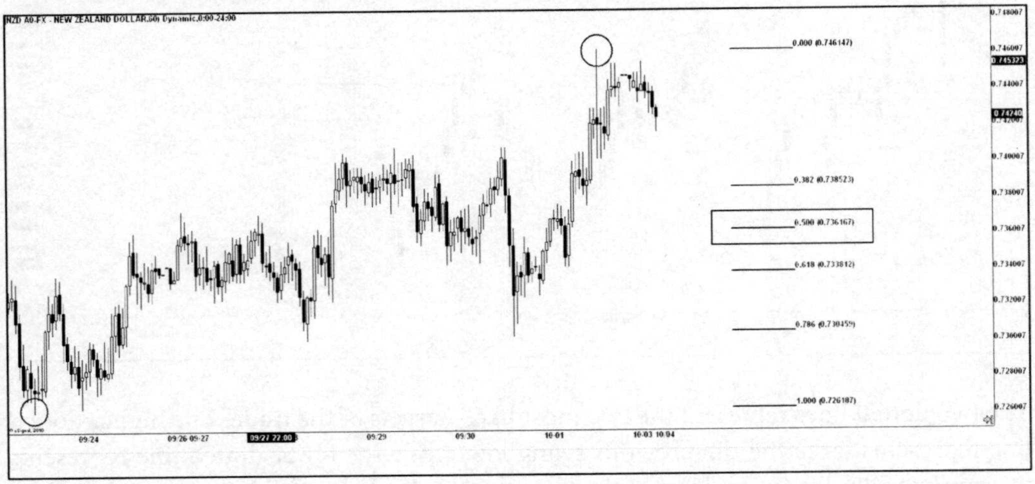

Now that we have plotted the Fibonacci retracement levels on the 1 hour chart, we can look at the 15 minute chart and confirm the overlapping level.

Figure 3.26 is the NZD/USD 15 minute chart. The circles highlight the high and low of the upward swing and the rectangle is drawn around the 61.8% Fibonacci retracement level, which has a price of .7362. This is just 1 pip different than the 50% level of the swing on the 1 hour chart.

Figure 3.26: the highlighted overlapping Fibonacci retracement level

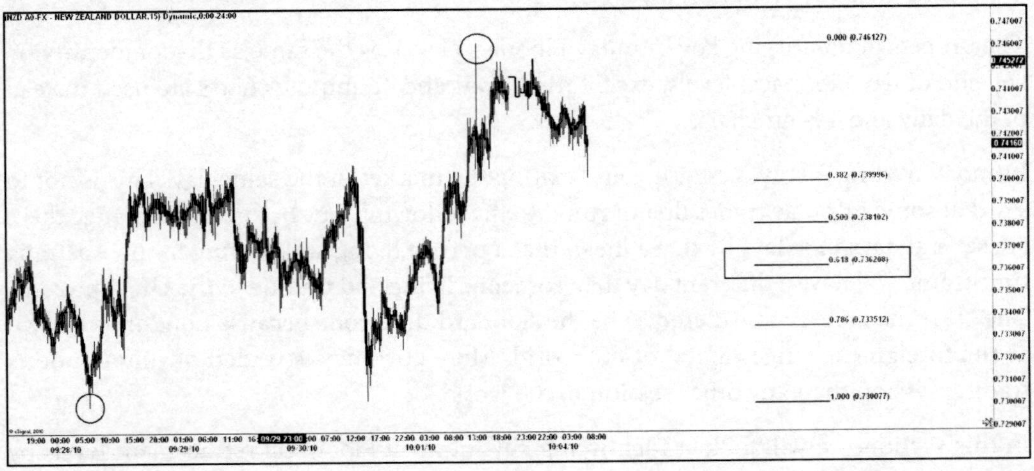

Given that the images from Figure 3.25 and 3.26 clearly show that the price action is moving up, intraday traders who have identified these overlapping Fibonacci retracement levels will be anticipating a strong bounce off this level.

Figure 3.27 shows what happens when the price retraces down to the overlapping Fibonacci level on the 15 minute chart.

Figure 3.27: price action responding to the overlapping Fibonacci retracement level

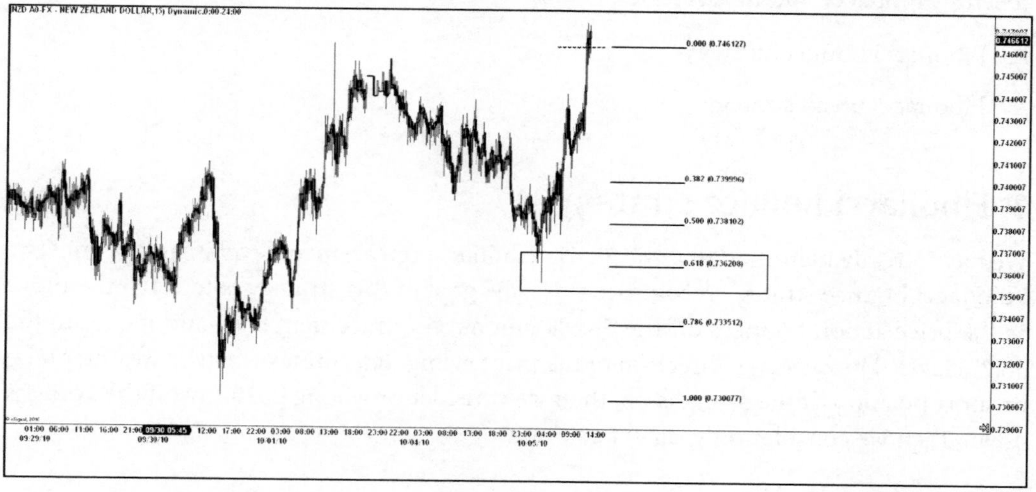

The rectangle in Figure 3.27 shows the strong bounce off the overlapping Fibonacci retracement levels. A typical target for a setup like this would be the 100% retracement level, as indicated by the dotted line.

Intraday traders who use the overlapping Fibonacci retracement technique regularly scan 1 hour and 15 minute charts of currencies that they are familiar with. Once they find these overlapping levels, they wait patiently for the price action to hit them and then enter trades in the direction of the Fibonacci swings that overlap.

ENTRY AND EXIT STRATEGIES

In this chapter, we first learned that Fibonacci retracement levels reveal hidden levels of support and resistance. We explored the five Fibonacci retracement levels and discovered the difference between major and minor Fibonacci levels. We then looked at the power of overlapping Fibonacci retracement levels and found out how to use them to identify key end of day and intraday prices. In the final part of this chapter we will learn two specific Fibonacci trading strategies:

1. Fibonacci bounce strategy
2. Fibonacci break strategy

1. Fibonacci bounce strategy

We have already identified that the 78.6% Fibonacci retracement level is significant. The Fibonacci bounce strategy recognises this. The goal of this strategy is to catch the move as the price action bounces off the 78.6% Fibonacci retracement level and moves to the 38.2% level. The expected direction of the price swing determines whether we enter long or short position. If the swing is up, then we consider only long positions. If the swing is down, then we consider only short positions.

Entry

Figure 3.28 is a GBP/CHF daily chart. The high and low of the swing is circled and the 78.6% level is highlighted with a rectangle.

Figure 3.28: highlighted 78.6% Fibonacci retracement level on example chart

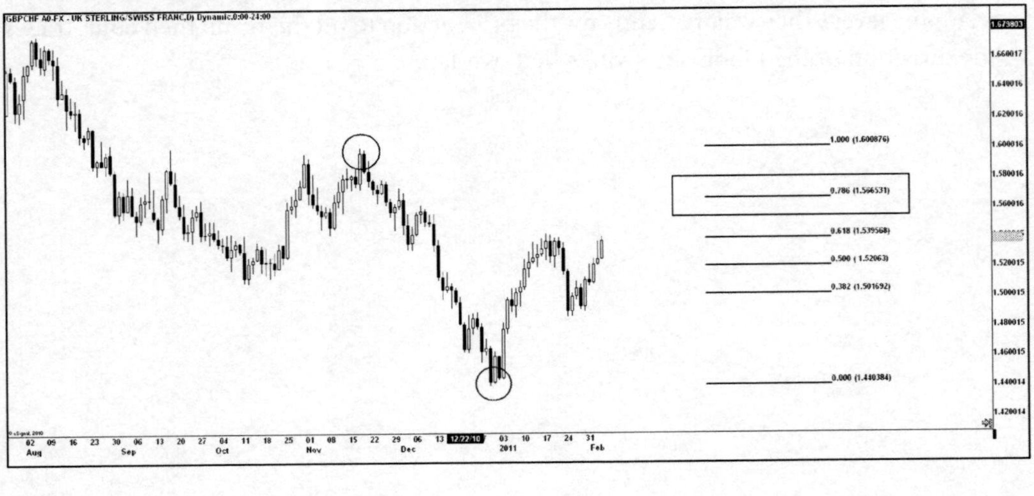

As the primary swing and the *visual flow* of the price action are both down, we are looking for a short position. The chart shows that the price action is currently making its way up towards the 78.6% Fibonacci retracement level. If the price gets there, we would expect it to bounce. Figure 3.29 zooms in on the continuation of the price action as it touches the 78.6% level.

Figure 3.29: close up of entry

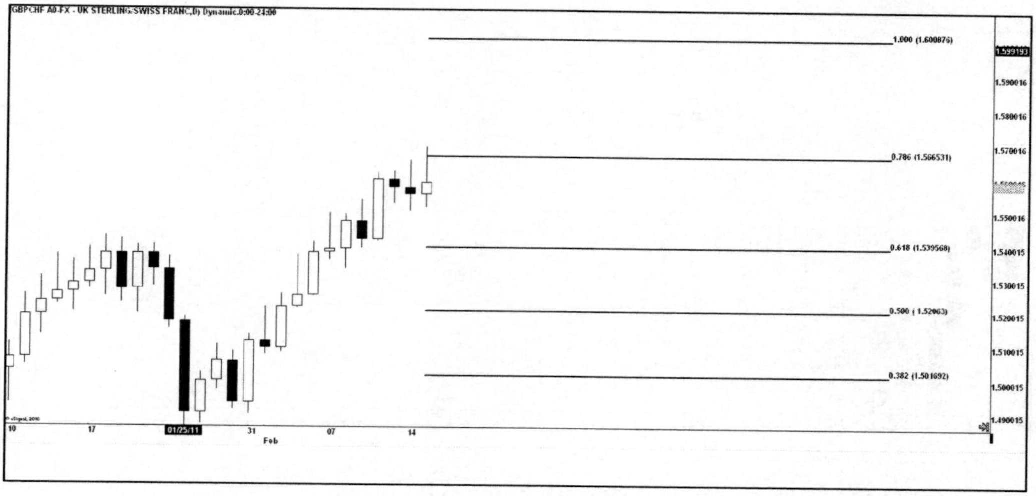

Once the 78.6% level has been touched, we can decide on an entry. We enter the moment that the candlestick that first touches the 78.6% level closes below it. If the candlestick that first touches the 78.6% level closes above it, there is no trade. We are not concerned, however, if the price action goes above the 78.6% level during the formation of this candlestick, as long as it closes below it.

Figure 3.30 zooms in again. The dotted line represents the exact entry price.

Figure 3.30: exact entry price revealed

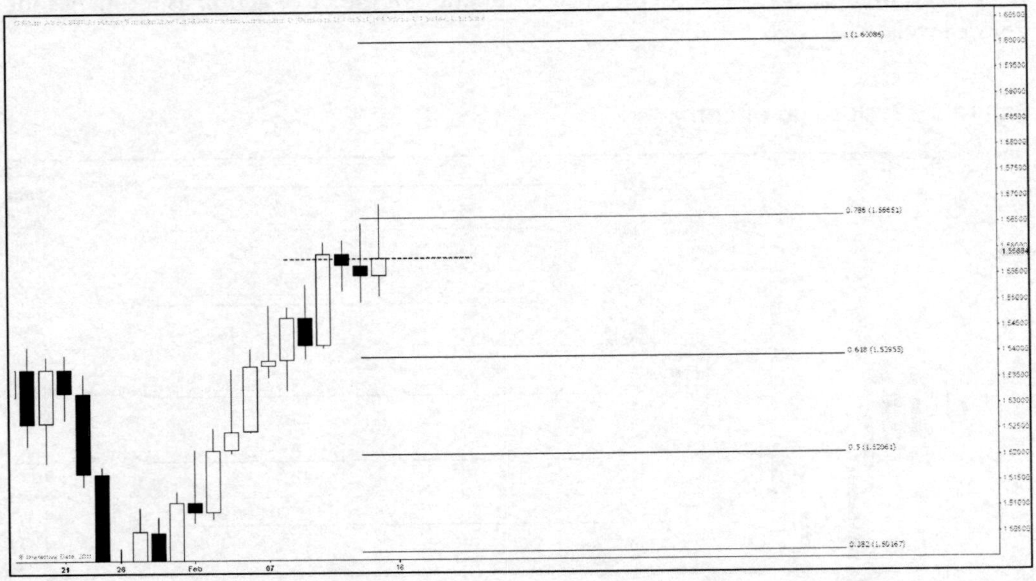

In summary, the four steps of entering a Fibonacci bounce trade are:

1. Confirm the direction of the swing – up or down.
2. Identify the 78.6% Fibonacci level.
3. Wait for the price action to retrace to the 78.6% Fibonacci retracement level.
4. Enter as the candlestick that touches the 78.6% Fibonacci retracement level closes below it for a short position, or above it for a long position.

Exit – Risk

Now that we know our entry, we need to identify where our stop loss should be placed. Here we have two options.

The first, more aggressive, option is to place the stop loss 5 pips above the 78.6% Fibonacci level. (If this were a long trade then the stop loss would be 5 pips below this level.) The dotted line in Figure 3.31 demonstrates this.

Figure 3.31: option one stop loss placement

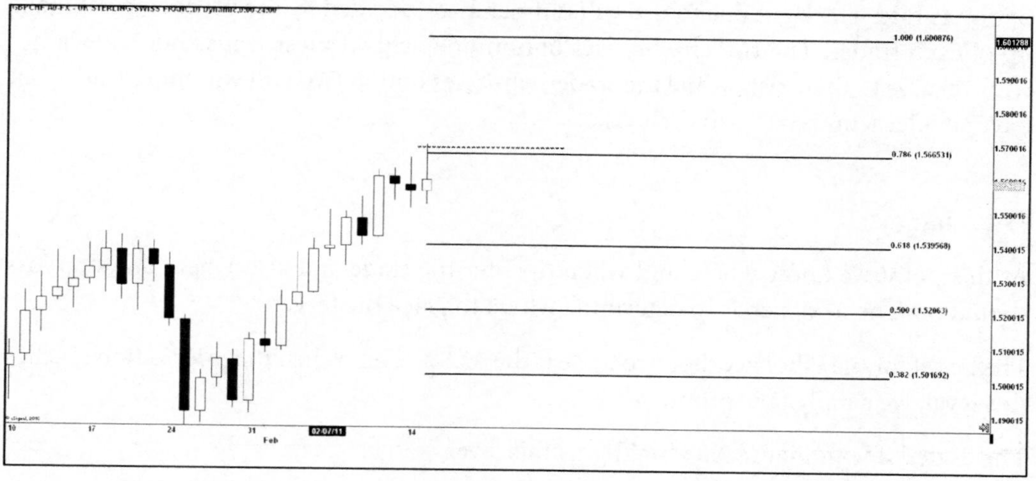

The image may seem to suggest that we have been stopped out of the trade, but this is not the case as the trade was not entered until the candlestick that touched the 78.6% Fibonacci retracement level closed.

The more conservative option is to place the stop loss 5 pips above the 100% retracement level. The stop loss is above this level because we are going short. For a long trade, the stop loss would be 5 pips below this level. Figure 3.32 shows this with a dotted line. The image has been zoomed out again so that it includes the 100% Fibonacci retracement level.

Figure 3.32: option two stop loss placement

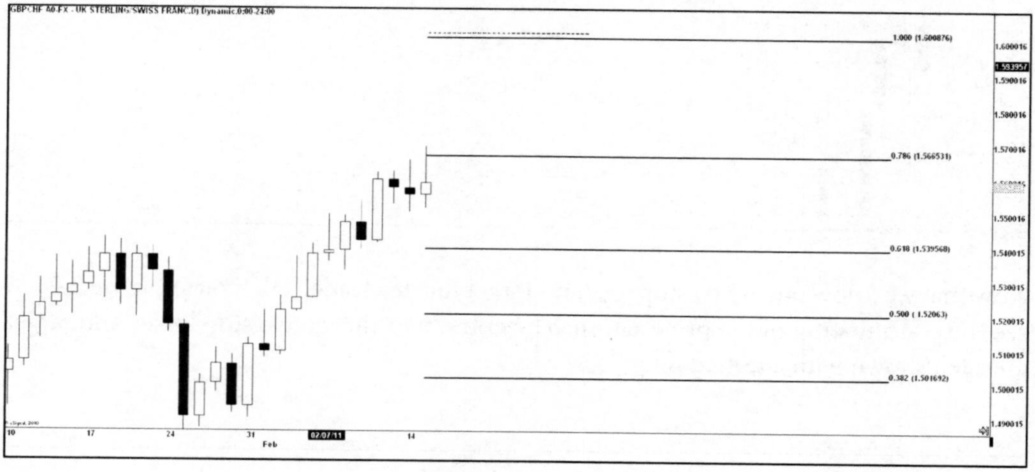

Notice that the second stop loss placement is far more conservative than the first. Either option is fine. The right one to use will ultimately be decided by the psychological make up of each trader. The trader who uses option one, will win less trades but have larger wins relative to their risk, while the trader who uses option two will win more trades but have smaller wins relative to their risk.

Exit – Target

At this point we know where and when to enter the trade and also where our stop loss should be. The next step is to determine where to place the target.

The target for the Fibonacci bounce trade is the 32.8% level. When the price action reaches this level, we simply take profit.

The dotted line in Figure 3.33 highlights this level.

Figure 3.33: example of target

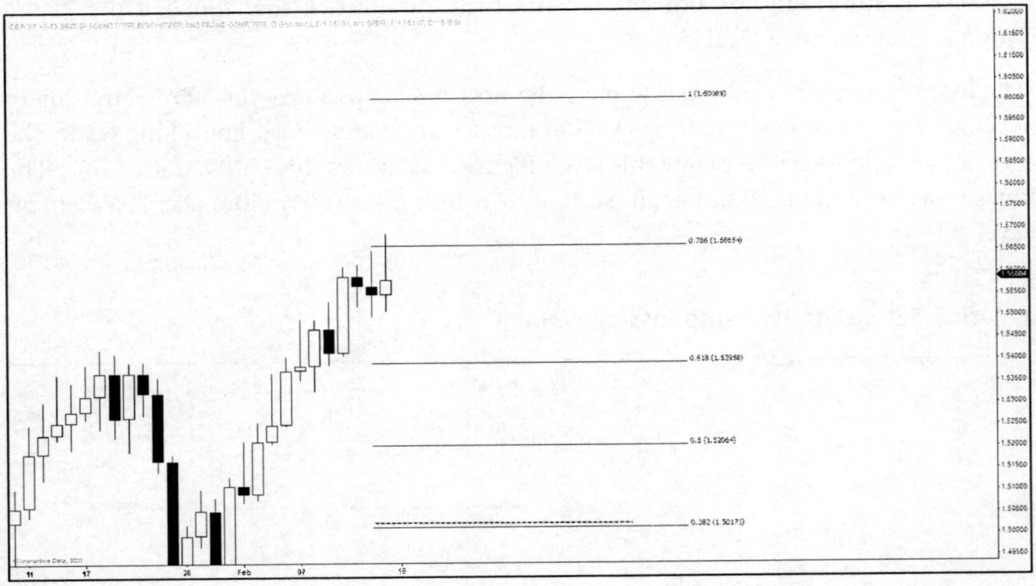

Now that we know our entry, stop loss and target for this trade, let's look at Figure 3.34 to see the continuation of the price action. The entry, two alternative stop losses and target are each shown with a dotted line.

Figure 3.34: example of entry, both stop loss options and target as it is reached

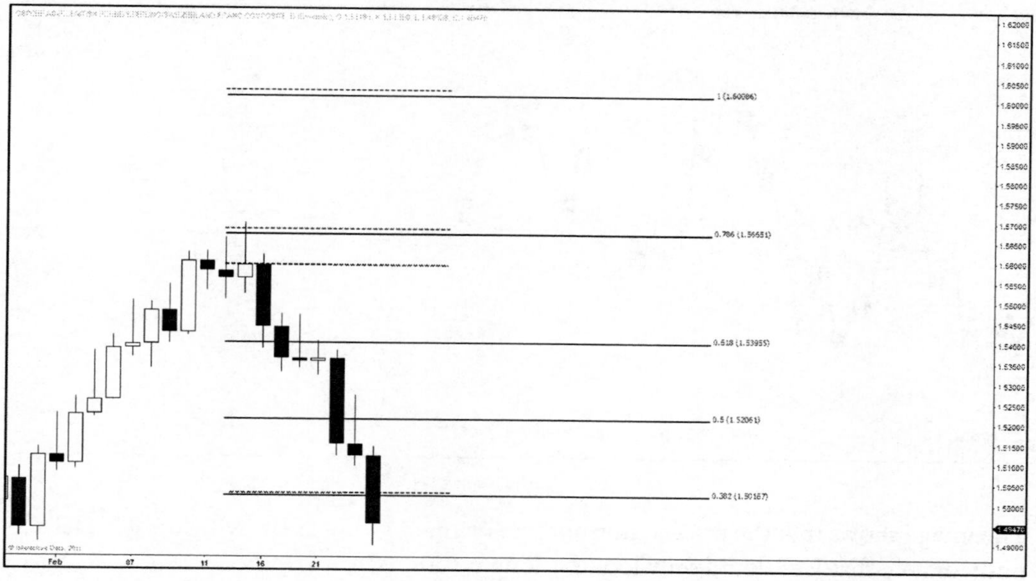

Figure 3.34 shows the price action's strong bounce off the 78.6% Fibonacci retracement level and the run that it then makes all the way down to the 38.2% level. By having all of the entry and exit levels highlighted on the same chart, we can see that the trader who chose the aggressive stop loss option would have profited nearly three times as much relative to the risk, as the trader who chose the more conservative option behind the 100% Fibonacci retracement level. In this case, taking a greater risk of being stopped out, led to a greater reward relative to the risk.

Let's go through an example of using the Fibonacci bounce strategy when going long. Figure 3.35 is a AUD/CAD 60 minute chart. As in the first example, the high and low of the swings are circled and the 78.6% Fibonacci retracement level has a rectangle around it.

Figure 3.35: highlighted 78.6% Fibonacci retracement level on example chart

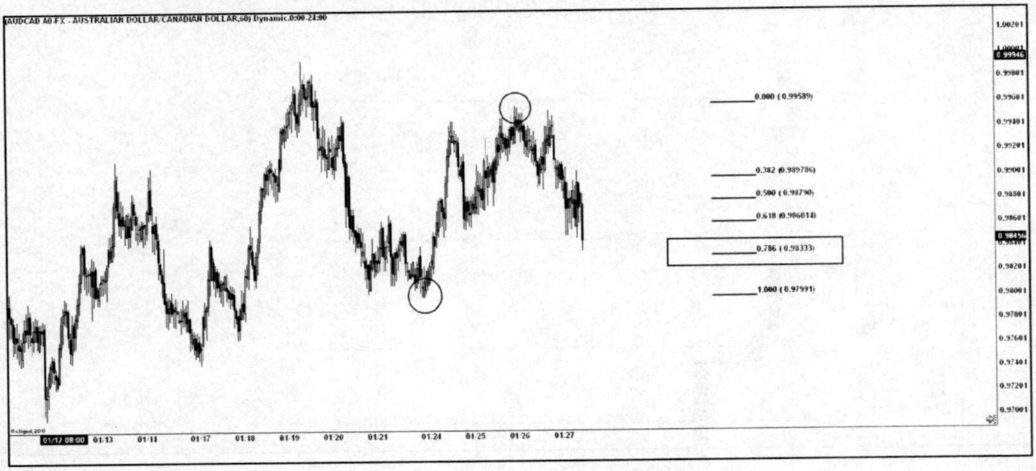

The image shows that the price action and the primary swing are moving up. This tells us immediately that we should only look for long positions.

Now let's zoom in to get a closer look at where to enter and exit the trade.

Figure 3.36 shows the long entry into the trade as the candlestick touches the 78.6% Fibonacci retracement level and then closes above it. The dotted line represents the exact entry level at the close of the candlestick.

Figure 3.36: exact entry

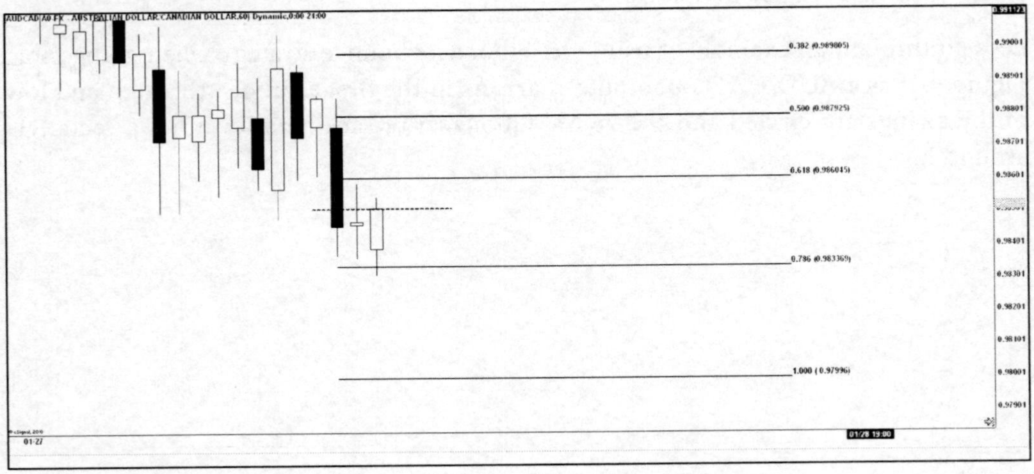

Figure 3.37 shows both the aggressive and conservative stop loss positions. The aggressive stop loss is placed 5 pips beneath the 78.6% Fibonacci retracement level, while the conservative stop loss is placed 5 pips beneath the 100% Fibonacci retracement level.

Figure 3.37: stop loss options

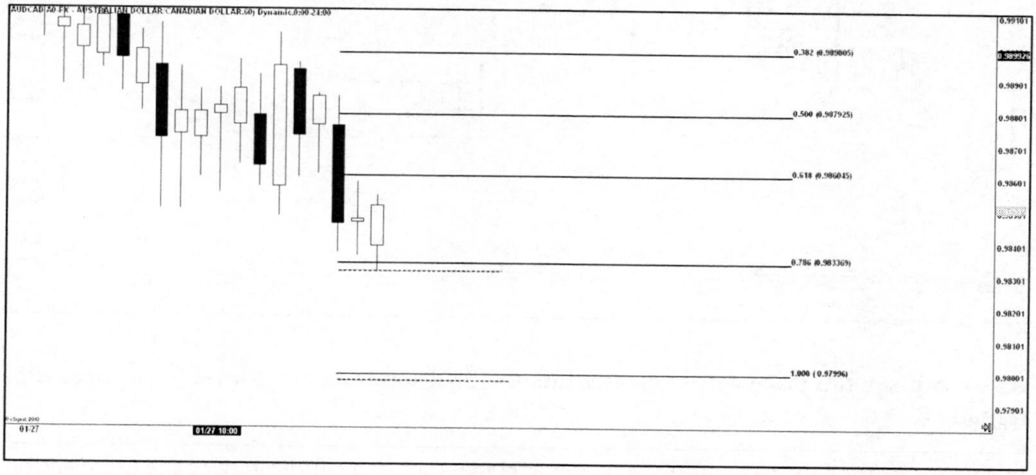

After we have determined our entry and stop loss positions, we go on to consider the target price. Figure 3.38 shows the target at the 38.2% Fibonacci retracement level, the level which will always be the target for this strategy.

Figure 3.38: target

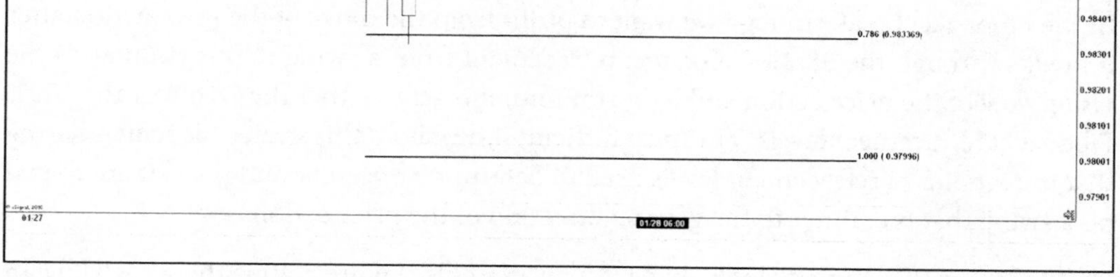

Now that we have determined our entry and exit levels, let's look at Figure 3.39 to see the continuation of the price action.

Figure 3.39: trade reaching target

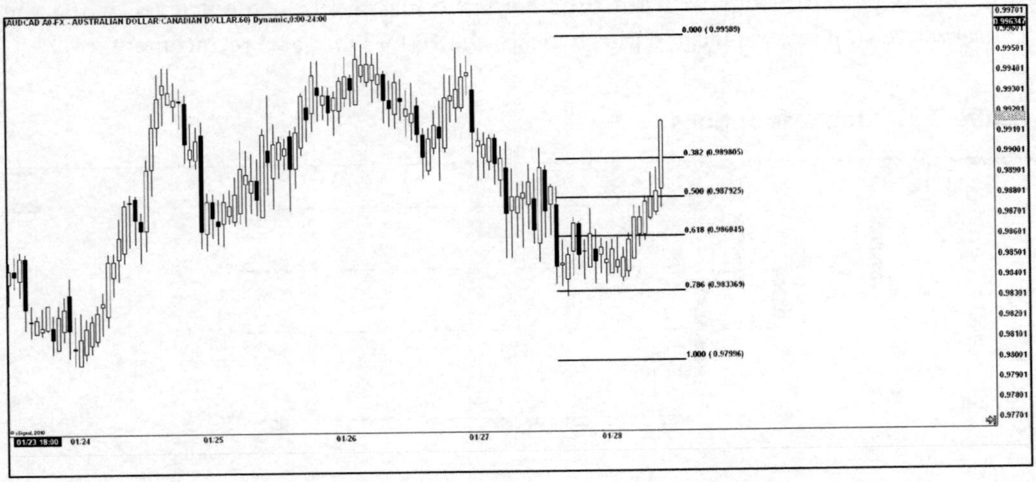

As we can see the price action clearly hits the 38.2% retracement level for a successful trade.

In summary, the Fibonacci bounce strategy triggers when a candlestick of the price action touches the 78.6% Fibonacci retracement level and closes on the relevant side – below it for a short trade and above it for a long trade. The two options in terms of the stop loss location are,

1. aggressively: 5 pips above the 78.6%% Fibonacci retracement level for short trades or 5 pips below it for long, or
2. conservatively: 5 pips above the 100% Fibonacci retracement level for short trades or 5 pips below it for long.

The target for this strategy is always the 38.2% Fibonacci retracement level.

2. Fibonacci break strategy

In the Fibonacci break strategy we want to profit from the move of the price action after it breaks through the 38.2% Fibonacci retracement from a swing that is counter to the *visual flow* of the price action and let it run until it reaches either the 78.6% or the 100% Fibonacci retracement levels. The most difficult thing about this strategy is remembering that the Fibonacci retracement levels used to determine the entry and the exit are drawn on a swing that is counter to the general direction of the price action.

Let's see what this strategy looks like with an example. Figure 3.40 is the EUR/USD 15 minute chart. The first image in this example is zoomed out a considerable distance to show the *visual flow* of the price action, which, in this scenario, is up. The high and low of our chosen downward swing are highlighted with circles.

Figure 3.40: initial example image

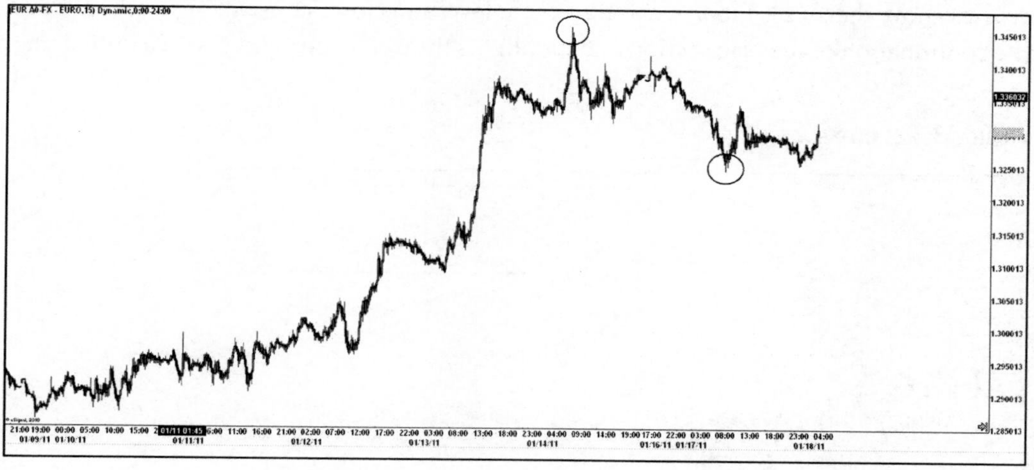

Now that we have seen the big picture, let's zoom in to focus on the downward swing and to see where the Fibonacci retracement levels fall. In Figure 3.41 the 38.2% Fibonacci retracement level has a rectangle around it. This is the level that will ultimately define our entry.

Figure 3.41: highlighted key Fibonacci level

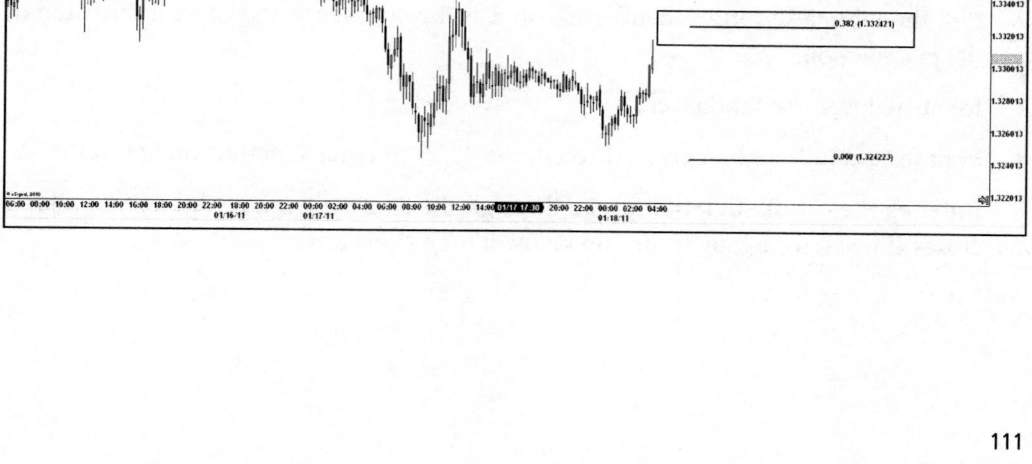

Entry

Although the swing that we are using to determine the Fibonacci retracement levels is down, we want to enter a long position because the dominant *visual flow* of the price action which led to the swing is up. The exact entry of the trade occurs when a candlestick crosses above the 38.2% Fibonacci retracement level and closes above it. Figure 3.42 shows the continuation of the price action and highlights the exact entry price with a dotted line.

Figure 3.42: entry

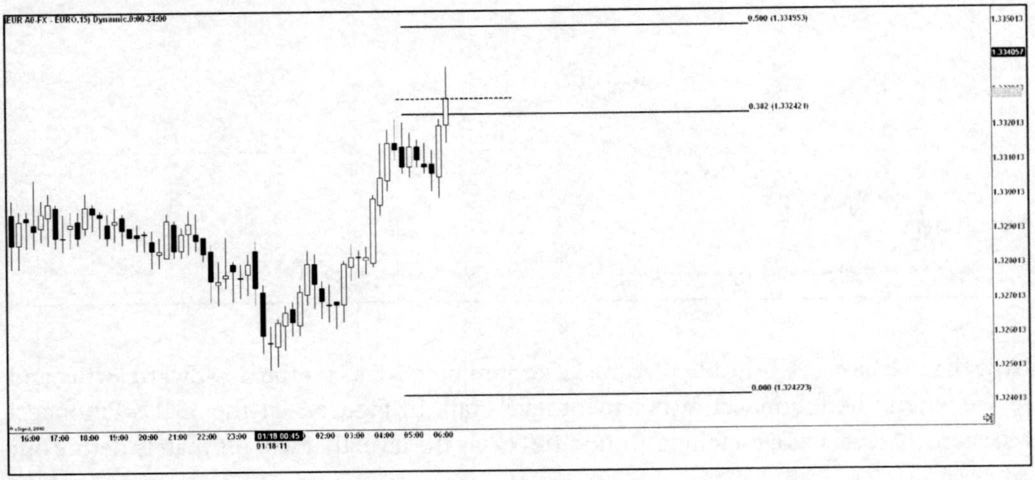

We enter the trade as soon as the candlestick closes up through the 38.2% Fibonacci level. This is the earliest indication that the downward swing, used to plot the Fibonacci retracement levels, has broken down and the dominant upward pressure of the price action is taking over again.

In summary, the five steps to entering the Fibonacci break trade are:

1. Confirm the general direction of the price action to determine the potential long or short position.
2. Plot the Fibonacci retracement levels on a swing counter to the general direction of the price action.
3. Identify the 38.2% Fibonacci level.
4. Wait for a candlestick to break through the 38.2% Fibonacci retracement level.
5. Enter as the candlestick that broke through the 38.2% Fibonacci retracement level closes above it for a long trade and below it for a short trade.

Exit – Risk

Now that we know our entry, we need to identify where our stop loss most be placed. Here we have two options.

The first option is to place the stop loss 5 pips below the 38.2% Fibonacci retracement level. This is a similar approach to the aggressive stop loss placement in the Fibonacci bounce strategy. The benefit of placing our stop loss here is that our reward to risk ratio is favourable – we are risking a small number of pips for the reward of a relatively large number of pips.

Figure 3.43 demonstrates the placement of the stop loss with a dotted line.

Figure 3.43: stop loss option one

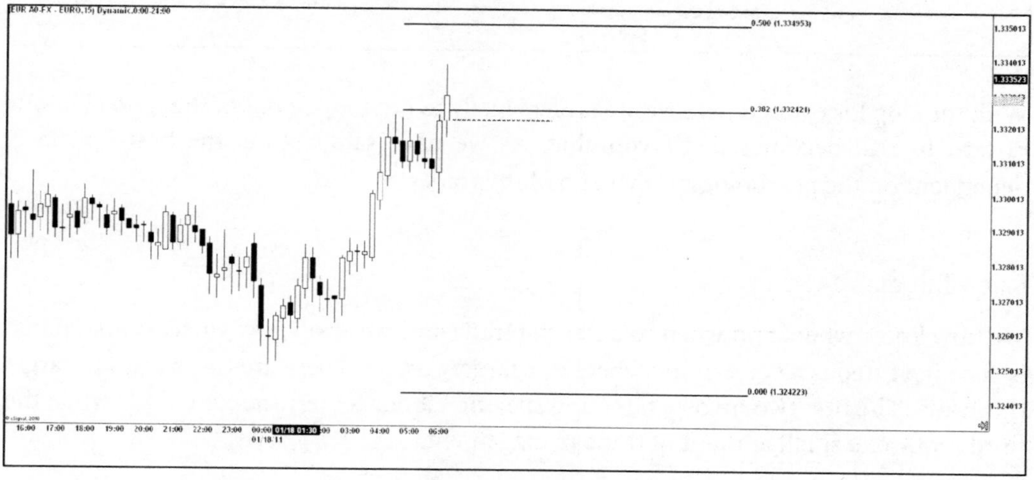

The second, more conservative, location for our stop loss is 5 pips below the low of the swing, which is the 0% Fibonacci level. Figure 3.44 shows this with a dotted line.

Figure 3.44: stop loss option two

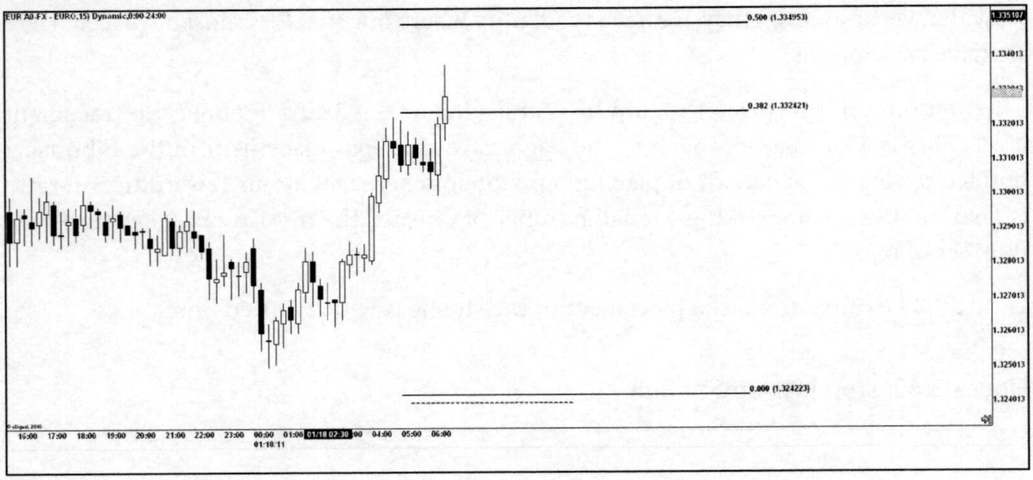

With the stop loss placed here we are far less likely to be stopped out of the trade, but our reward to risk becomes less favourable. As we have said before, the best option is dependent on the psychological makeup of the trader.

Exit – Target

We now know where and when to enter the trade and we also know where our stop loss is. The next step is to determine where our target will be. There are three ways to target this trade. The first two involve targeting specific Fibonacci retracement levels while the third requires a small amount of trade management.

The first way to target the trade is to take profit at the 78.6% level. We have discussed the importance of this level throughout this chapter and now understand that the price action is likely to have some form of reaction upon reaching this level. Again, this is due to the large number of institutional traders who consider this level significant, therefore causing the price action to respond to it. Taking profit here is considered the most conservative target of the three. Figure 3.45 shows this target with a dotted line.

Figure 3.45: target option one

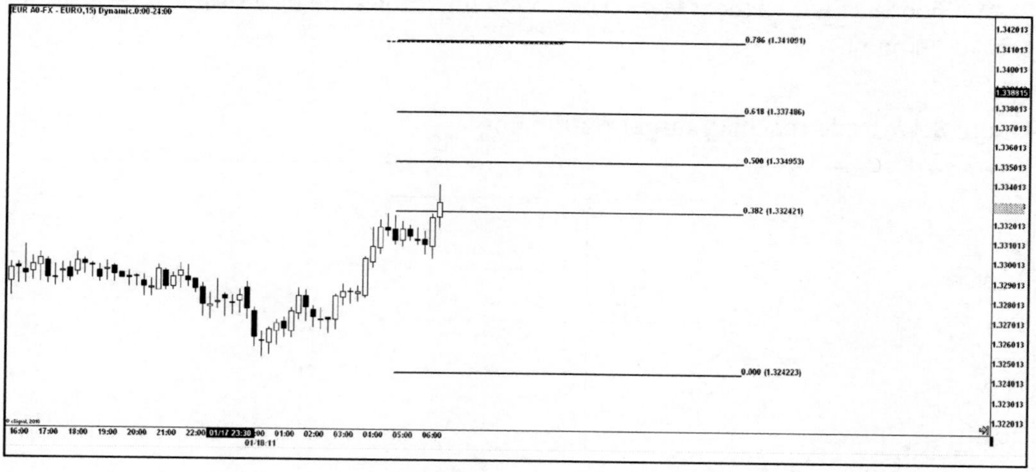

The second, and most aggressive, option for targeting this trade is to take profit at the 100% Fibonacci retracement level. This is more risky as it depends on the price action retracing all the way back to the high of the swing. When the price action hits the 100% level, we exit the trade for a profit. Figure 3.46 shows this target with a dotted line.

Figure 3.46: target option two

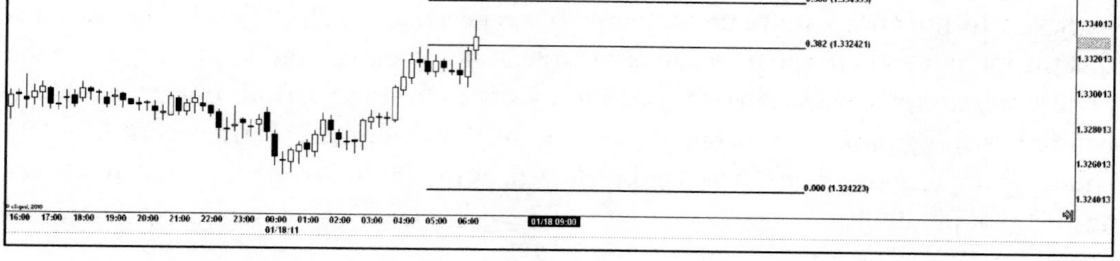

The third target option is a combination of the two. When the price action hits the 78.6% level, instead of taking profit, as in option one, or simply letting the trade continue, as in option two, we move our original stop loss to the breakeven point. This way, if the price action bounces off of the 78.6% Fibonacci retracement level, we are safe against a loss. If, however, the price action continues beyond the 78.6% Fibonacci retracement level, we can still benefit. Figure 3.47 shows the continuation of the price action as it reaches the 78.6% Fibonacci retracement level. The dotted line shows the new stop loss level at the breakeven point.

Figure 3.47: trade reaching target option one

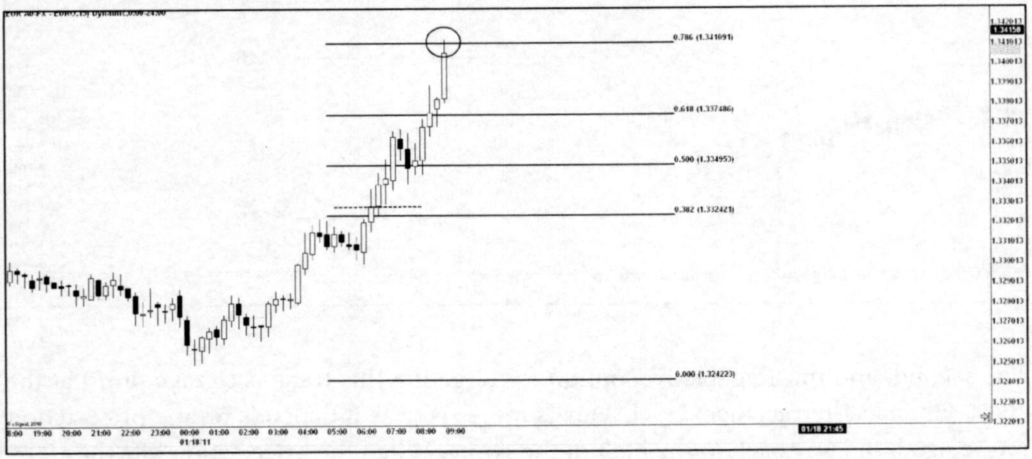

As it stands, if we had targeted this trade according to option one, we would have already taken profit as the price action has hit the 78.6% level. If we had targeted this trade according to option two as shown in Figure 3.47, we would still be trading with no risk, as our stop loss is now at breakeven and we are simply waiting for the price action to make its way up to the 100% Fibonacci retracement level. If we had decided to target this trade according to option three, then we would currently be running a winning position with our stop loss in its original place, either aggressive or conservative, while we wait for the price action to hit the 100% retracement level. Some may wonder why we would ever choose option three over option two. Ultimately, both options are targeting the same 100% level, so why not always move the stop loss to breakeven at the 78.6% level? The reason is that the foreign exchange market can be volatile. A news release could suddenly cause the price action to spike back down for just a few seconds to stop the trade out at breakeven, before returning back to its original push to the 100% Fibonacci retracement level. By choosing not to move the stop loss to breakeven, as in option three, we protect ourselves against that possibility.

Let's go through another example from start to finish. This time we will be looking at a short setup.

Figure 3.48 is a USD/JPY 60 minute chart.

Figure 3.48: example chart revealing visual flow of the price action

The first step in trading the Fibonacci break strategy is to decide the *visual flow* of the price action. Figure 3.48 shows the price action moving down. This tells us that we are looking for short setups. Next, we identify a swing that is counter to the *visual flow* of the price action to use to plot our Fibonacci retracement levels. The high and low of the upward swing to be used in this example are circled in Figure 3.49.

Figure 3.49: highs and lows used to determine Fibonacci retracement levels

The next step is to draw the Fibonacci retracement levels and mark the 38.2% level. Figure 3.50 zooms in on the price swing and highlights the 38.2% Fibonacci retracement level with a rectangle.

Figure 3.50: highlighted 38.2% Fibonacci retracement level

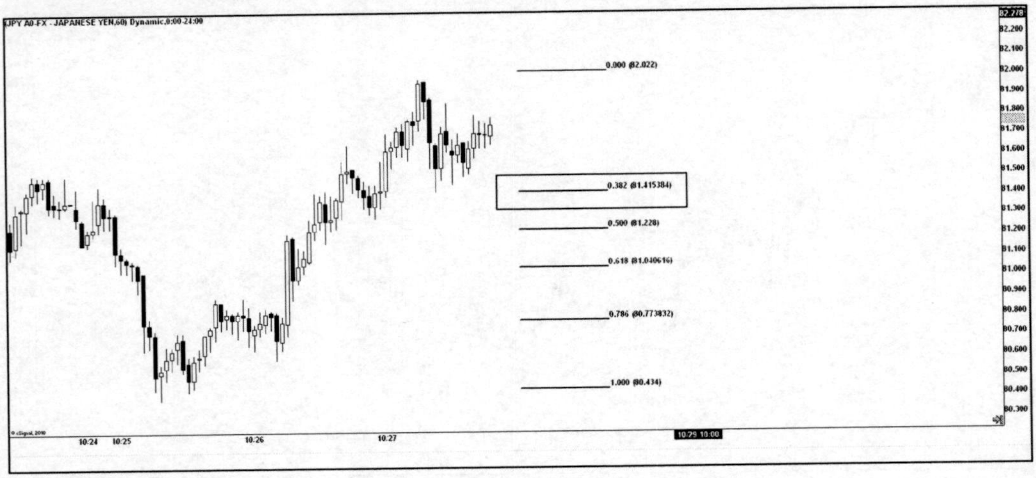

We are now waiting for the price action to go down to the 38.2% Fibonacci level. Once it gets there we need a candlestick to penetrate it and then close beneath it. Figure 3.51 shows the continuation of the price action and the entry into the trade. The image has been zoomed in to show the exact entry, represented by the dotted line.

Figure 3.51: entry

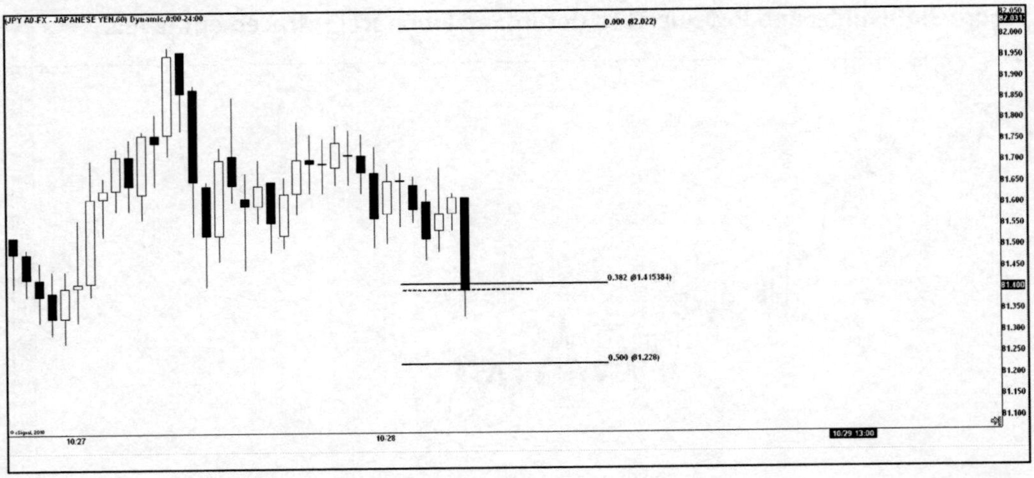

We can see that the entry took place as soon as the candlestick closed down through the 38.2% Fibonacci retracement level.

Now that the entry has been decided, we can look at each stop loss option. Figure 3.52 shows option one, the more aggressive option, with the stop located just 5 pips above the 38.2% Fibonacci retracement level.

Figure 3.52: stop loss option one

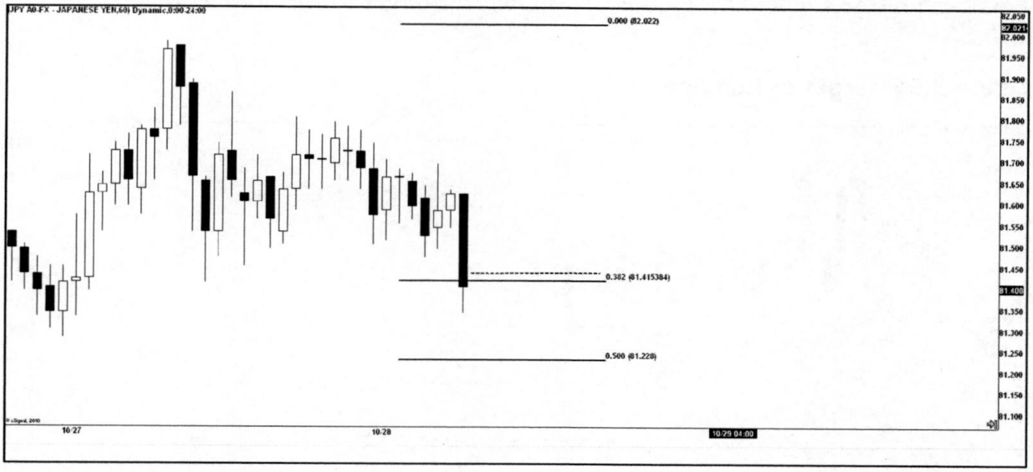

You can see just how tight this stop loss is. The price of the entry can also be a factor when determining your stop loss. If, for instance, the entry to the trade is very close to the 38.2% Fibonacci retracement level, you may want to go for the more conservative option. If, however, the close of the candlestick that breaks the 38.2% Fibonacci level is further away from the 38.2% Fibonacci level, you may feel more comfortable with the aggressive stop loss.

The second option for the stop loss is 5 pips above the peak of the swing, which is the 0% level. Figure 3.53 shows this with a dotted line.

Figure 3.53: stop loss option two

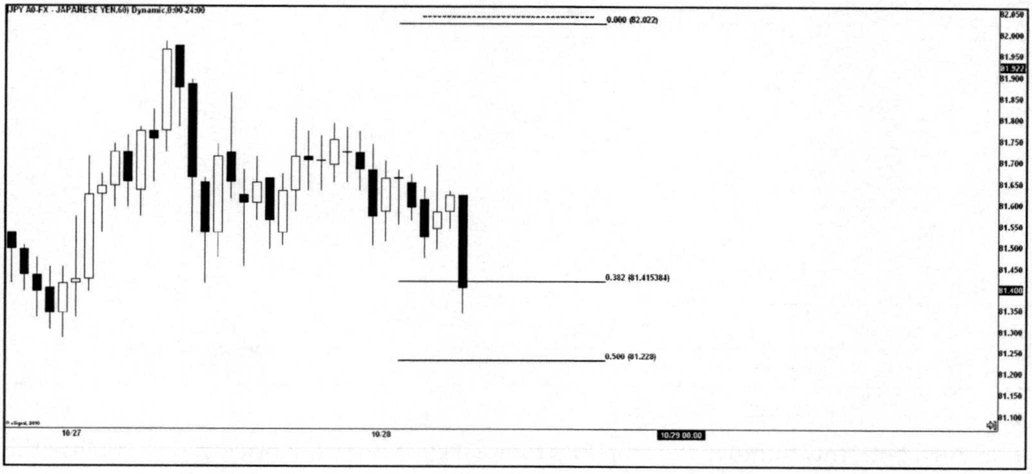

Next we look to target the trade. Let's start off with the conservative target of the 78.6% Fibonacci retracement level. Figure 3.54 shows this target with a dotted line.

Figure 3.54: target option one

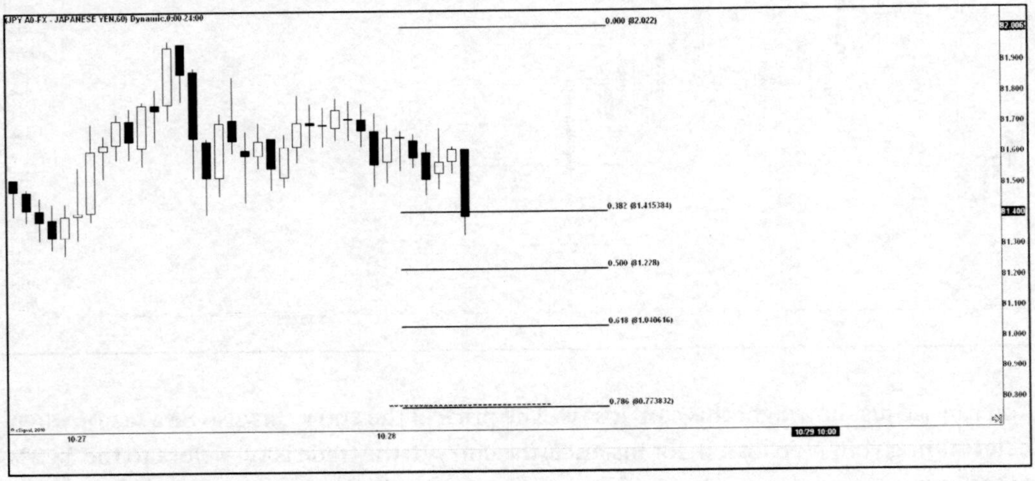

The second option, placing the target at the 100% Fibonacci retracement level, is highlighted in Figure 3.55. We consider this to be more aggressive as we are trying to capture almost double the number of pips.

Figure 3.55: target option two

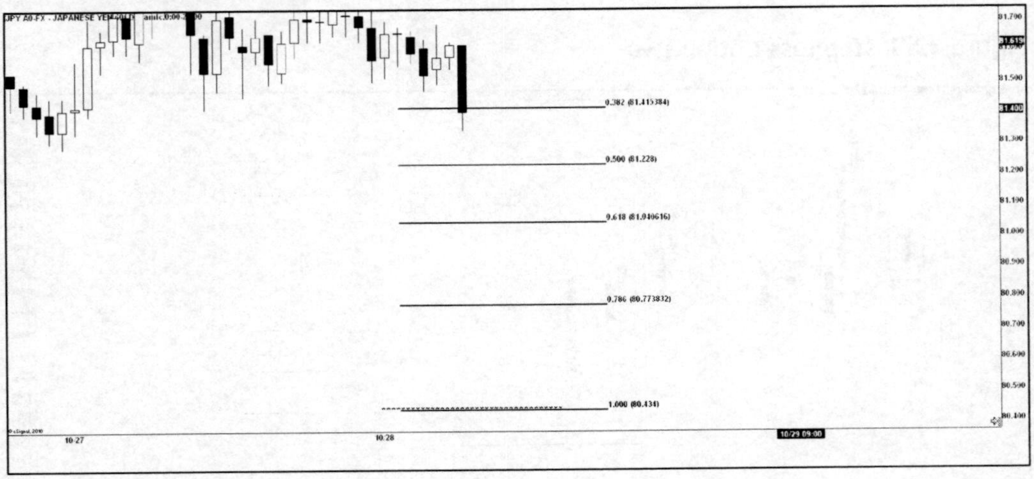

The third option is to move the stop loss to breakeven once the price action reaches the 78.6% level. Figure 3.56 shows the continuation of the price action, and the stop loss moved to the breakeven point with a dotted line.

Figure 3.56: trade reaching target one

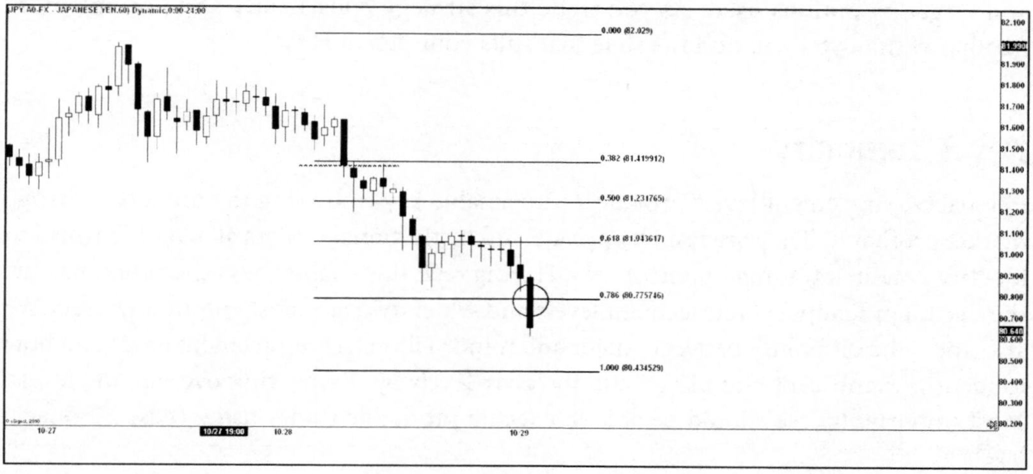

So, depending on our approach, let's see where we are so far. If we had targeted conservatively, we would now be out of the trade, having banked our profit once the price action hit the 78.6% level. If we were targeting the trade more aggressively we would currently be running a profitable position with our stop loss in the original location and would be waiting for the price action to hit our target at the 100% Fibonacci retracement level. If we decided to use the breakeven stop loss target option as shown in Figure 3.56, we would currently be running a profitable position with no risk of losing on the trade.

Given that there are two options for stop loss placement, and three different ways to target this style of trade, there are several possible combinations. Instead of going through each one, let's take a look at the end result of the trade.

Figure 3.57: trade reaching target two

The trade has now come to a profitable close regardless of the combination of stop loss and targeting options used. As you trade this strategy consistently and become more familiar with it, you will find the style that suits your personality.

Key 3 Summary

Fibonacci retracement levels provide an invaluable key to trading the foreign exchange market profitably. They are used by private and institutional traders all over the world to identify potential trading opportunities. Having read this chapter, you should now know the five main Fibonacci retracement levels and which two are most commonly used. We also know the difference between major and minor Fibonacci retracement levels and how to identify significant end of day and intraday levels by discovering overlapping levels. Most importantly, we should be able to execute profitable trades using these Fibonacci levels.

KEY 4
SYMMETRICAL TRIANGLES

Like the three keys that we have already discussed, symmetrical triangles can be used to identify highly successful trading opportunities based on specific patterns in the price action.

THE THEORY

Primary strength: clear message – indecision

A symmetrical triangle can be like a family get together. Once the family comes together, someone needs to decide what everyone should do. At some point, someone is likely to suggest going out for dinner. Normally everyone agrees to a suggestion like this. After all, who doesn't like going out to eat? The question that arises next, however, is not so easy to answer. It is the question of where the group should go to eat. At this point, no one is willing to give a straight answer. Everyone knows exactly where they want to go but are trying to be polite and easy-going, no one wants to step up and take charge. At first this is not a problem, as everyone is just happy to see each other and catch up on old business. Not only that, they are happy to relax for a few minutes after travelling to the meeting place. After a while, however, tensions begin to develop. Everyone starts getting hungry until eventually someone speaks up and makes the decision. Now, because everyone is hungry and tired of sitting around, they all make a strong, decisive move to the designated restaurant.

This is similar to the message a symmetrical triangle gives. The price action gets to a point where it settles down and begins to consolidate. The buyers are unwilling to make the decision to push the price action up. The sellers are equally unwilling to make their move and push the price action down. This is signified by the price action forming lower peaks and higher troughs, thus creating a symmetrical triangle. Once the frustration of the price action gets too strong, however, a decisive move is made by either the buyers or the sellers. Once this decision is made, everyone follows and the market makes a very strong, decisive move. As traders watching these events unfold, it is impossible to know which "restaurant" the price action will choose, either up or down, but we do know which move we would be happy to trade – the move that is in the direction of the trend that led into the symmetrical triangle.

Let's take a look at the characteristics of the symmetrical triangle to get a better understanding of how it is formed and what it looks like.

Symmetrical triangle characteristics

The two main characteristics of symmetrical triangles are:

1. Converging trend lines caused by the price action forming lower peaks and higher troughs.
2. Consolidating price action caused by the converging trend lines.

Figure 4.1 shows the price action of a USD/JPY 15 minute chart.

Figure 4.1: price action for example of a symmetrical triangle

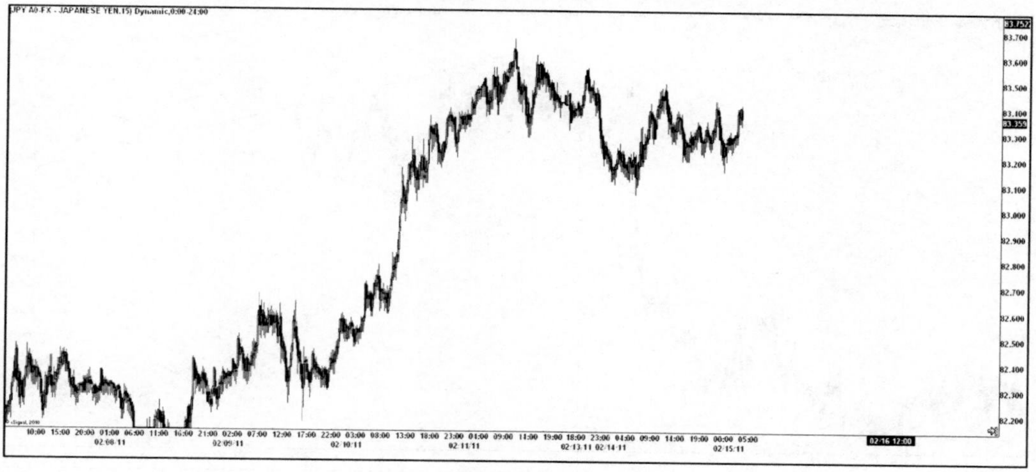

First, we identify that the recent peaks of the price action are getting lower. Figure 4.2 connects these lowering peaks with a trend line.

Figure 4.2: partial symmetrical triangle

Second, we identify that the recent troughs of the price action are getting higher. Figure 4.3 connects the troughs with another trend line. By drawing these two trend lines, a symmetrical triangle has been formed.

Figure 4.3: example of a symmetrical triangle

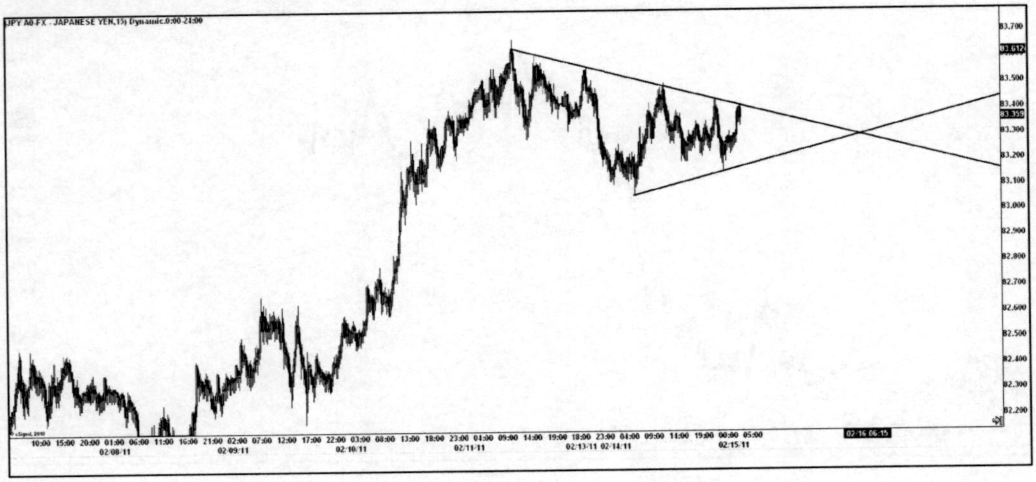

Image 4.3 also shows how the price action consolidates and tightens as it makes its way through the triangle. As the price action that preceded the formation of the triangle was moving up, we can anticipate that the eventual break out of this triangle will also be up.

Let's identify another symmetrical triangle. Figure 4.4 is another example from a USD/JPY 15 minute chart. This time the price action is trending down.

Figure 4.4: price action for example of a symmetrical triangle

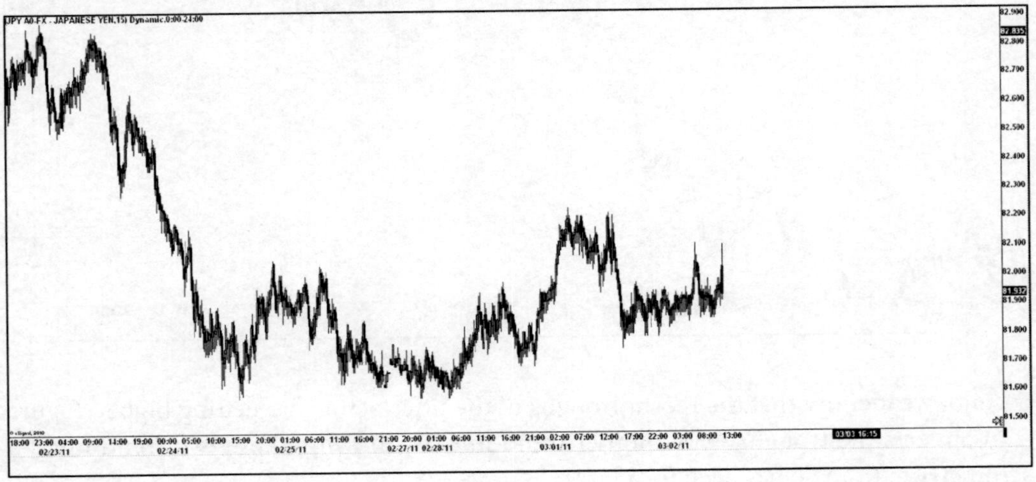

We notice that the recent peaks are getting lower, while the recent troughs are getting higher. In Figure 4.5 one trend line connects the peaks and another trend line connects the troughs.

Figure 4.5: symmetrical triangle

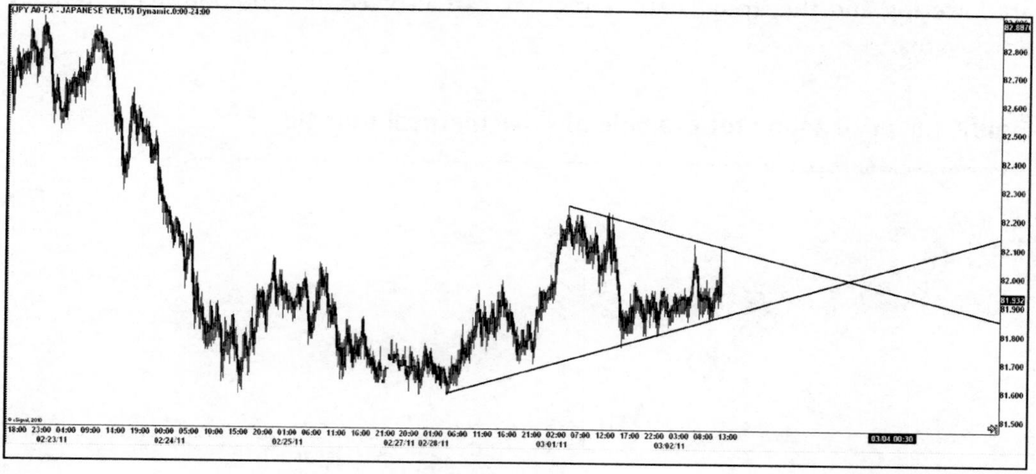

Now we can see the symmetrical triangle clearly. The preceding price action was in a downward trend, so we can anticipate a breakout through the bottom line of this triangle.

Symmetrical triangles are made up of two converging trend lines. The price action within the triangle consolidates forming a peak which represents a period of indecision. Eventually the price action is likely to make a decisive breakout of the triangle in the direction of the trend that led into the formation of the symmetrical triangle. Symmetrical triangles do not actually need to be truly symmetrical. They must simply be made up of two converging trend lines as opposed to a single trend line converging with a horizontal line of support or resistance. The convergence of a trend line and a horizontal line forms a different chart pattern with its own set of rules (which I do not cover in this book).

Symmetrical triangle types

There are two types of symmetrical triangles. The first is the major symmetrical triangle and the second is the minor symmetrical triangle. Like major and minor Fibonacci retracement levels, the difference is based on the time frame of the symmetrical triangles.

Major symmetrical triangles

Major symmetrical triangles are found on either daily or 4 hour charts. These triangles are generally used by end of day traders to identify market entry and exits points, or by intraday traders to determine the direction in which to place shorter term positions.

Figure 4.6 is the EUR/AUD daily chart. From this image we can see that the current peaks are lowering and the troughs are rising. We can also see that the dominant trend is downwards.

Figure 4.6: price action for example of a symmetrical triangle

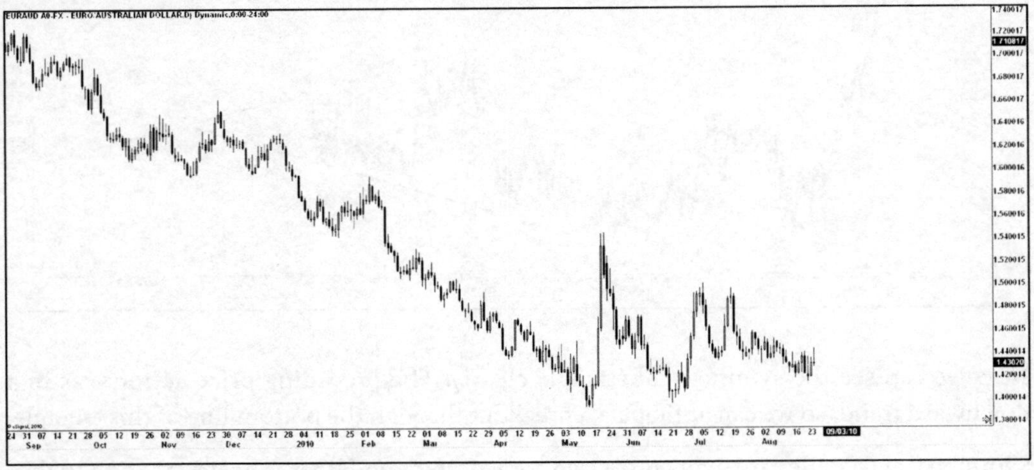

Image 4.7 shows the symmetrical triangle formed by the converging trend lines. Before looking at it, try and imagine the symmetrical triangle on the bare price action on Figure 4.6. It is important to develop the skill of spotting this pattern.

Figure 4.7: symmetrical triangle

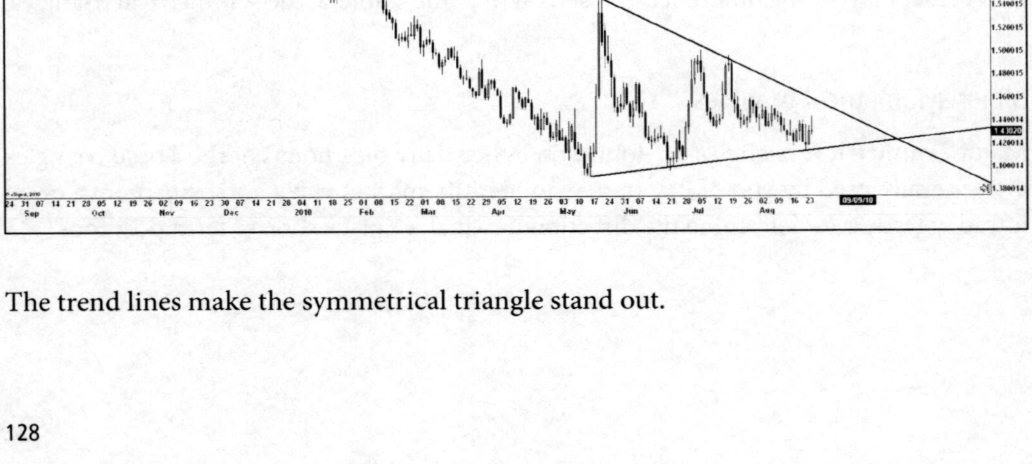

The trend lines make the symmetrical triangle stand out.

There is an interesting story behind this chart. Prior to the formation of this symmetrical triangle, the EUR/AUD currency pair had been in a very strong, downward trend for 14 months. This means that the Euro had been weakening against the Australian dollar for over a year. The large spike shown in Figure 4.7 was the result of a new taxation law being announced in Australia that would have a dramatic impact on some of its largest companies. This caused a sudden weakness in the Australian dollar, including against the Euro. The triangle shows the struggle and the indecision that followed for the next few months. Would the dominant downward trend take control again, pushing the price back down, or would the buyers in the market take advantage of the kick-start given by the new fundamental information and push the price upwards? Figure 4.8 has been zoomed in to show the continuation of the price action.

Figure 4.8: price breaking out of a symmetrical triangle in the direction of the trend

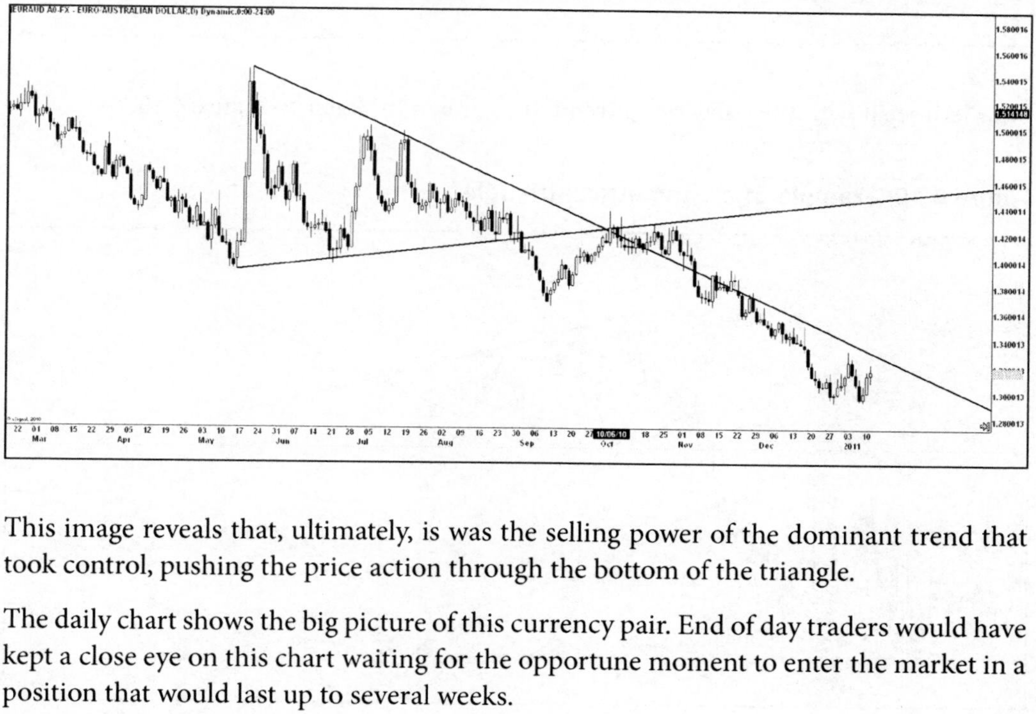

This image reveals that, ultimately, is was the selling power of the dominant trend that took control, pushing the price action through the bottom of the triangle.

The daily chart shows the big picture of this currency pair. End of day traders would have kept a close eye on this chart waiting for the opportune moment to enter the market in a position that would last up to several weeks.

Let's look at another example of a major symmetrical triangle. Figure 4.9 is the GBP/USD 4 hour chart. A symmetrical triangle has formed after a strong upward push which lasted for over a month. Visualise it with nothing but the price action.

Figure 4.9: price action for symmetrical triangle example

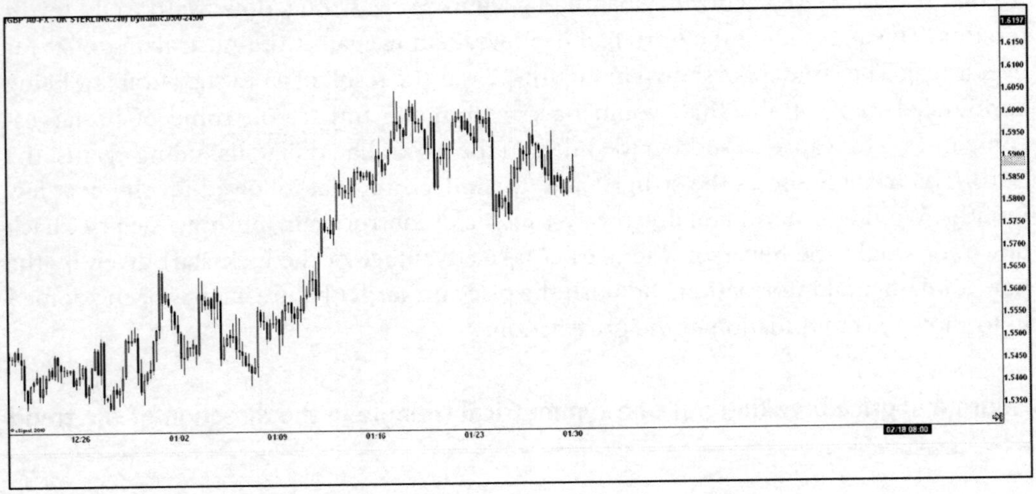

Now let's see it with the converging trend lines drawn in. Refer to Figure 4.10.

Figure 4.10: example of a symmetrical triangle

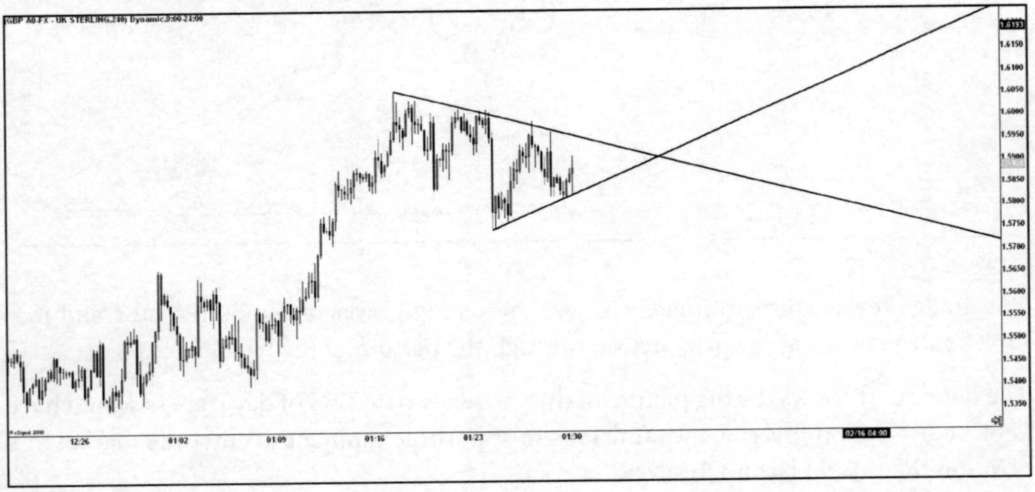

Again, end of day traders would be watching this chart closely, waiting for an opportunity to enter a trade once the price action has broken out of the symmetrical triangle. As trend traders, we would only enter the trade if the price action broke through the upper trend line, as that is the move which is consistent with the trend. Although intraday traders do not usually enter trades using the 4 hour chart, the majority of them would still be looking at this symmetrical triangle for an indication of where the price action will be trading in the short to medium term.

If the price action breaks out of the upper trend line, the intraday trader would be looking for potential long trading opportunities on the 1 hour and 15 minute charts. If the price action breaks out of the bottom of the triangle, the intraday trader would be looking for possible short trading opportunities. You could argue that the symmetrical triangle on the 4 hour chart would be the same as the symmetrical triangle on the 1 hour chart. This is true in some cases, but not always. The trader who is analysing the 1 hour chart may use different peaks and troughs to draw the converging trend lines. This would make the geometry of the symmetrical triangles slightly different and, in turn, would change the entry, stop loss and target prices.

To repeat, major symmetrical triangles are found on daily and 4 hour time frames. They are used primarily by end of day traders looking to identify trading opportunities they hope to hold for several weeks. Occasionally, the intraday trader may refer to the 4 hour chart, which is a close relation to the intraday charts, for clarification on short to medium term trends.

Minor symmetrical triangles

Whereas major symmetrical triangles are located on daily and 4 hour charts, minor symmetrical triangles are only drawn on 1 hour and 15 minute charts.

Figure 4.11 is a minor symmetrical triangle found on a USD/CHF 60 minute chart.

Figure 4.11: price action for symmetrical triangle example

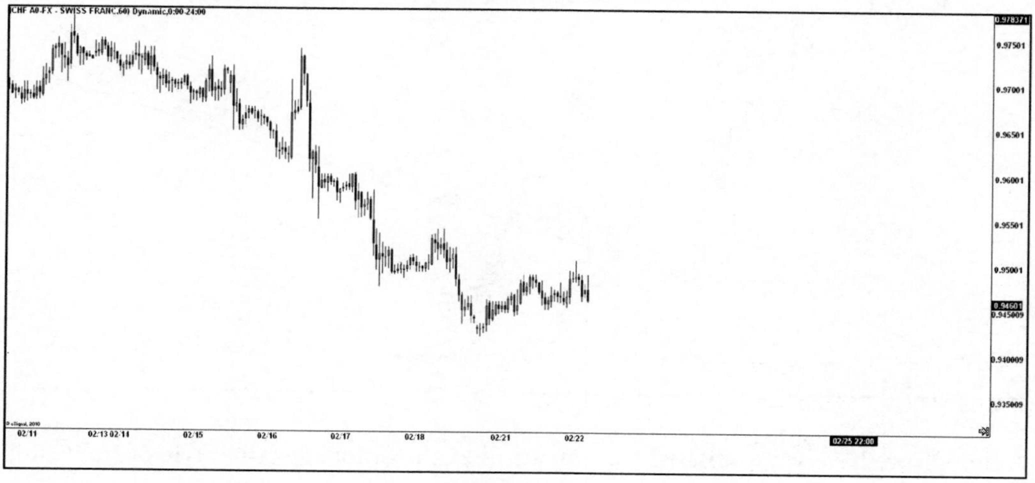

Identify the symmetrical triangle on the bare price action and then confirm it by looking at Figure 4.12.

Figure 4.12: example of a symmetrical triangle

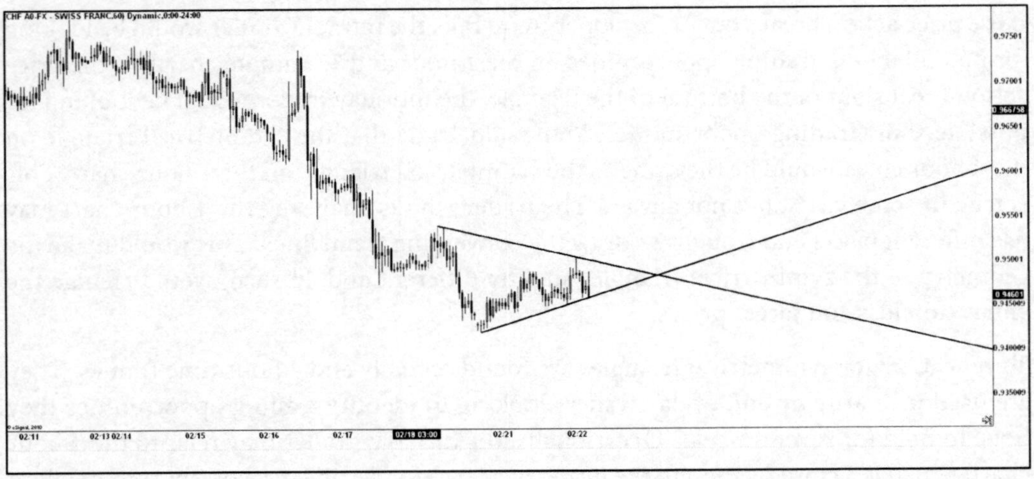

We can see here that the price action is tightening up as it consolidates and travels towards the apex of the symmetrical triangle. At this point, the intraday trader would be looking for an efficient entry point once the price action breaks out of the bottom of the symmetrical triangle. Figure 4.13 shows the continuation of the price action as the indecision comes to an end and the breakout occurs.

Figure 4.13: price action breaking out of the symmetrical triangle

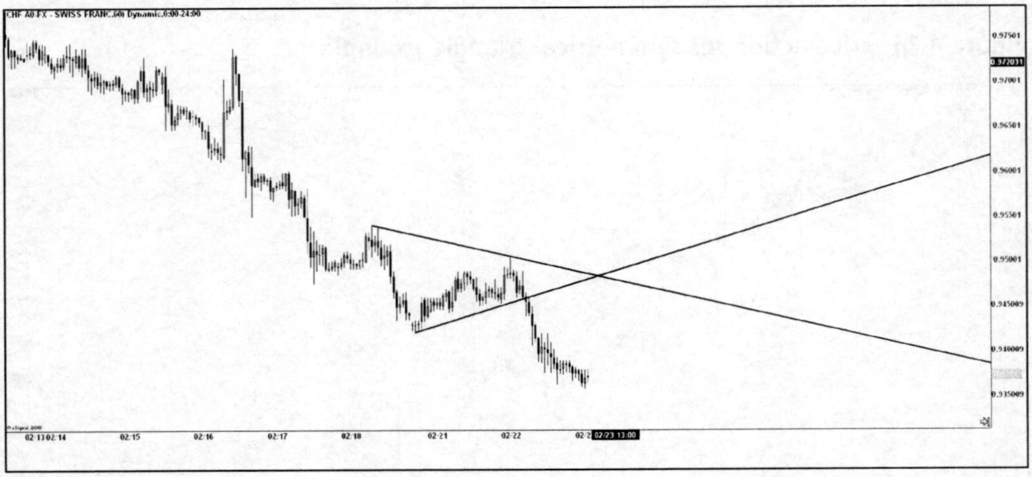

Although we have yet to discuss the entry and exit positions for this style of trade, it is worth noting that the price action breaks out of the symmetrical triangle and reaches its target in the same day. This is exactly what the intraday trader is looking for.

Let's look at another example of a minor symmetrical triangle. Figure 4.14 shows a GBP/USD 15 minute chart. This time the price action is trending up.

Figure 4.14: price action for symmetrical triangle example

Identify the symmetrical triangle on the bare price action and then confirm it by looking at Figure 4.15.

Figure 4.15: symmetrical triangle

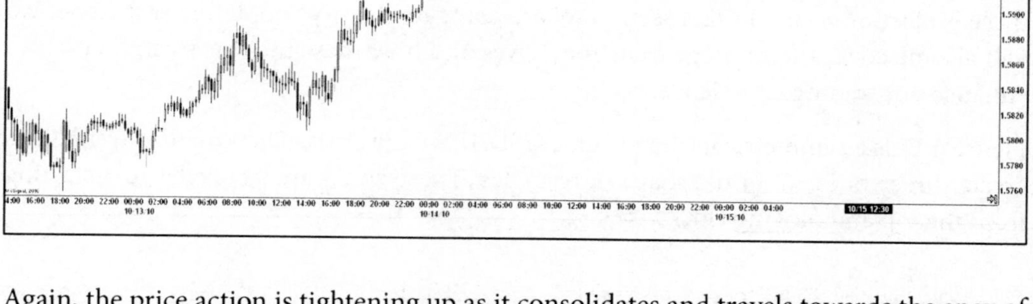

Again, the price action is tightening up as it consolidates and travels towards the apex of the symmetrical triangle. At this point, the intraday trader would be looking for an efficient entry point once the price action breaks through the top of the triangle. Figure

4.16 shows the continuation of the price action as the indecision comes to an end and the breakout occurs.

Figure 4.16: price action breaking out of the symmetrical triangle

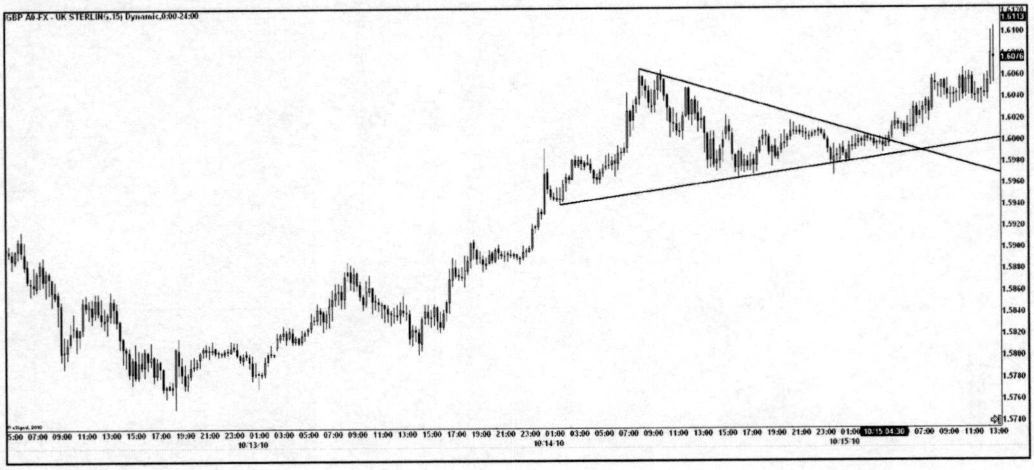

As in the last example, the price action broke out of the triangle in the direction of the original trend and reached its target in the same day.

Minor symmetrical triangles are found on 1 hour and 15 minute charts. They are the result of lowering peaks and rising troughs which form a triangular pattern as the price action consolidates. These triangles are used by intraday traders to determine entry and exit positions in the foreign exchange market.

Symmetrical triangle zone projection

The extended converging trend lines that form a symmetrical triangle intersect to create three projecting zones. In this section we are going to identify and define each zone. We will also discover the message each zone gives and how these messages can be used to enhance our trading experience.

Figure 4.17 is a symmetrical triangle on a USD/JPY daily chart. The extended trend lines create three zones, all in the shape of triangles. These zones are labelled 1 to 3 starting from the top and moving clockwise.

Figure 4.17: labelled zones created by the projected lines of the symmetrical triangle

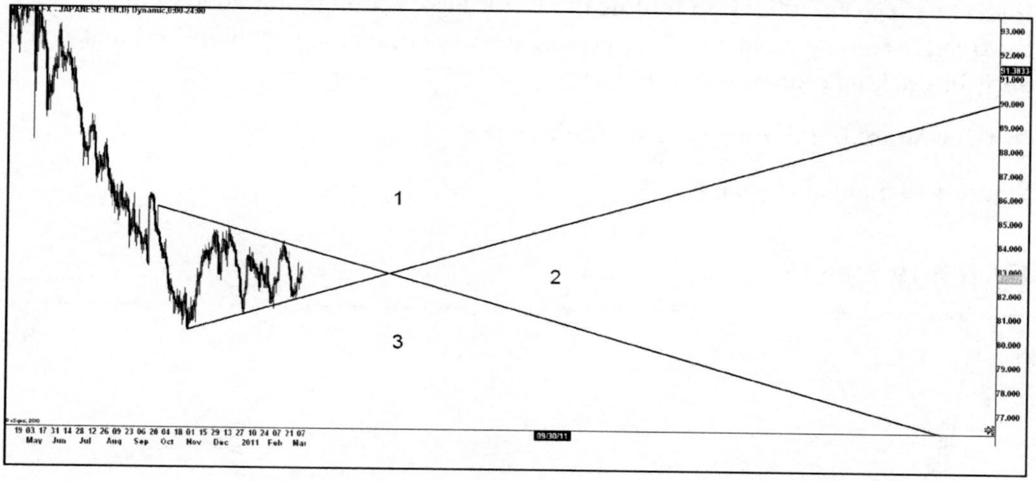

Now that the zones are labelled, we can define their purpose. The roles of zones 1 and 3 are dependant on the trend that precedes the symmetrical triangle. The role of zone 2 never changes.

Let's start by defining these zones according to the downward trend of USD/JPY daily chart. First we must identify the trend of the price action before the occurrence of the symmetrical triangle. Figure 4.18 makes it clear that the trend was down. Once we know the trend, we can define each zone. We will start with zone 1. Refer to figure 4.18.

Figure 4.18: zone 1

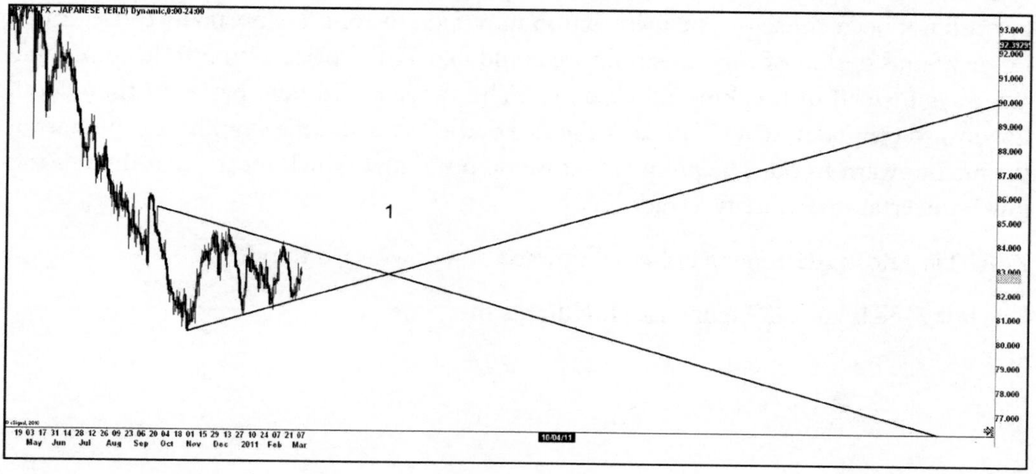

Zone 1 represents the breakdown of the triangle, contrary to the overall trend. As trend traders we have no interest in trading in zone 1. Price action in this zone would indicate the trend is coming to an end. This creates an environment of instability and makes the decision-making process very difficult.

In a downward trend, zone 1 is a no-trade zone.

Figure 4.19 highlights zone 2.

Figure 4.19: zone 2

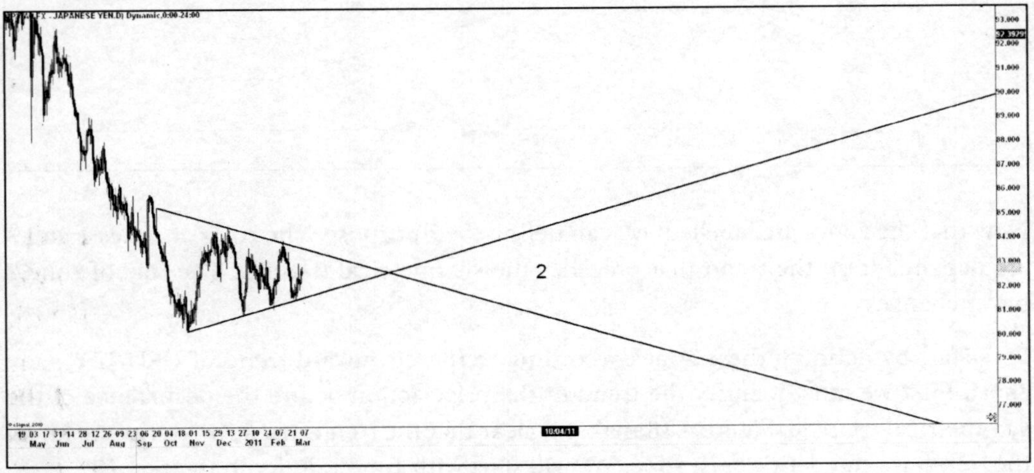

Zone 2 represents a continuation of the indecision which originally caused the symmetrical triangle. (Continuing the analogy from earlier in the chapter, a restaurant has still not been chosen.) The price action moving into zone 2 is normally the start of a range bound period of time meaning we could expect the price action to keep moving sideways instead of breaking up or down. The range could be a pause in the overall downward trend before it resumes or the end of the trend and the support for the start of the next upward trend. The point is that we do not know, which means that there is too much uncertainty to justify a trade.

Zone 2 is a no-trade zone in either an upward or a downward trend.

The last zone is zone 3. Figure 4.20 highlights this zone.

Figure 4.20: zone 3

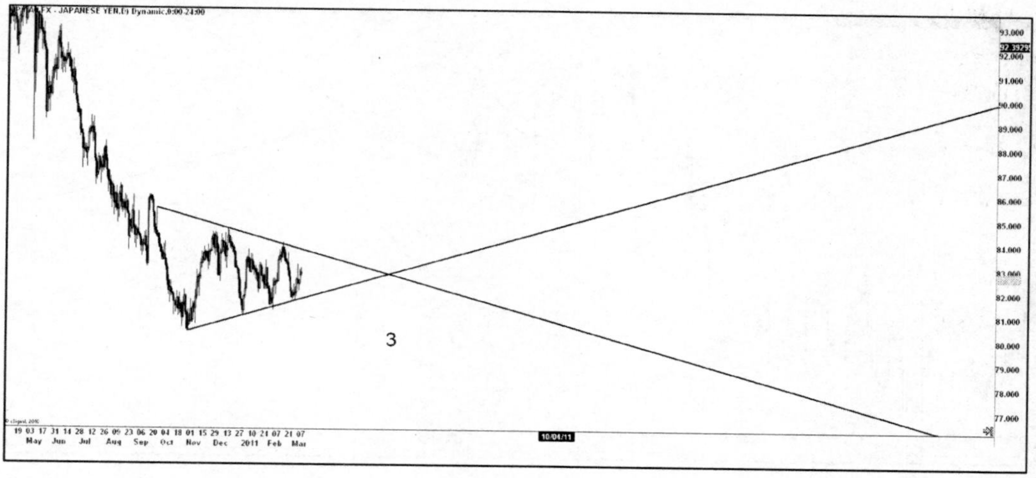

When the price action enters zone 3, we would consider potential short trades. This is because zone 3 is consistent with the overall downward trend. Once the price action enters this zone, we know that the symmetrical triangle that formed was nothing more than a pause in the overall trend.

In a downward trend, zone 3 is the only zone in which to look for potential trades. This is not to say, however, that we enter a short position as soon as the price action enters zone 3. Our entry needs to be much more specific than that. The foreign exchange market can be very volatile and there are many false breakouts. We will define the exact entry requirements later in this chapter when we cover the symmetrical triangle break strategy.

In Figure 4.21, a symmetrical triangle has formed at the end of an upward trend on a GBP/USD 4 hour chart. This image shows how the roles of zones 1 and 3 are reversed when the price action is trending up.

Figure 4.21: zones 1, 2 and 3 in an uptrend

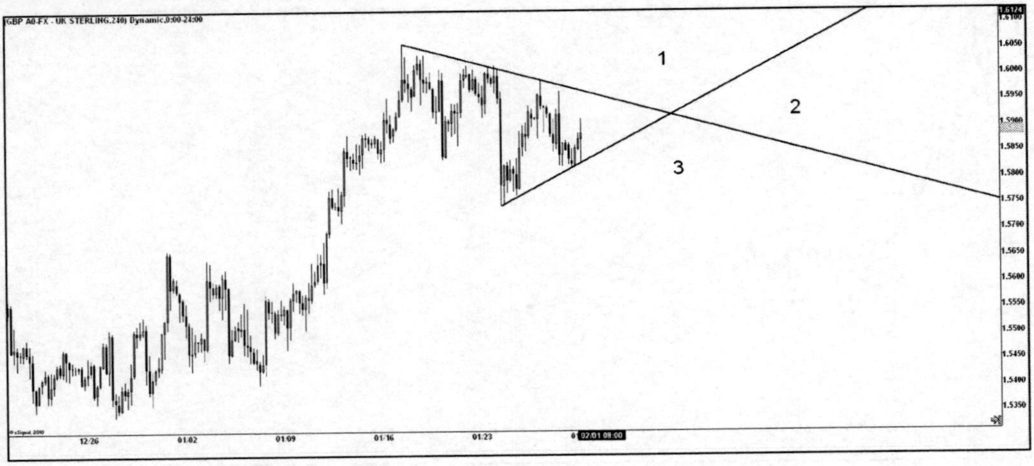

It is clear from Figure 4.21 that zone 1 is now the zone that we can trade in and zone 3 is a no-trade zone. This is because zone 1 is consistent with the upward trend leading into the symmetrical triangle, while zone 3 indicates a weakening upward trend and possibly the beginning of a new downward trend. Zone 2 keeps its usual role as the zone of indecision, representing the beginning of a range bound period before the continuation of the upward trend or the resistance that ultimately triggers a new downward trend.

When trading symmetrical triangles we must refrain from entering trades in zones 2 and 3 when going long and in zones 2 and 1 when going short. The zone that is consistent with the trend that precedes the symmetrical triangle is the only safe zone in which to identify trading opportunities. In an upward trend, the safe zone is 1 and in a downward trend the safe zone is 3.

ENTRY AND EXIT STRATEGIES

We began this chapter by defining not only what makes a symmetrical triangle, but also what the message the symmetrical triangle gives. We then went on to break down the characteristics of a symmetrical triangle and demonstrate the process of clearly identifying and drawing it on our charts. From there, we explored major and minor symmetrical triangles and saw how projecting the trend lines which formed our symmetrical triangles created zones.

It is now time to look at two symmetrical triangle trading strategies:

1. Symmetrical triangle bounce strategy
2. Symmetrical triangle break strategy

Both strategies clearly define the entry, risk exit and target exit of the trade.

1. Symmetrical triangle bounce strategy

Symmetrical triangles are made up of two converging trend lines. One of the trend lines runs in the direction of the dominant trend, while the other runs counter to it. In the symmetrical triangle bounce strategy, we trade the price action's bounce off the trend line of the triangle which is in agreement with the trend that preceded the formation of the symmetrical triangle. As with all of the strategies that we have looked at so far, this is a continuation strategy which we trade with the trend.

Entry

Figure 4.22 is a GBP/USD 60 minute chart. This is our example chart for the symmetrical triangle bounce strategy.

Figure 4.22: symmetrical triangle for trade example

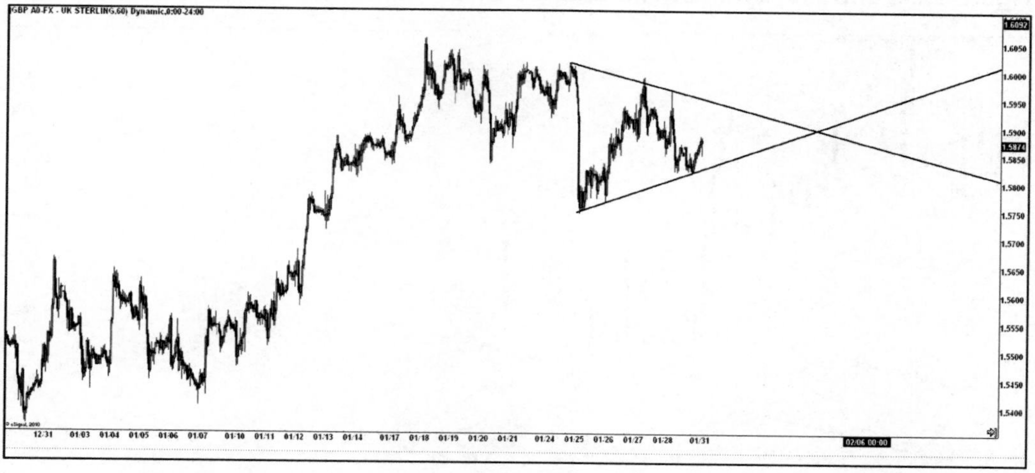

The first thing that we notice is the upward push of the price action leading into the symmetrical triangle. This tells us that we should look for a long opportunity. As the trend is up, we would expect a bounce to occur off the bottom trend line of the triangle, as this trend line is consistent with the trend. Figure 4.23 has been zoomed in so that we can better look at the setup we are waiting for.

Figure 4.23: zoomed symmetrical triangle

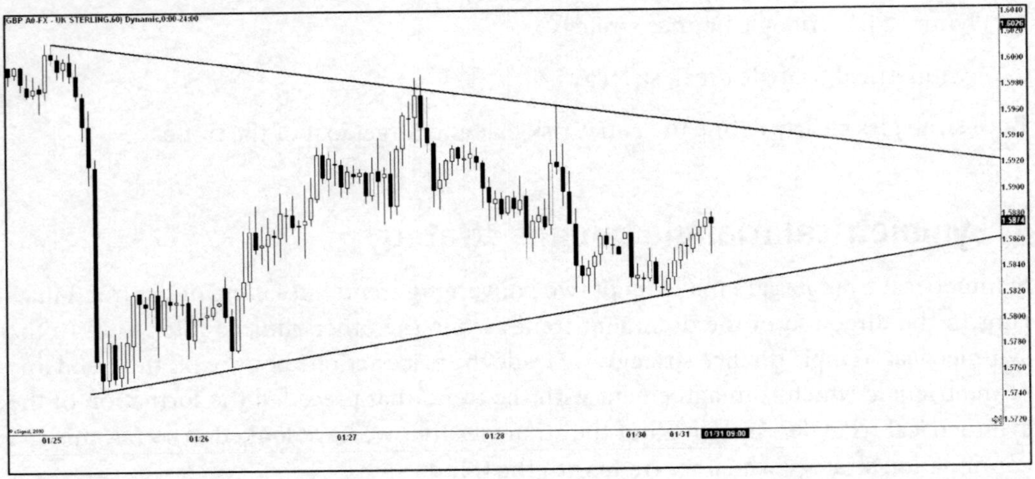

The entry for this strategy is defined by a candlestick touching the significant trend line of the symmetrical triangle, in this case the bottom line as the overall trend is up, and closing above this line, inside the triangle. We enter the trade immediately on the close of this candle. Figure 4.24 has been zoomed in further to show the continuation of this chart and the exact entry point for the trade.

Figure 4.24: entry for symmetrical triangle bounce strategy

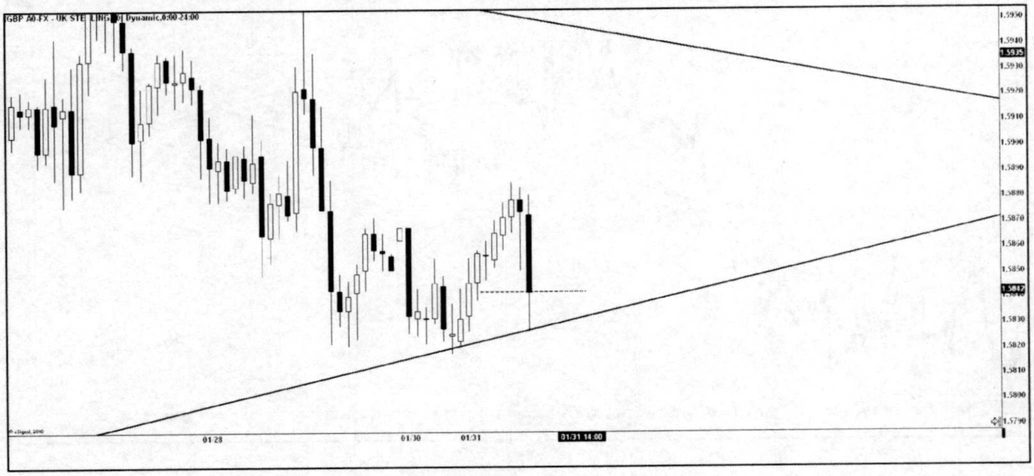

The dotted line indicates the entry point. Notice how the candlestick retraces to the bottom trend line, touches it and then closes above it. If the wick of the candlestick had gone straight through the trend line but still closed above it, we would also enter the trade.

If, however, the candlestick had gone through the trend line and closed below it, the trade would be off as this may signal the breakdown of the triangle.

The reason we did not use the previous touch on the bottom trend line of the triangle for our entry is because, at that point, the triangle did not exist. It was, in fact, that small swing low that created the trend line that formed the triangle.

In summary, the four steps of entering the symmetrical triangle bounce strategy are:

1. Identify the symmetrical triangle and draw the two converging trend lines to establish the triangle and create the projection zones.
2. Confirm the direction of the price action preceding the formation of the symmetrical triangle and use this information to determine whether to look for long or short positions and which trend line the price action needs to touch. If going long, the candlestick must touch the bottom trend line. If going short, it must touch the top.
3. Wait for a candlestick to touch the significant trend line of the symmetrical triangle.
4. Enter as soon as a candlestick closes on the appropriate side of the trend line that it touched. If going long, the candlestick must close above the bottom trend line of the triangle. If going short it must close below the top trend line.

Exit – Risk

Now that we know the entry point, we can define the stop loss. The stop loss is placed 5 pips below the low of the previous touch on the bottom trend line. If we were going short it would be placed 5 pips above the high of the previous touch on the top trend line. Figure 4.25 shows the position of the stop loss with a dotted line.

Figure 4.25: stop loss placement

This is a fairly safe place for the stop loss as it is beneath the previous swing low and the trend line. An alternative would be to place the stop loss 5 pips below the price action's touch of the trend line which was used to determine the entry. We may want to do this if the previous touch of the trend line is relatively far away from our entry, making our reward to risk unfavourable.

This strategy requires stop loss management as the trade progresses. We will look at the details of this once we have defined the target.

Exit – Target

The target, for the symmetrical triangle bounce strategy, is the first touch on the counter trend line which is the opposite trend line to the one used for the bounce. Refer to the dotted line in Figure 4.26.

Figure 4.26: target placement

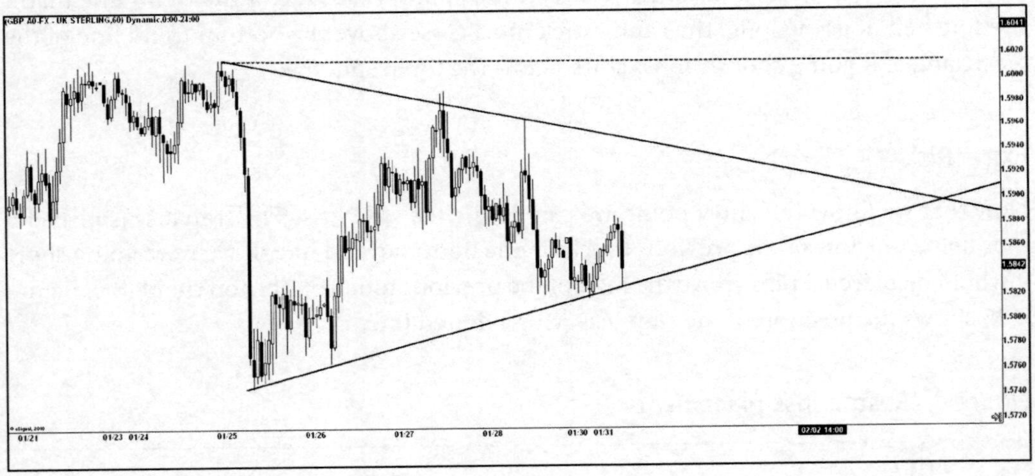

Notice how the target is simply the exact price of the first touch on the counter trend line. It is basically the point where the counter trend line of the triangle begins.

In Figure 4.27, the three dotted lines represent the entry, stop loss and target of the trade. In this image, we can see that there is a clear problem that must be addressed.

Figure 4.27: location of entry, stop loss and target for trade

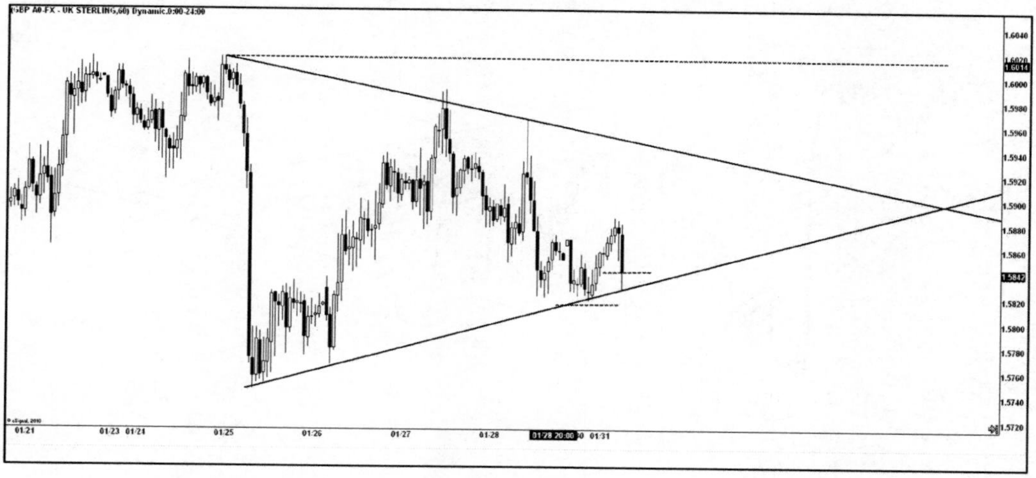

The problem is that there is a trend line running between our target and our entry. In other words, for the price action to hit our target, we need it to break through the top trend line of the symmetrical triangle.

How can we know if this trend line will break so that we can achieve our target?

Unfortunately, we cannot know for sure if the trend line will hold or break. All we can do is manage around it. The first thing that we could do is simply to take profit once the price action hits the trend line. This would be a viable option for this trade, but will not always work. For instance, if the entry occurs deep into the triangle near its apex, then there may be very little profit if we exit once the counter trend line has been touched. A better option would be to bring the stop loss to the breakeven point once the price action has reached the counter trend line. By doing this, we remove the risk of losing on the trade if the trend line holds, while remaining in a position to reap the rewards if the trend line breaks. Figure 4.28 shows the continuation of the price action. Notice how once it reaches the counter trend line, the stop loss is moved to the same price level as the entry. Notice that the target is unchanged.

Figure 4.28: example of when to move stop loss to breakeven

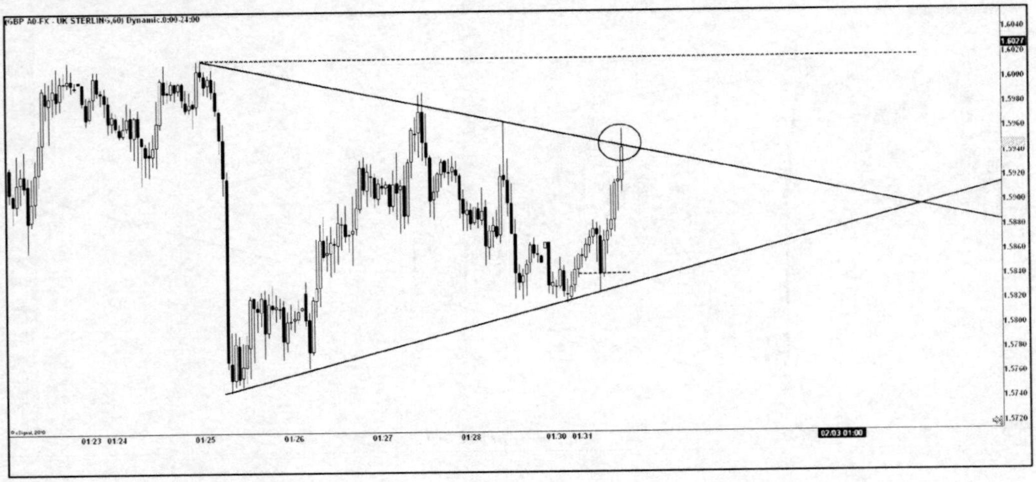

Trailing the stop loss once the counter trend line has been reached is responsible trading. This technique takes into account the clear technical level standing in the way of the price action reaching its target and removes the risk of the trade.

Figure 4.29 shows the continuation of the trade as it reaches the target.

Figure 4.29: trade reaching target

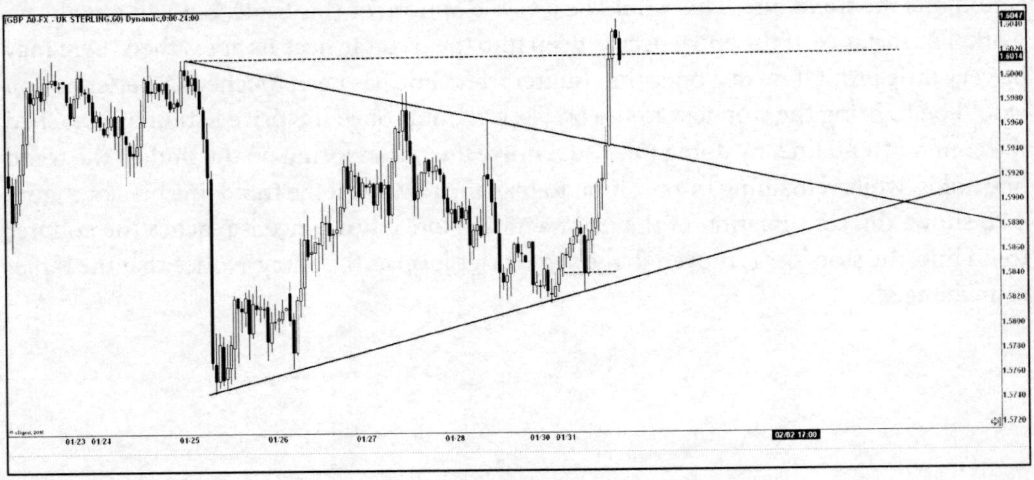

In this case, the target was hit and the trade exited.

Let's look at another example of the symmetrical triangle bounce strategy. Figure 4.30 is a USD/CHF 60 minute chart.

Figure 4.30: example chart

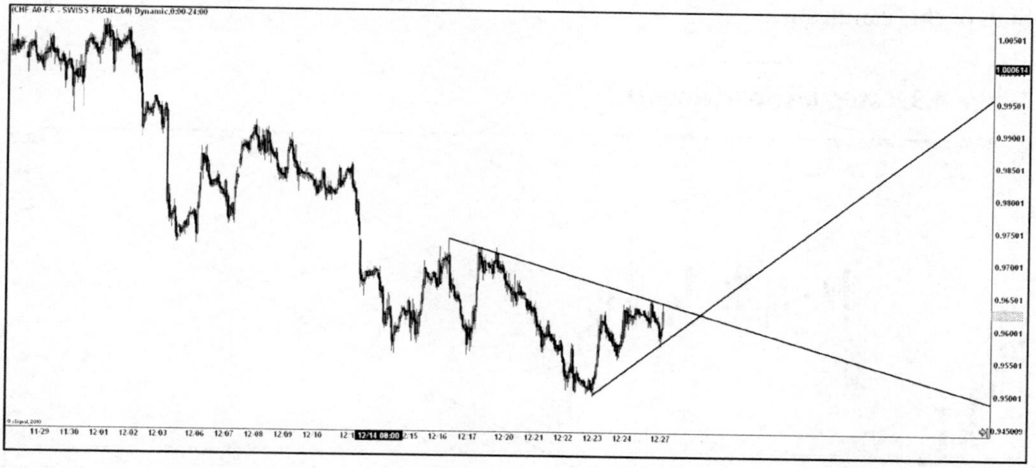

The image makes it clear that the symmetrical triangle is at the bottom of a downward trend. As the trend is down, we are looking for a potential short position where the price action bounces off the top trend line of the triangle. Figure 4.31 is zoomed in on the entry.

Figure 4.31: entry

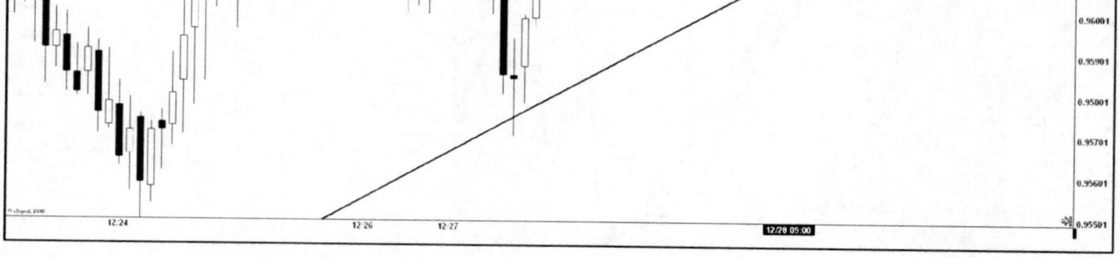

The entry is defined by the candle which touched the upper trend line and closed below it. In this example, we can see that the wick of the candle extended outside of the triangle. Remember, this is not a problem as long as the close of the candlestick is beneath the trend line. The dotted line reveals the entry.

Now that our entry is determined, we can position our stop loss. As the high of the wick of the candlestick that determined our entry is higher than the high of the previous touch of the trend line which would normally determine our stop loss, we want to use the wick of the candlestick to set our stop loss. Figure 4.32 shows the stop loss 5 pips above the high of this candlestick.

Figure 4.32: stop loss placement

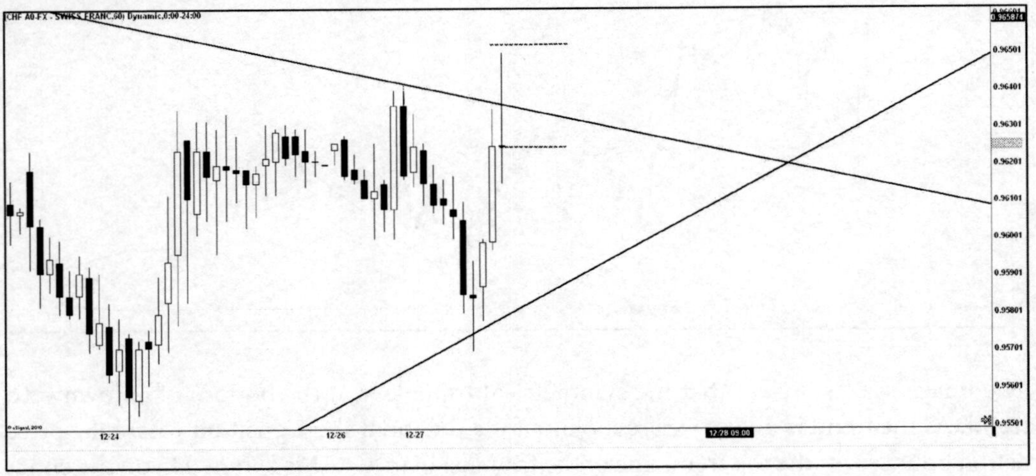

Next we set the target for the trade. This will be the first touch of the price action on the counter trend line. Figure 4.33 is zoomed back out to highlight the target.

Figure 4.33: target placement

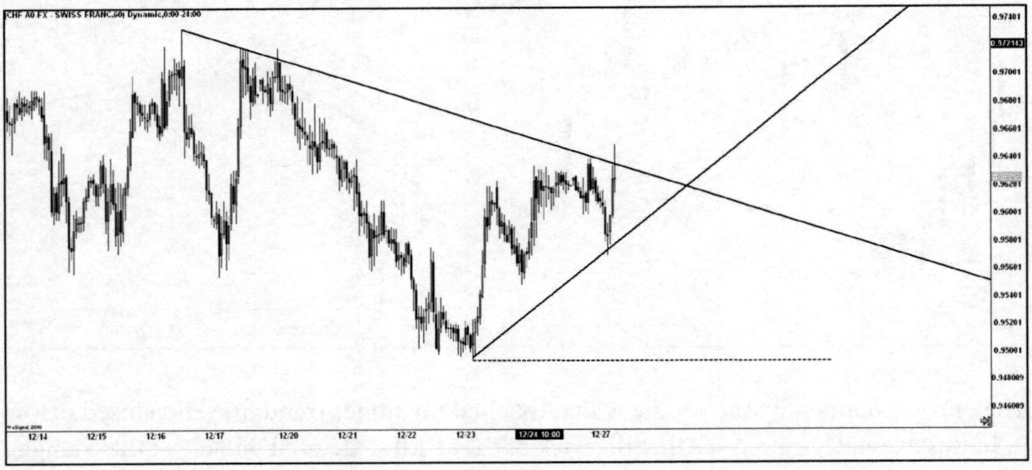

At this point, the trade is live and our stop loss and target orders are in place. Figure 4.34 zooms in again and shows the movement of the stop loss to break even as the price action touched the counter trend line. We move the stop loss here to eliminate the risk of the price action bouncing off the counter trend line and stopping the trade out for a loss. The stop loss and entry now overlap.

Figure 4.34: example of when to move stop loss to breakeven

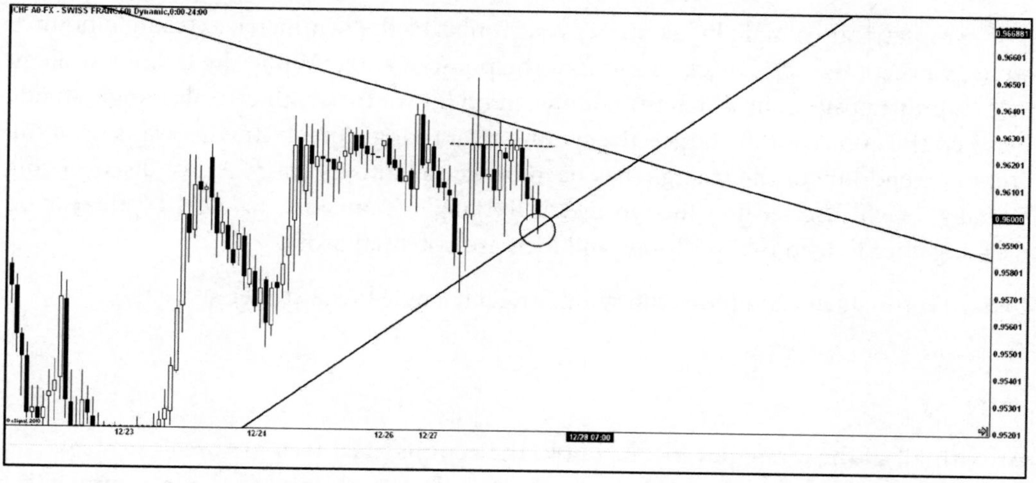

Figure 4.35 shows the continuation of the price action as our target is reached.

Figure 4.35: trade reaching target

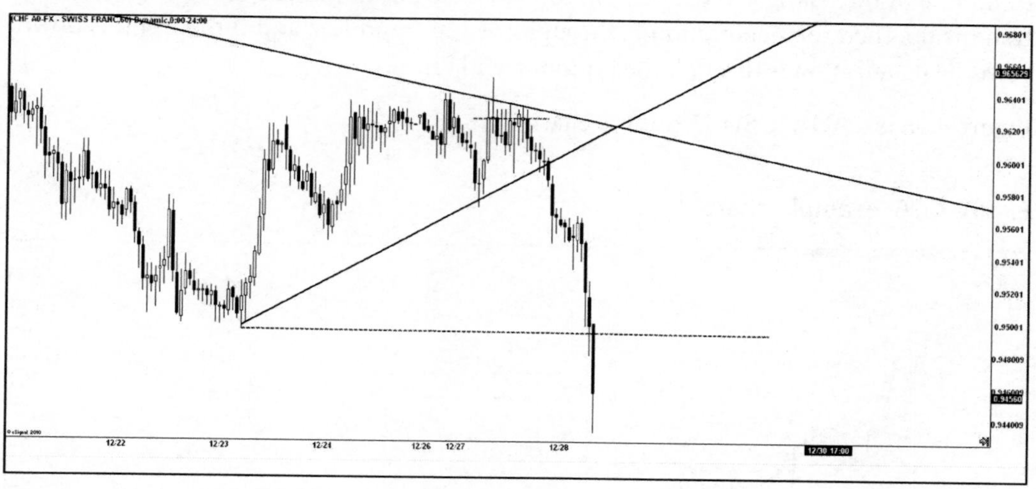

The target was hit and the trade exited.

The symmetrical triangle bounce strategy is a very efficient way to trend trade. The entry is defined by the bounce off the trend line of the triangle which is consistent with the preceding trend. The stop loss is the previous touch on the same trend line plus or minus 5 pips, depending on whether we are going long or short. The target is the first touch of the counter, or opposite trend, line of the symmetrical triangle. The stop loss is brought to the breakeven point once the price action reaches the counter trend line, just in case it holds and stops the price action from reaching our target.

2. Symmetrical triangle break strategy

The symmetrical triangle break strategy is similar to the symmetrical triangle bounce strategy except that it is more cautious at the point of entry. While the bounce strategy gets us into a position in which the counter trend line of the symmetrical triangle stands between the entry and the target, the symmetrical triangle break strategy waits until the counter trend line of the triangle has been broken before its entry. As we discover this strategy we will also see how the symmetrical triangle bounce and break strategies can be used together to load into positions and increase potential profit.

Let's go through an example of the symmetrical triangle break strategy.

Entry

As with all of the strategies in this book, the symmetrical triangle break strategy is a continuation strategy to be traded with the trend. We understand that a symmetrical triangle is made up of two trend lines – one is consistent with the trend preceding the formation of the symmetrical triangle and the other is counter to it. The entry point of the symmetrical triangle break strategy occurs when a candlestick penetrates the counter trend line of the triangle and closes on the other side of it, outside of the triangle. If the trend is up, then the penetration is through the top trend line and if the trend is down, then the penetration is through the bottom trend line.

Figure 4.36 is a AUD/USD 15 minute chart.

Figure 4.36: example chart

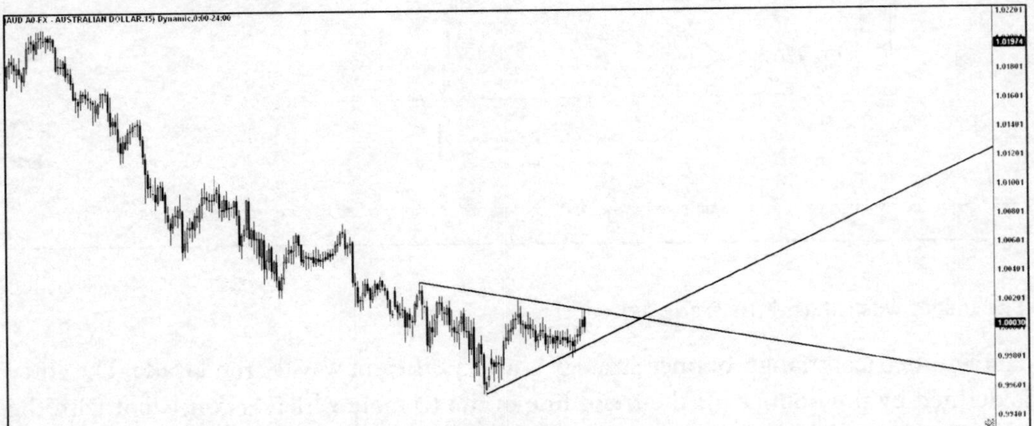

The first thing to notice is the clear downward trend of the price action. This tells us immediately that we should only look for short trades. Next, we are waiting for one of the candlesticks to penetrate the counter trend line and close on the outside of the symmetrical triangle. Once this happens, we enter the short position immediately. Figure 4.37 zooms in to show a close up of the entry point. The dotted line pinpoints the exact entry at the close of the penetrating candlestick.

Figure 4.37: entry

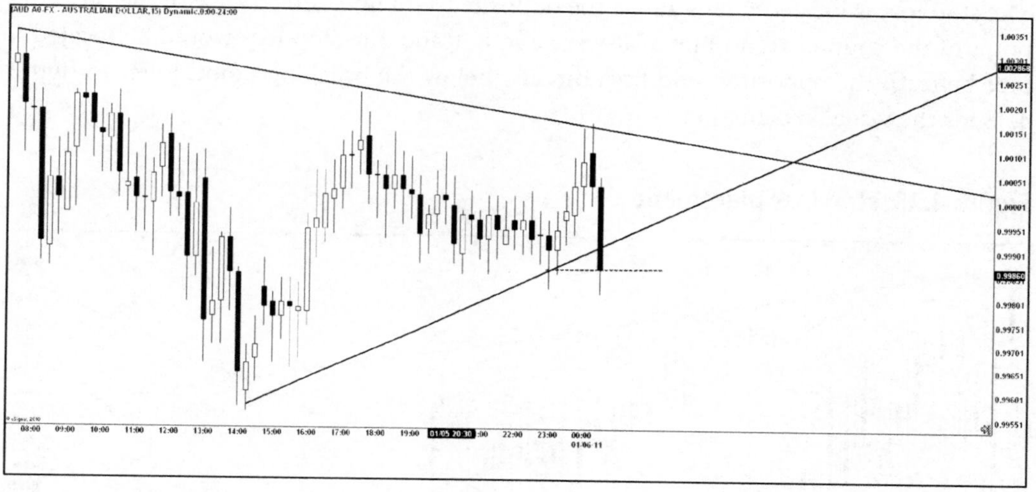

As shown in this image, the entry point occurs at the moment the candlestick penetrates the counter trend line of the symmetrical triangle and closes below it. It is clear that the entry of the symmetrical triangle break strategy is far more cautious than that of the symmetrical triangle bounce strategy, which would have required the short entry to be several pips higher. If we had entered earlier, however, using the bounce strategy, we could now enter again and add to the position by trading the break strategy. By doing this, we have two trades running but only the risk of losing on one of them. This is because our stop loss from the bounce strategy would already be placed at the breakeven point. This is an advanced way to load into a position.

In summary, the four steps to entering the symmetrical triangle break strategy are:

1. Identify the symmetrical triangle and draw the two converging trend lines to establish the triangle and create the projection zones.
2. Confirm the direction of the price action which preceded the formation of the symmetrical triangle and use this information to determine whether to look for long or short positions and to identify which trend line the price action needs to touch.
3. Wait for a candlestick to penetrate the counter trend line of the symmetrical triangle. If the setup is long, the candlestick must penetrate the top trend line. If going short it must penetrate the bottom one.

4. Enter as soon as the candlestick closes on the appropriate side of the trend line that it penetrated. If the setup is long, this will be the top trend line. If it is short it will be the bottom trend line.

Exit – Risk

The stop loss is located 5 pips above the opposite trend line, directly above the breaking point of the counter trend line. If it were a long trade, the stop loss would be located 5 pips beneath the opposite trend line, directly below the breaking point. Refer to figure 4.38 for the visual explanation.

Figure 4.38: stop loss placement

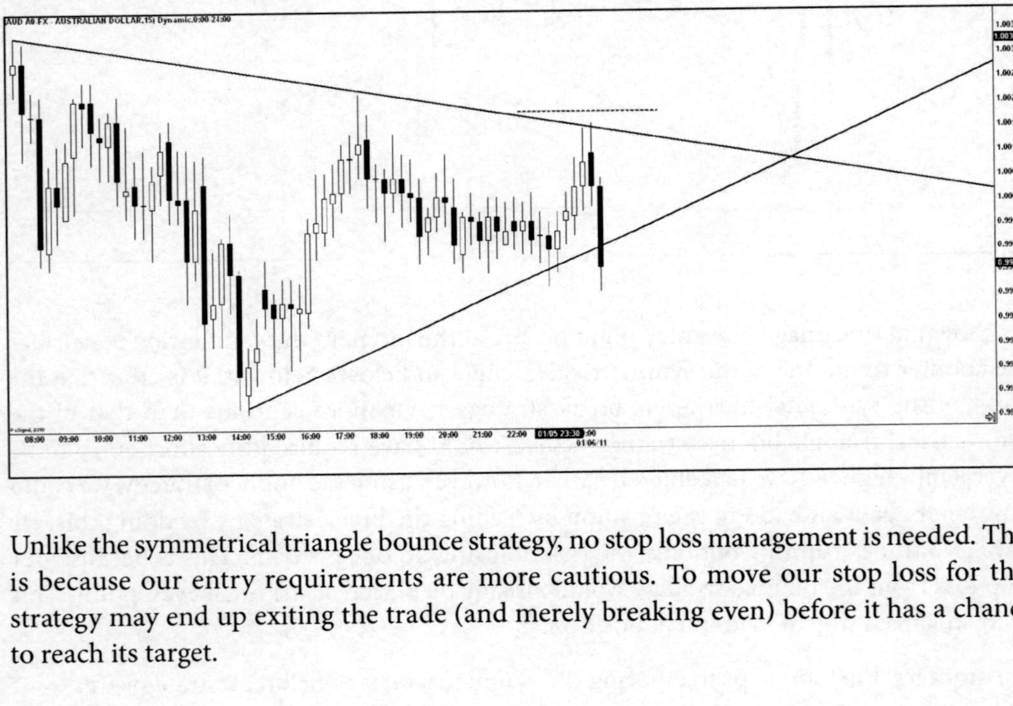

Unlike the symmetrical triangle bounce strategy, no stop loss management is needed. This is because our entry requirements are more cautious. To move our stop loss for this strategy may end up exiting the trade (and merely breaking even) before it has a chance to reach its target.

Exit – Target

The target of the symmetrical triangle break strategy is identical to that of the symmetrical triangle bounce strategy. We target the price of the first touch of the counter trend line of the symmetrical triangle. This happens to be the same trend line which we used to define our entry. So, for the symmetrical triangle break strategy, the counter trend line has a role in defining both our entry and our target. Figure 4.39 demonstrates the location of the target.

Figure 4.39: target placement

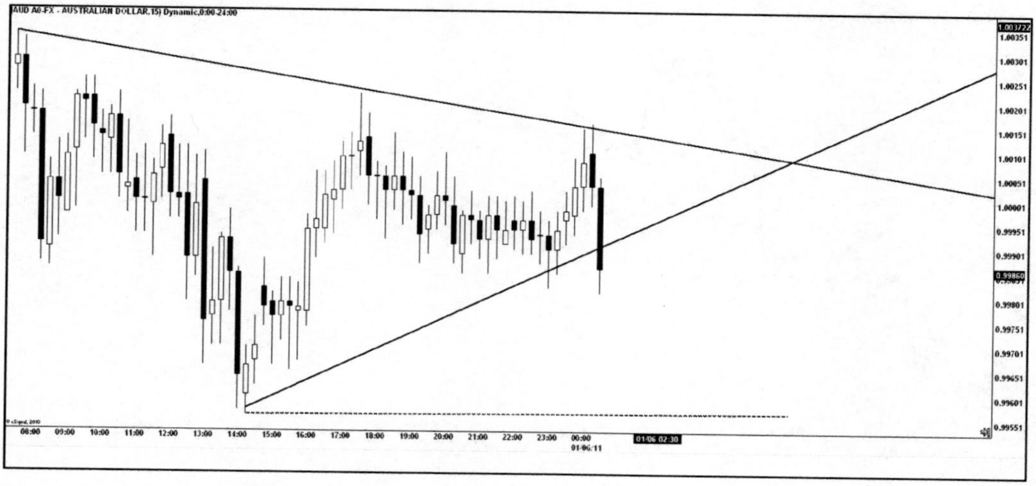

We have now defined the entry, and both exits, of this strategy. Figure 4.40 shows the continuation of the price action as it hits the target, with all three price levels of the trade highlighted.

Figure 4.40: trade reaching target

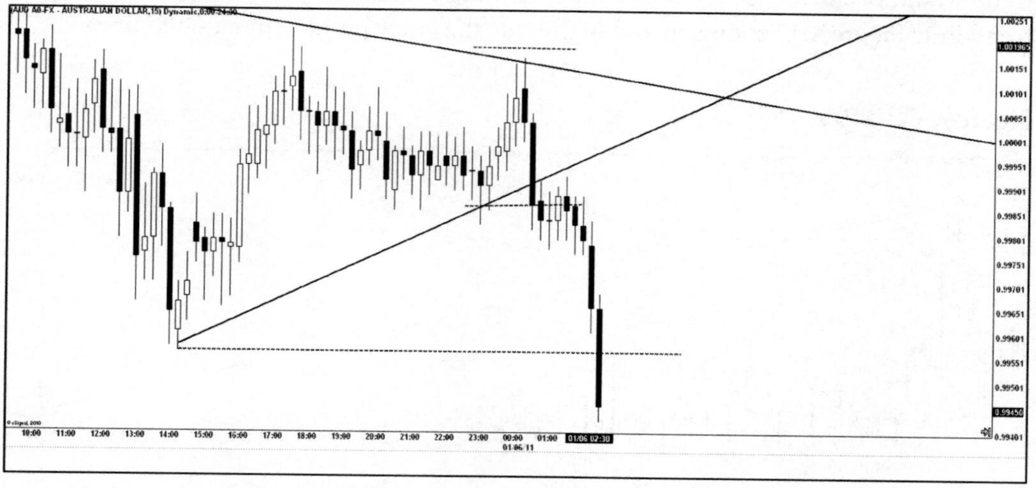

In this case, the target was hit and the trade exited.

Let's move on now and look at another example of the symmetrical triangle break strategy. Figure 4.41 is a EUR/AUD 15 minute chart.

Figure 4.41: example chart

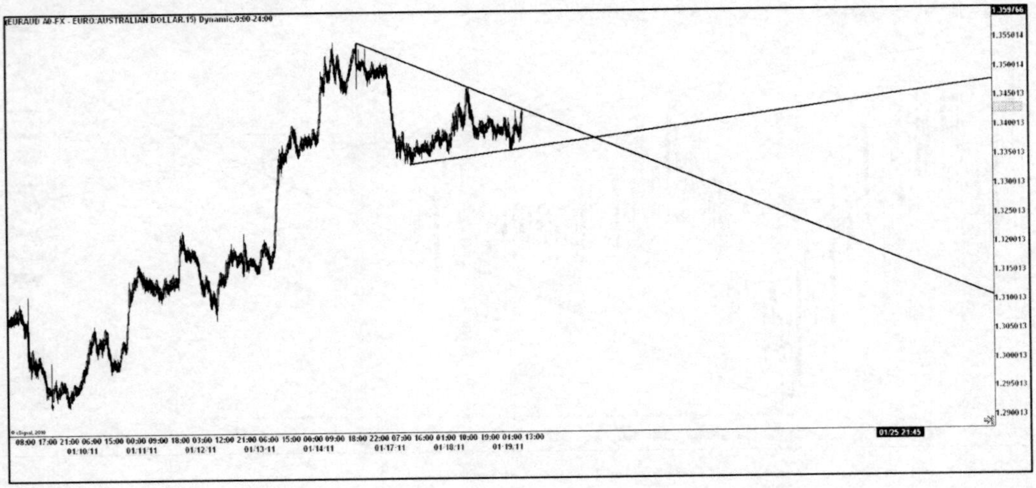

The price action is in an overall upward trend, which leads into the symmetrical triangle and tells us that we are only looking for long positions. The price action is also consolidating deep into the apex of the triangle, so a breakout is likely to occur at any moment. As we are trading the symmetrical triangle break strategy, we are only interested if the price action breaks through the counter trend line and enters zone 1. Entry into this trade would occur the moment that a penetrating candlestick closed above the counter trend line. Figure 4.42 zooms in and highlights the entry point with a dotted line.

Figure 4.42: entry

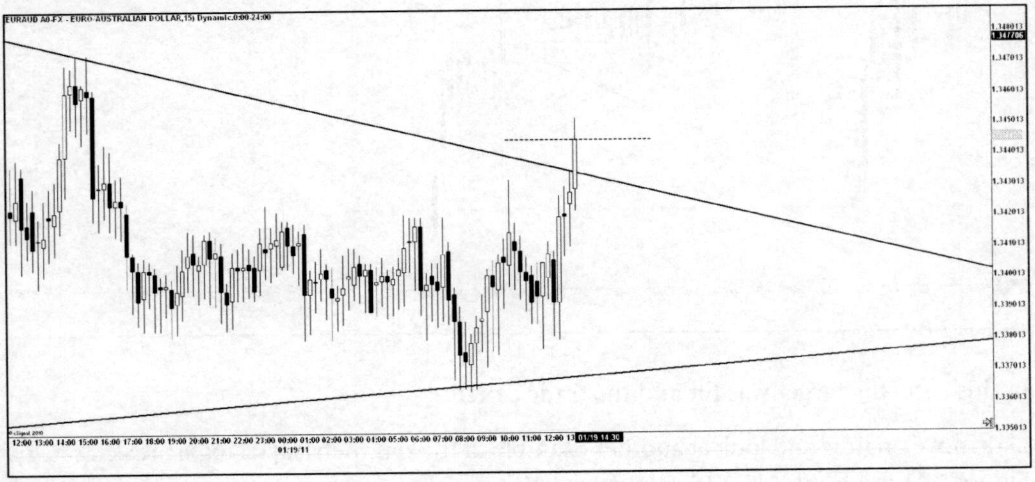

Notice that our entry was not the previous candlestick. Although this candlestick penetrated the counter trend line, it didn't close above it. We, therefore, did not consider the trend line to be broken as this could have easily been a false breakout.

Having finalised the entry, we place our stop loss 5 pips beneath the opposite trend line in the same time period as this entry. Figure 4.43 shows the location of the stop loss.

Figure 4.43: stop loss placement

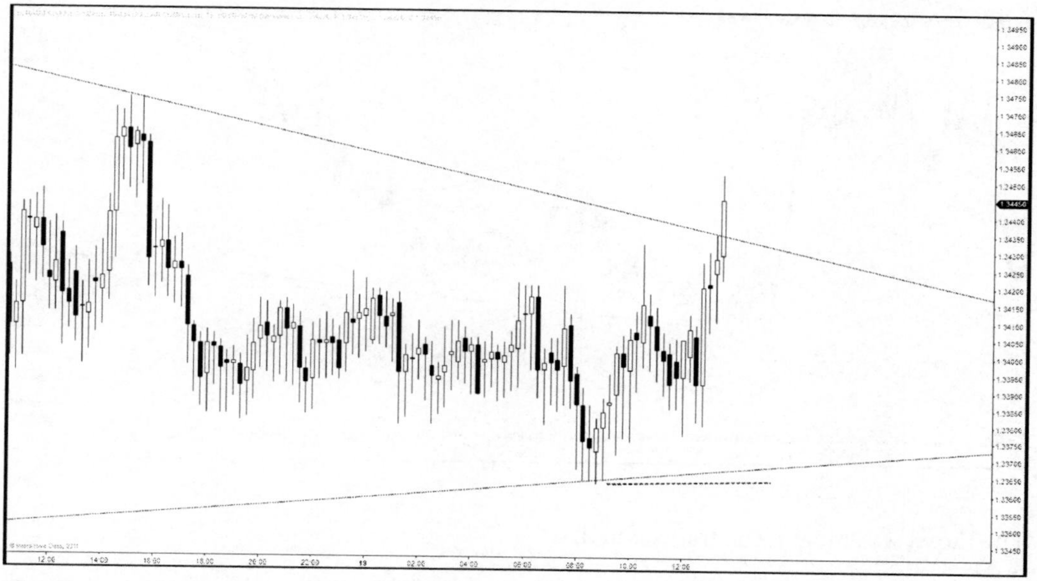

Last, we place our target at the first touch of the price action on the counter trend line of the symmetrical triangle. Figure 4.44 zooms out and reveals the target with a dotted line.

Figure 4.44: target placement

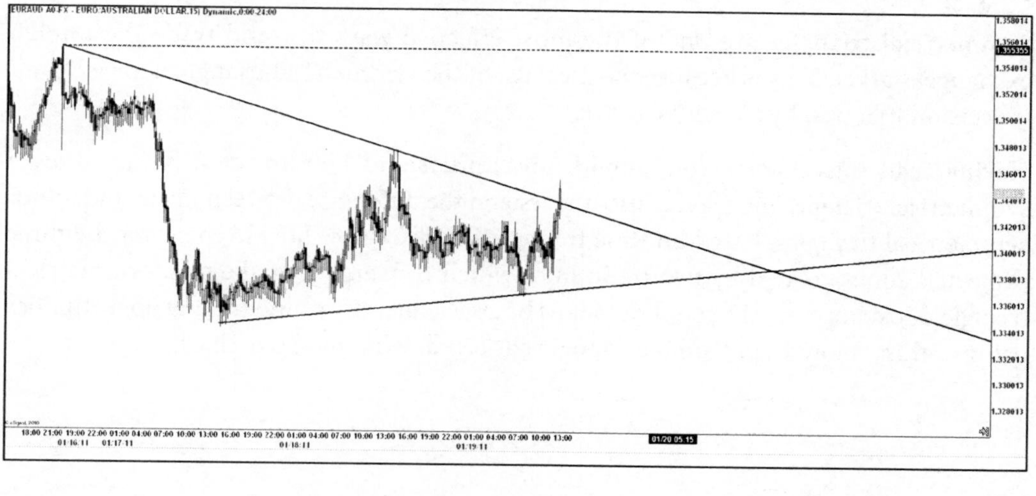

In this image, we can see how the first touch of the counter trend line of the symmetrical triangle is used as the price for our target.

Figure 4.45 shows the trade, with the entry and both exits highlighted, as well as the continuation of the price action.

Figure 4.45: entry, stop loss and target levels

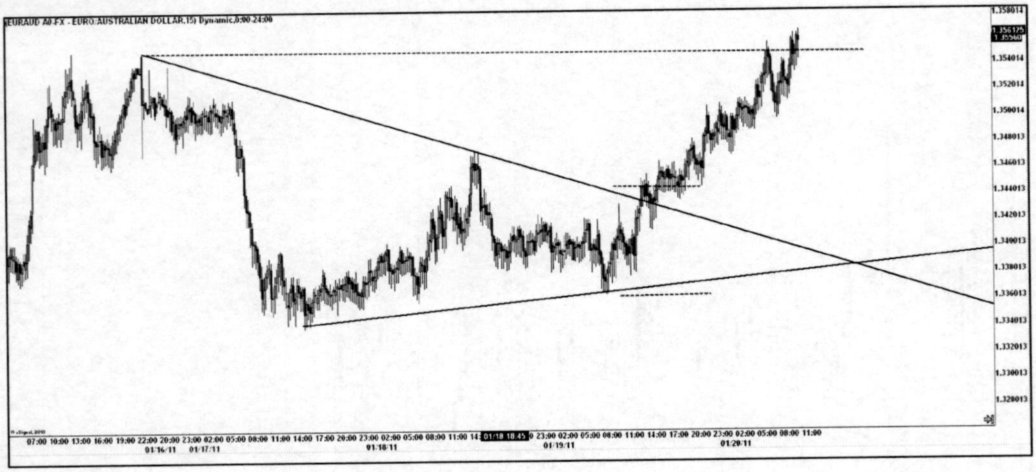

The target was hit and the trade exited.

The last two examples clearly demonstrate the indecision of the price action as it moves through the triangle, leading to a very decisive breakout of the triangle as price then moves towards its target.

Key 4 Summary

Symmetrical triangles are one of the most effective ways to trend trade the foreign exchange market. This is because the message of the symmetrical triangle is very clear – indecision followed by a decisive move.

Having read this chapter you should now understand how to identify and draw a symmetrical triangle. You should also understand the difference between major and minor symmetrical triangles, based on time frames. You also know how to interpret the three projected zones created by two trend lines which converge to make up a symmetrical triangle. Most importantly, you should now be able to identify sound trading opportunities using nothing more than a simple triangle pattern drawn onto your chart.

USING THE KEYS EFFECTIVELY

The purpose of this chapter is to focus on other technical factors that can increase the profitability of these strategies. To do this we must explore the environment, or larger picture, of the currency pairs that make up the foreign exchange market. In particular we are going to find out which currencies are the most suitable for each strategy.

Which currency pairs should we trade?

Before looking for potential trading opportunities using any of our strategies, we need to establish which currency pairs we should trade. As we have learned, the daily chart provides us with the strongest overview of the direction of the dominant trend of any particular pair. If there is not a clear trend on the daily chart then it is safest to stay away from that currency pair altogether.

Novice traders can feel uncomfortable neglecting a currency pair as they fear that they may miss their chance to place a trade and, ultimately, their chance of making money. Traders who adopt this type of mind set are rarely ever successful. They are constantly chasing trades, not because they believe that there is a viable trading opportunity, but simply because they fear they may miss a big chance.

The daily chart is a critical tool in helping us to decide which currency pairs have a strong trend which may lead to potential trading opportunities.

There are two main characteristics of a strong trend on a daily chart. The first is an obvious trend line and the second is the relationship between the price action and the 50 and 200 period exponential moving averages (EMAs). In an upward trend, there will be an upward trend line and the price action will be trading above the 50 and 200 EMAs. In a downward trend, there will be a downward trend line and the price action will be below the 50 and 200 EMAs.

Let's look at an example. Figure 5.1 is the EUR/USD daily chart. The thin wavy line is the 50 EMA. The thicker wavy line is the 200 EMA.

Figure 5.1: chart with exponential moving averages to determine trend

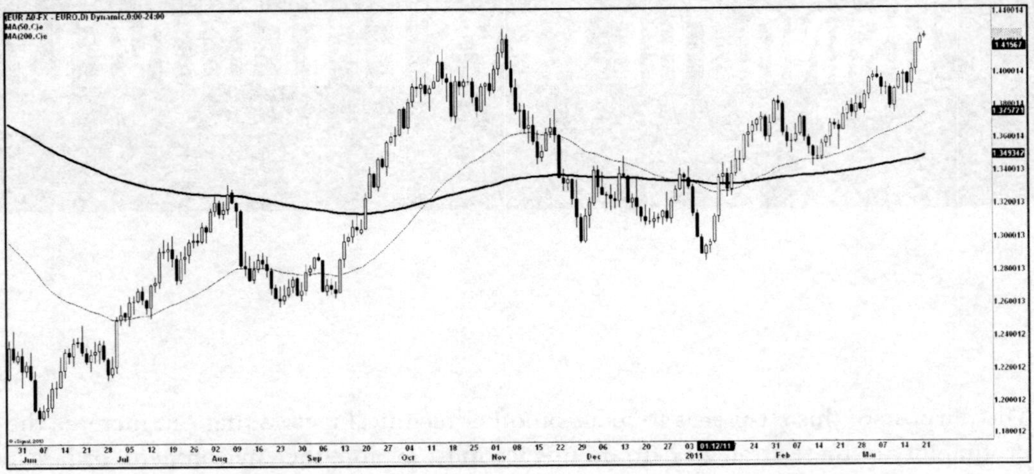

It is clear from Figure 5.1 that the price action is currently trading above both EMAs. We also need to look for at least one upward trend line. Figure 5.2 includes the most obvious trend line.

Figure 5.2: addition of trend line to help determine trend

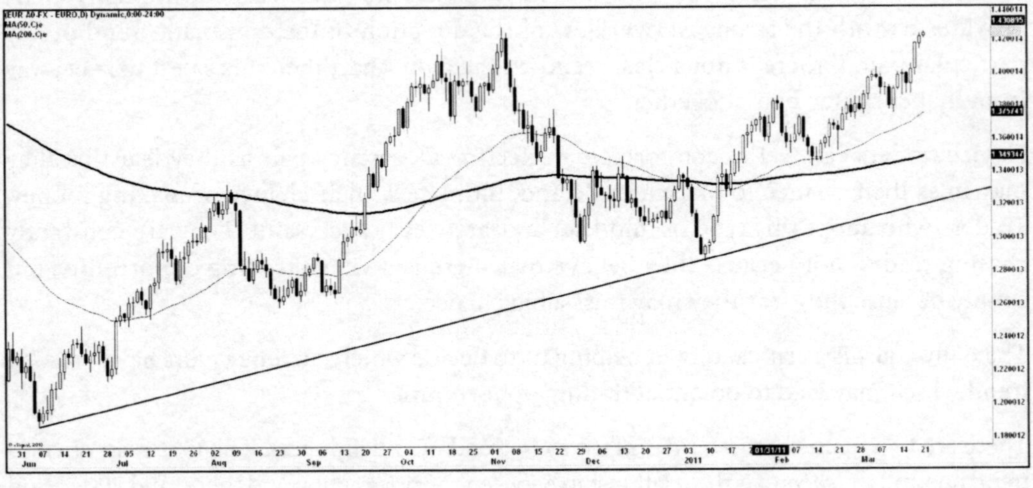

From this image, we can confidently say that we believe the EUR/USD currency pair to be in a strong overall upward trend on the daily chart. Therefore, if we see a setup on one of our strategies on a smaller time frame such as the 4 hour, 1 hour or 15 minute chart that is also occurring in an uptrend, we know that we also have the weight of the larger time frame pushing for the desired result. If, however, we see a trade setting up on one of the smaller time frames which is running counter to the daily trend, it is not as safe to trade as it is disagreeing with the dominant daily trend.

A common way to link the trends of multiple time frames is to group them into two categories – the daily and 4 hour charts for medium to long term trades and the 1 hour and 15 minute charts for the shorter term intraday trades. In other words, before trading a strategy on the 4 hour chart, we would check if the trend on this chart is in agreement with that of the daily chart. Similarly, before executing a strategy on the 15 minute chart, we would check for trend agreement on the 1 hour chart. In fact, the safest time for an intraday trader to execute any trend-based strategy is when all four time frames are in agreement.

Let's look at an example involving the EUR/USD pair. We already know that the daily chart is trading above both of its significant EMAs. Now we need to check the other time frames for trend agreement. Figure 5.3 is the EUR/USD 4 hour chart.

Figure 5.3: chart with trend line and exponential moving averages

Figure 5.3 shows us that the 4 hour EUR/USD is also trending up, with a definite trend line and the price action above both significant EMAs.

Figure 5.4 is the EUR/USD 1 hour chart.

Figure 5.4: chart with trend line and exponential moving averages

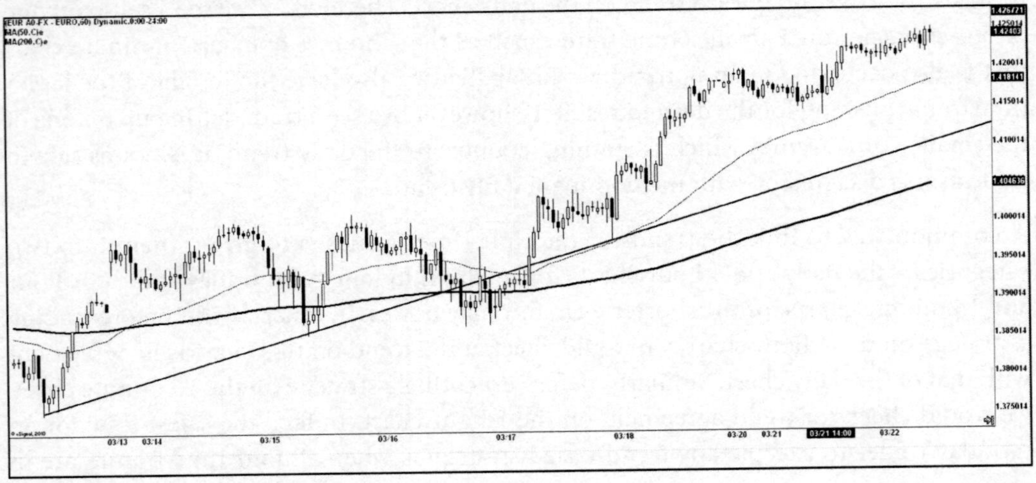

The hourly chart is in agreement with both the daily and 4 hour charts. The price action is trending up, trading above its EMAs with a trend line running through it.

Figure 5.5 is the EUR/USD 15 minute chart.

Figure 5.5: chart with trend line and exponential moving averages

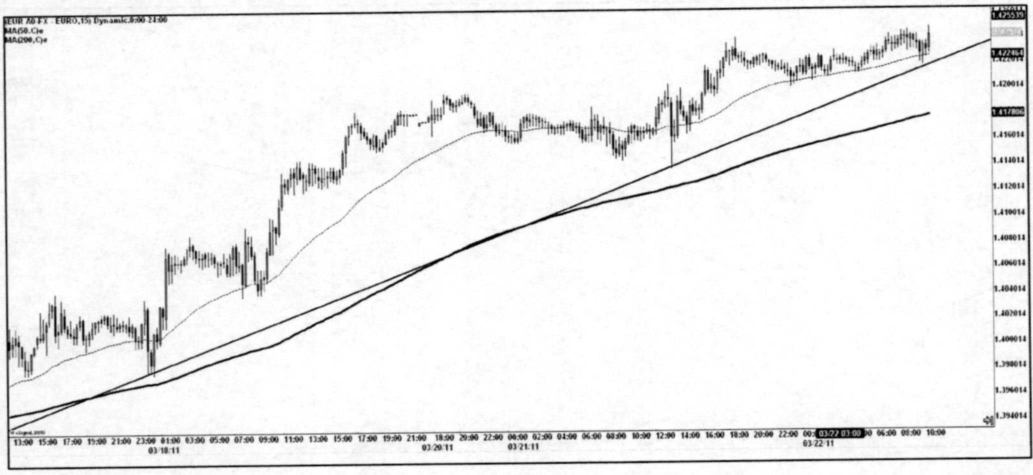

Finally, we can see that the 15 minute chart is also in a strong uptrend. This is confirmed by the presence of a trend line and the location of the price action in relation to the 50 and 200 EMAs.

From this analysis we conclude that the EUR/USD is currently in an incredibly strong uptrend. If we are looking for medium to long term trades using the daily or 4 hour charts, or short term intraday trades using the 1 hour and 15 minute charts, we can be completely confident of the upward trend.

Now let's take a look at a currency pair that we should pass over. Remember, we first use the daily chart to determine the overall trend. Figure 5.6 is the EUR/JPY daily chart.

Figure 5.6: chart with exponential moving averages

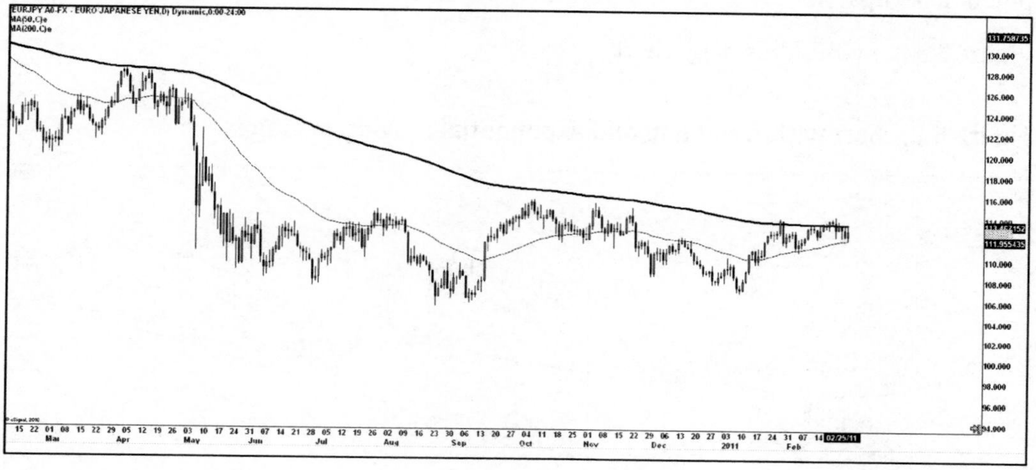

The first thing that we should notice is the consolidation of the price action between the moving averages. The price action is undecided about whether it wants to trend up or down. Figure 5.7 reveals horizontal support and resistance levels that confirm that lack of direction of the price action.

Figure 5.7: chart with exponential moving averages and levels of support and resistance

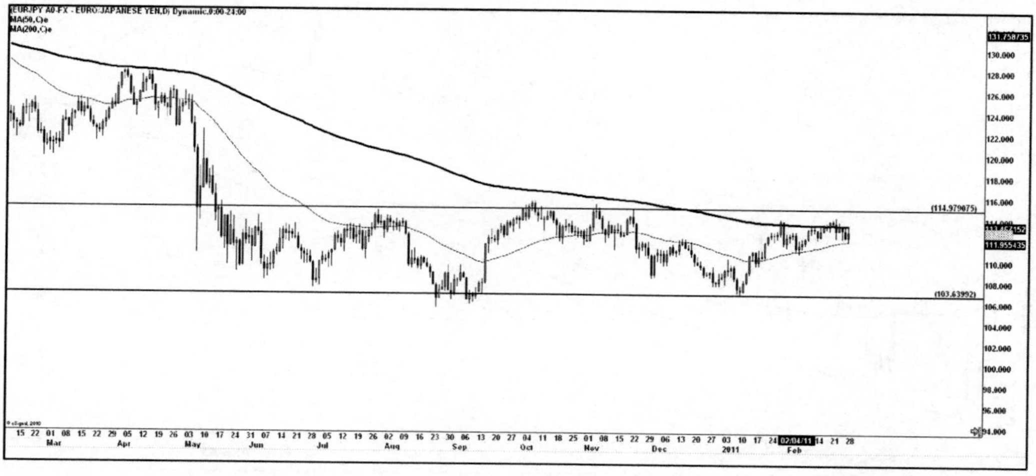

Our analysis of this daily chart indicates that there is no dominant overall trend on this particular currency pair. Until the price action clearly breaks out of this sideways channel, we should steer clear of trading this currency pair. Trend trading works best when there is a clear trend!

Figures 5.8 and 5.9 are images of two daily charts which are trending upwards. Remember, a clear trend on a daily chart encourages us to look through the other time frames for potential setups.

Figure 5.8 is a GBP/USD daily chart.

Figure 5.8: chart with trend line and exponential moving averages

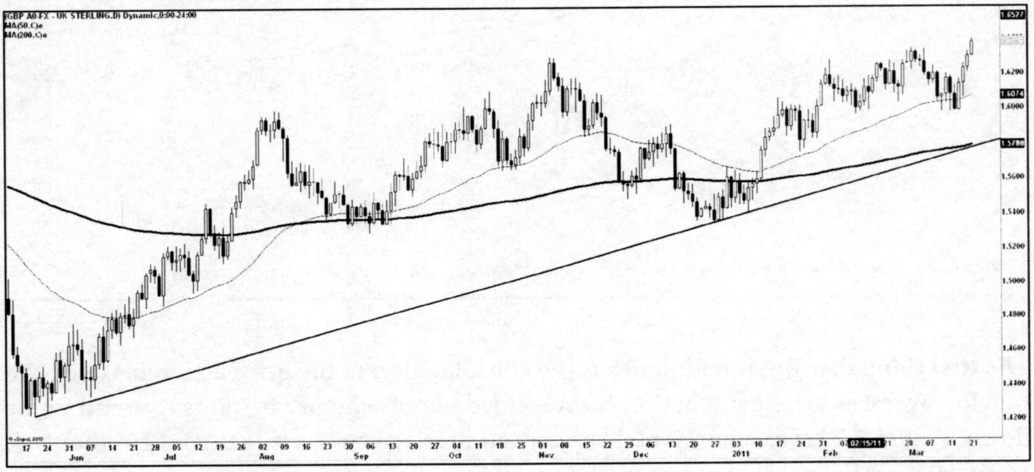

Figure 5.9 is a AUD/USD daily chart.

Figure 5.9: chart with trend line and exponential moving averages

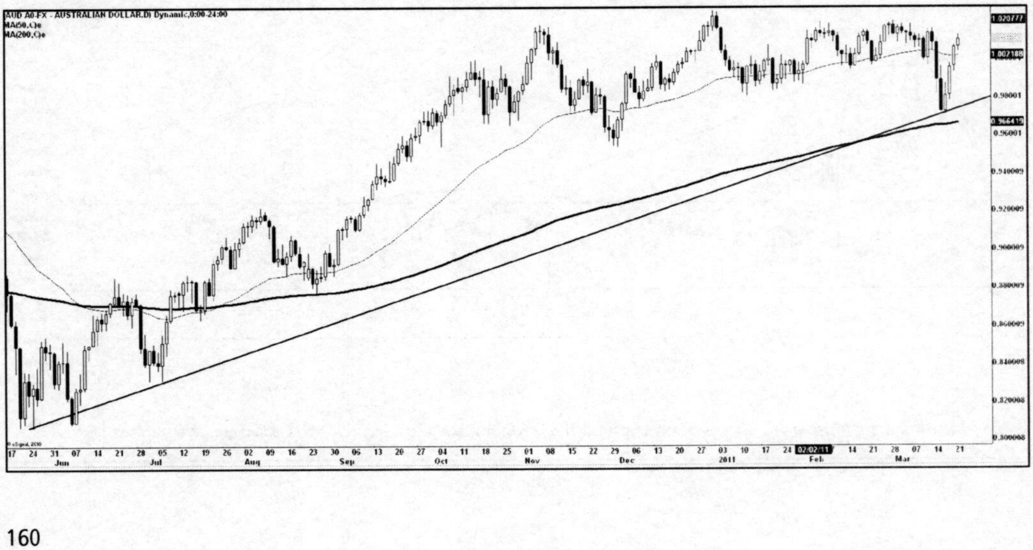

Notice that the price action is above the EMAs and a strong upward trend line is present on each chart.

Figures 5.10 and 5.11 are strong downward trending daily charts.

Figure 5.10 is a USD/CHF daily chart.

Figure 5.10: chart with trend line and exponential moving averages

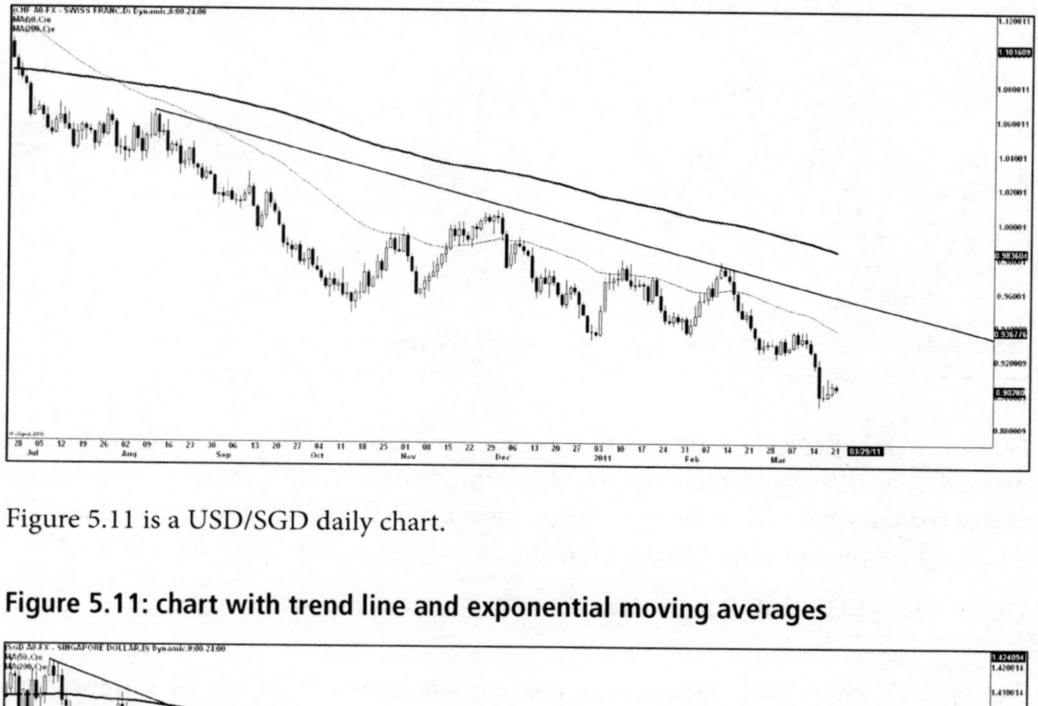

Figure 5.11 is a USD/SGD daily chart.

Figure 5.11: chart with trend line and exponential moving averages

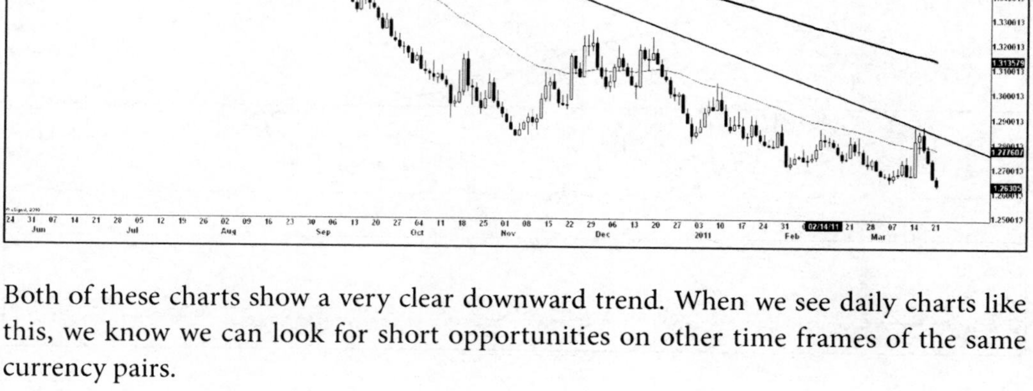

Both of these charts show a very clear downward trend. When we see daily charts like this, we know we can look for short opportunities on other time frames of the same currency pairs.

Now let's have a look at some daily charts that would immediately tell us to move on.

Figure 5.12 is a EUR/CAD daily chart.

Figure 5.12: chart with exponential moving averages to determine trend

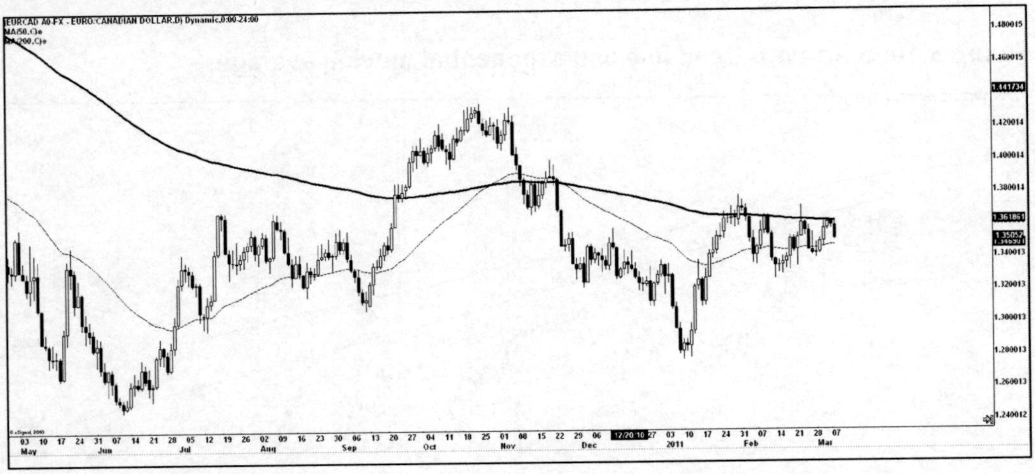

We can see that the price action is stuck between the moving averages, meaning there is no clear trend. We would, therefore, avoid entering trades on any of the other time frames of this currency pair. Once the price action breaks out of this consolidation and decides which side of the moving averages it is going to trade on, we can come back to it.

Figure 5.13 is a GBP/AUD daily chart.

Figure 5.13: chart with exponential moving averages and levels of support and resistance

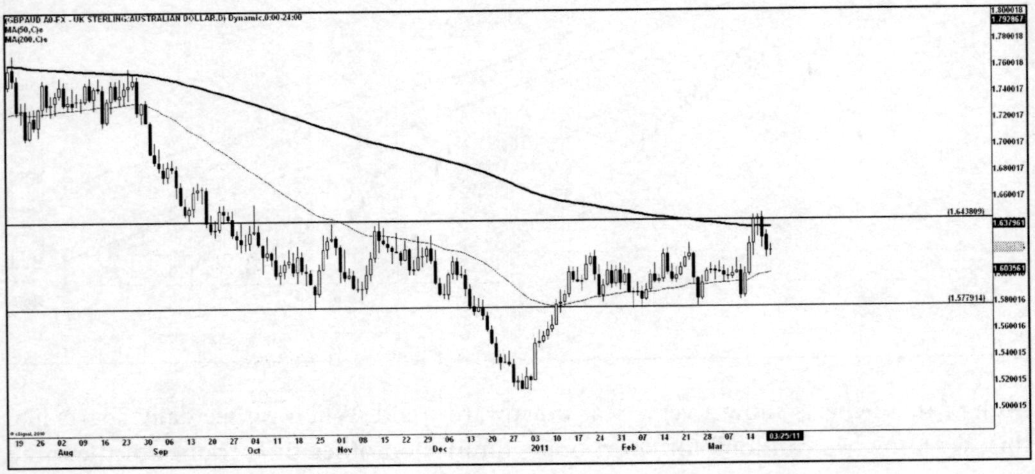

Right away, we notice that the price action is currently trading between its EMAs. Not only that, but there are also some horizontal levels of support and resistance that would need to break down before this daily chart can give us a clear message about its trend.

In summary, the daily chart is the first place that we look when filtering through currency pairs to discover potential trading opportunities. This is true regardless of whether we are short-term, medium-term or long-term traders. If the daily chart is clearly trending and there is trend agreement on the other time frames, we can trade with a higher level of confidence.

The trend strength of the cross rates

Commodities such as oil and gold are denominated in USD because it is considered to be the major global currency. For the same reason, major currency pairs always include the USD. Cross rates, on the other hand, are known as synthetic exchange rates which combine the exchange rates of two major currency pairs and do not include the USD. Cross rates can provide us with some reliable trends to trade.

Let's take a look at a commonly traded cross rate, the EUR/JPY. Let's take a look at an example.

Figure 5.14 is the EUR/JPY daily chart from August 2008 to January 2009.

Figure 5.14: chart with exponential moving averages to determine trend

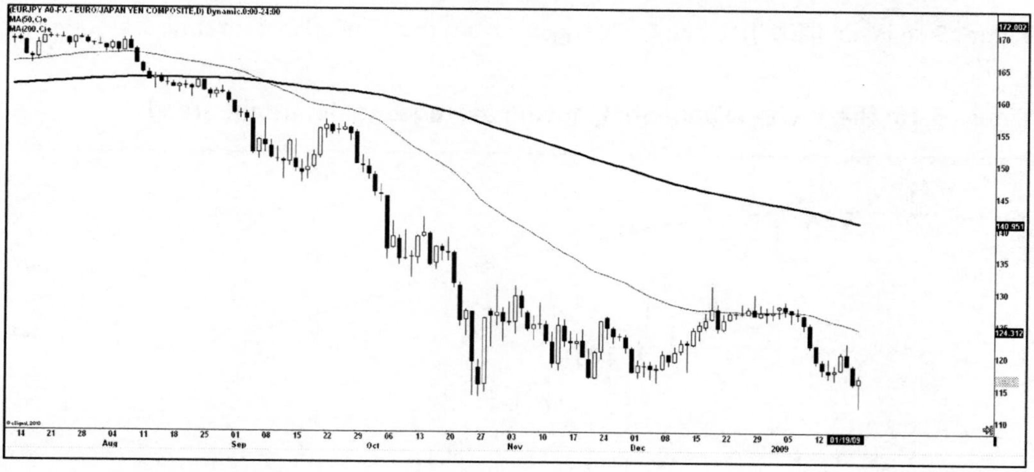

The downward trend of the EUR/JPY indicates that the Euro was weakening against the Japanese Yen over this period of time. Remember, when a chart is trending down, the base currency is trending down relative to the term's currency. Based on this we can expect to find either the Euro weakening against the USD, on the EUR/USD chart, or the Japanese Yen to be strengthening against the USD, on the USD/JPY chart also over the same time period. This is one way to explain the strong downward trend on the EUR/JPY chart.

To see if this is the case, let's check the daily charts of the EUR/USD and the USD/JPY. Figure 5.15 is the EUR/USD chart from this period of time.

Figure 5.15: chart with exponential moving averages to determine trend

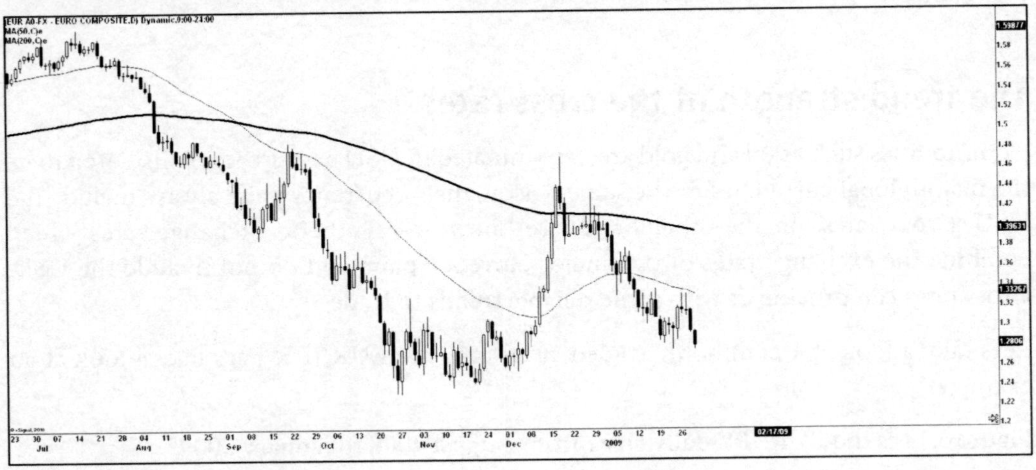

The downward trend on this chart is just what we expected to see.

Figure 5.16 is the USD/JPY daily chart, again from the same period of time.

Figure 5.16: chart with exponential moving averages to determine trend

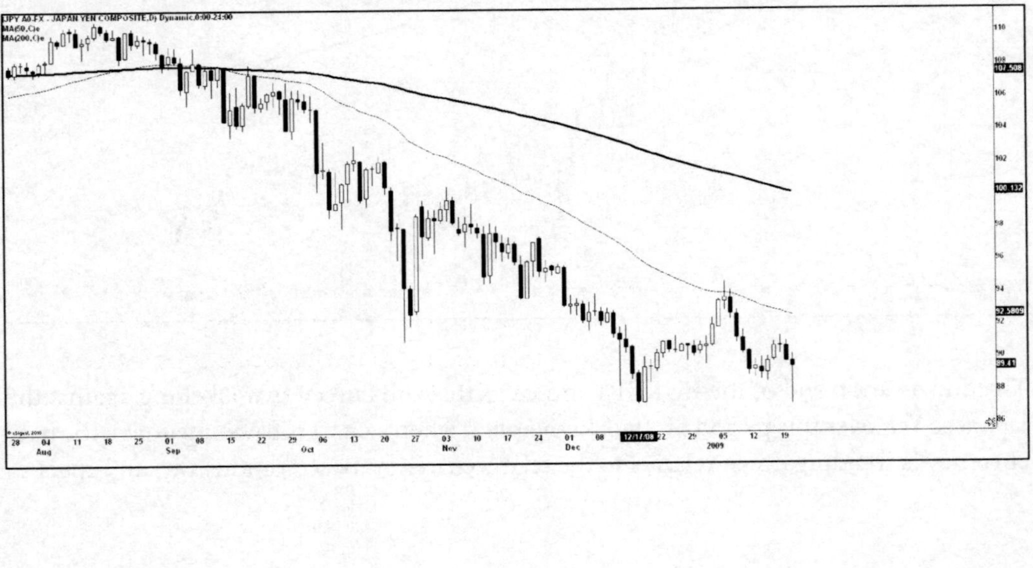

This chart also shows us what we expected to see - the JPY strengthening against the USD. Do not be confused here. This currency pair is known as an inverse pair, meaning the USD is the base currency instead of the terms currency. So when the USD/JPY chart is trending down, the USD is weakening and the JPY is strengthening against it.

When two currencies are trending strongly in opposite directions against the USD, the cross rate of those currencies is likely to create a very strong trend therefore creating more trading opportunities. Identifying such trending cross rates should be part of our daily trading routine, as we look through our daily charts to find trending currency pairs. Once we have found a few pairs which are trending, we need to check whether any of these trends are opposites. If they are, then the cross rate chart of the two currencies with opposite trends can be used to identify potential trading opportunities.

The locked chart

In this book so far we have covered a total of eight different trading strategies, relating to four trend trading keys. In this chapter, we have discussed the filtering process used to identify the standard and cross currency pairs most suitable for executing our strategies. Now, we are going to discuss a general approach to breaking down the price action on a *locked chart*.

A *locked chart* is a chart which only shows the raw price action. There are no indicators, trend lines or Fibonacci levels. The message of the chart is locked up in the price action. As trend traders we must use our keys to gain access to the chart's message.

Having been given four valuable keys, it may be difficult to know which one to try to unlock the chart with first. We need a process for implementing the techniques that we have learned so far. The best place to start is with key 1, using trend lines to analyse the chart. Then move on to key 2, channels and then key 3 Fibonacci retracement levels and then key 4, symmetrical triangles.

Do all of this on the same chart. This way we will see the locked chart, begin to give a clear message. Once the message has been unlocked, our eyes can quickly identify particular aspects of the price action that are critical for trend trading. For instance, we would notice if the price action was making consistently higher peaks in an upward trend or consistently lower troughs in a downward trend.

All eight strategies covered across the four keys of trend trading are sufficient individually. As time goes on, and you have learned to use each type of strategy, it is likely that a personal preference will develop. There is no problem at all with focusing on the ones that we like. After all, we like to do what we like. That is not to say that an understanding of all of the strategies and the concepts which they represent, will no longer be relevant. Being comfortable with all four keys and the strategies that relate to them, will allow us to identify when the strategies overlap each other.

Multiple key confirmations

A multiple key confirmation is when two or more of our trend trading keys point to the same price level. This price level could be the entry, stop loss or target of a trade. The point is when more than one key gives us the same message, this message becomes stronger.

Why are multiple confirmations so powerful?

Multiple key confirmations are powerful because when they occur there is a greater chance that we are trading the same trade as the majority of the market. Previously, we learned that we want to be in the same trading positions as institutional traders who are moving large amounts of money around. For instance, if we see that a symmetrical triangle bounce strategy is overlapping the 78.6% Fibonacci level we know the desired bounce is more likely. This is because some traders will be trading the symmetrical triangle bounce while others will be trading the Fibonacci retracement bounce. We know, therefore, that we stand a good chance of trading with the majority of the market because, regardless of which strategy they are using, we are using both. Chances are that others also spotted the multiple key confirmation, which will have increased their confidence to trade and, ultimately, confirmed the move even more. Basically, multiple key confirmations increase the visibility of a trading opportunity, increasing the amount of money being traded at a particular price level.

Deciding which key to turn?

When multiple keys point to the same entry of a trade, the question of which key to use will arise. This is a relevant question as, although the entry may be the same for each key, the management of the trade after the entry is different. Unfortunately, there is no set answer to this question. Instead, there are three further questions that we need to ask ourselves to help us to decide:

1. Which is the most objective key?
2. Which is the key of preference?
3. Which is the more conservative key?

The most objective key refers to the key that requires the least amount of subjective reasoning or discretion when executing the trade. Objective trading opportunities, which are based solely on technical levels, are normally more predictable and therefore much safer to trade.

The key of preference refers to the key that we naturally prefer and are most comfortable trading. This may sound unscientific, but the reality is that we are likely to make better decisions if we are managing a trade based on a strategy that we know well.

The more conservative key refers to the key that is more efficient in its entry, stop loss and target price levels. For instance, if the keys are both pointing to a long entry, which entry provides us with a better price? Which key provides the safest stop loss in terms of distance from our entry and support levels of protection? Which key suggests a more realistic target based on the entire picture of the chart?

Asking these three questions helps us to analyse the chart logically and objectively and to establish consistent and relevant thinking patterns.

Examples of multiple key confirmations

Let's take a look at an example of a multiple key confirmation.

The example in Figure 5.17 is an a locked EUR/USD 15 minute chart. It is considered locked as it shows only the raw price action.

Figure 5.17: example chart of raw price action

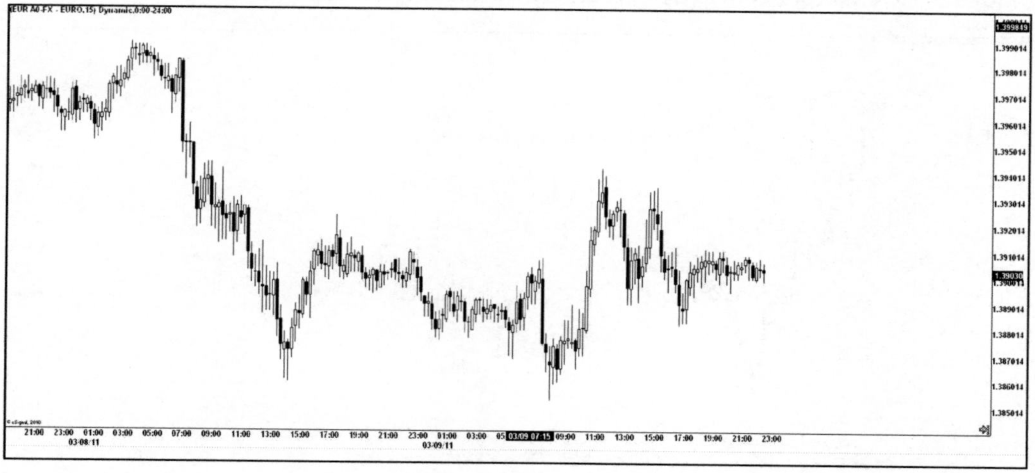

The first thing that we notice about this chart is that the price action is moving down. From this we know that we will be looking for short opportunities. As the price action is moving down let's see if we can identify any downward trend lines.

Figure 5.18: example chart with trend line

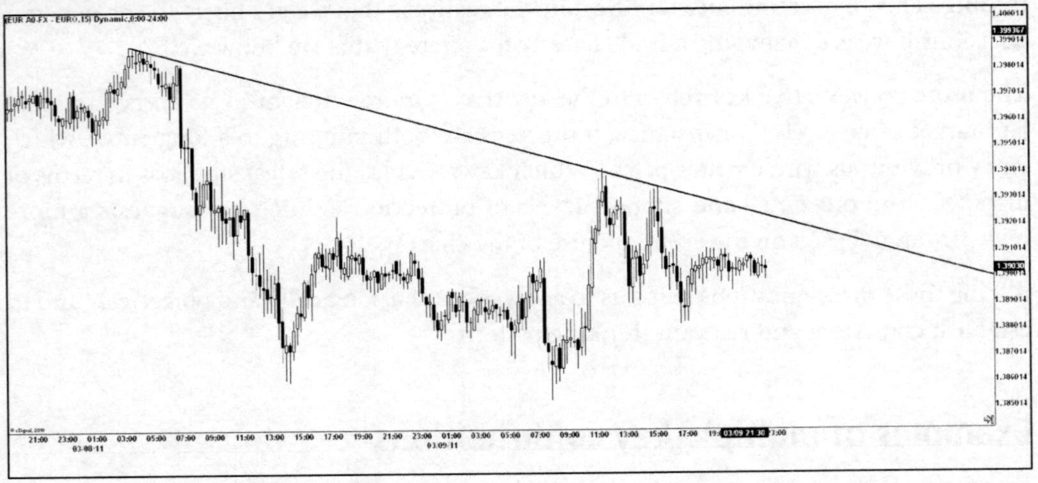

Figure 5.18 reveals that there is certainly a strong single-sided downward trend line. At this point, we would be alert for the standard trend line bounce strategy. Before we do that, however, let's see if there are any other setups occurring on this chart.

Figure 5.19: example chart with Fibonacci retracement levels

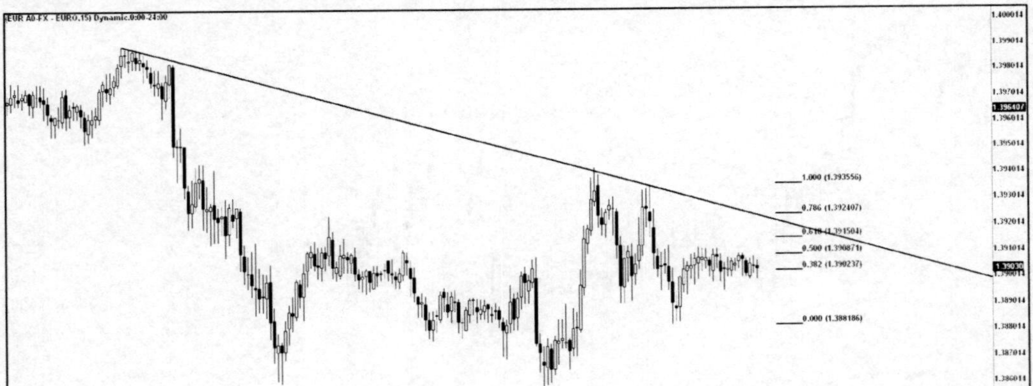

Figure 5.19 shows that there is also the potential for a Fibonacci bounce trade off the significant retracement level of 78.6%. Notice that the trend line and the 78.6% level are basically overlapping. Let's keep going and see if any other trades are setting up on this chart.

Figure 5.20: example chart with symmetrical triangle revealed

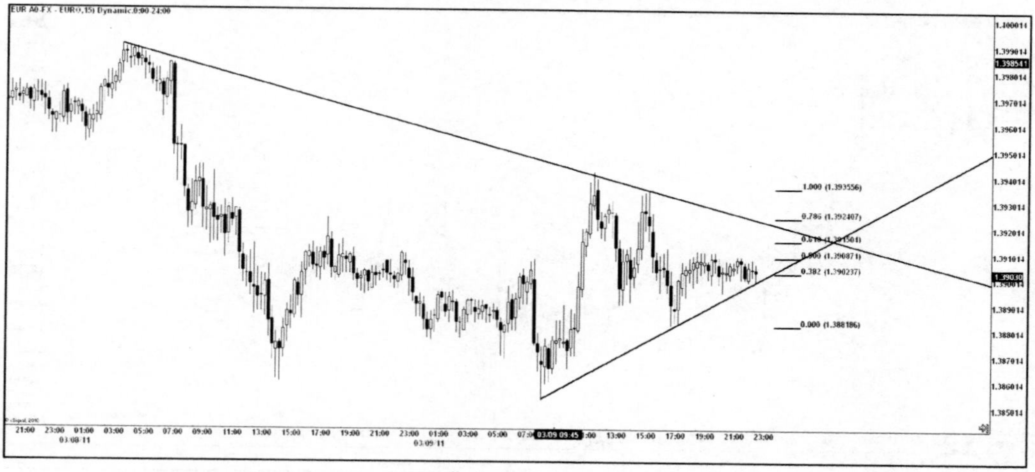

In Figure 5.20, we can see that there is also a symmetrical triangle bounce strategy setting up.

Let's slow down for a moment and look at each of the three setups individually. We will start with the trend line bounce, as shown in Figure 5.21.

Figure 5.21: example chart with trend line

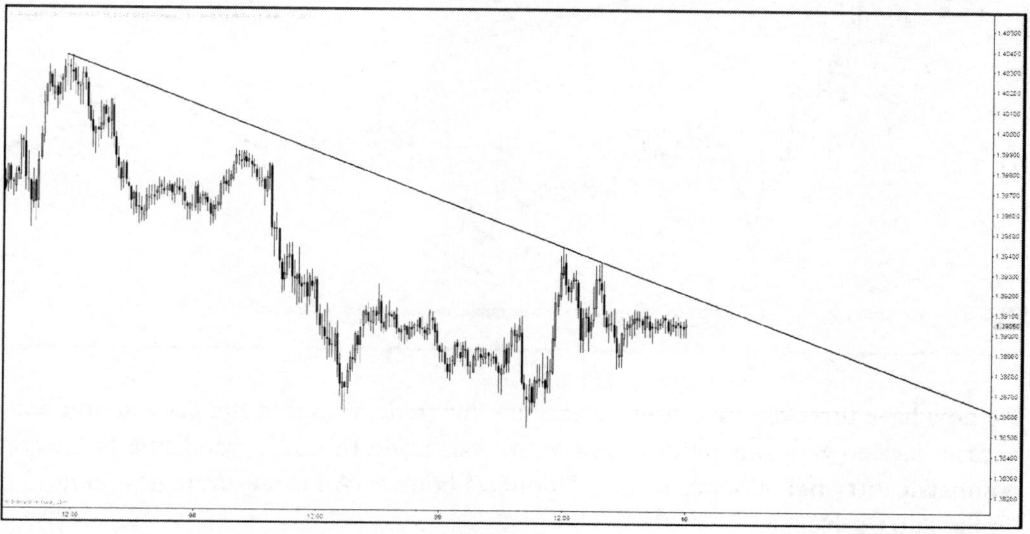

Next, we will look at the Fibonacci setup on its own, shown in Figure 5.22. The 78.6% Fibonacci retracement level is highlighted with a rectangle.

Figure 5.22: example chart with Fibonacci retracement levels

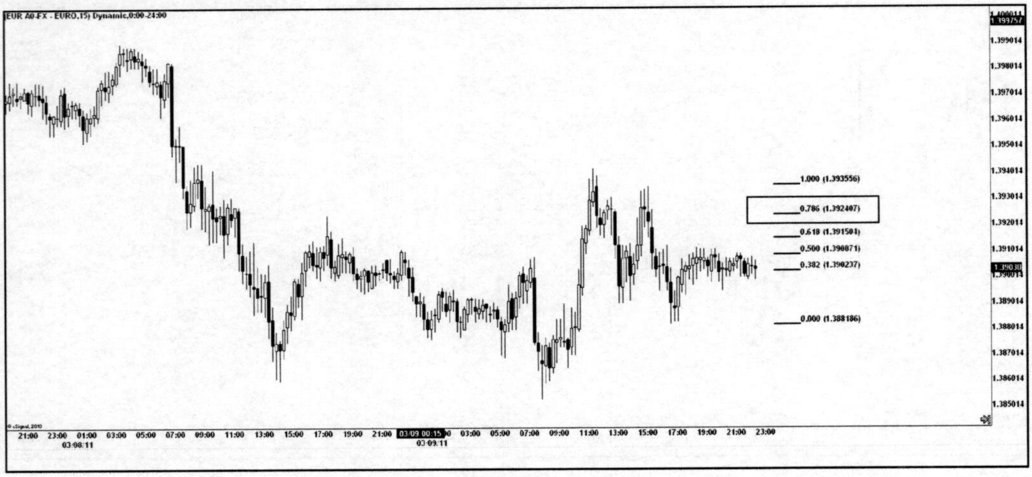

Finally, we will isolate the symmetrical triangle in Figure 5.23.

Figure 5.23: example chart with symmetrical triangle revealed

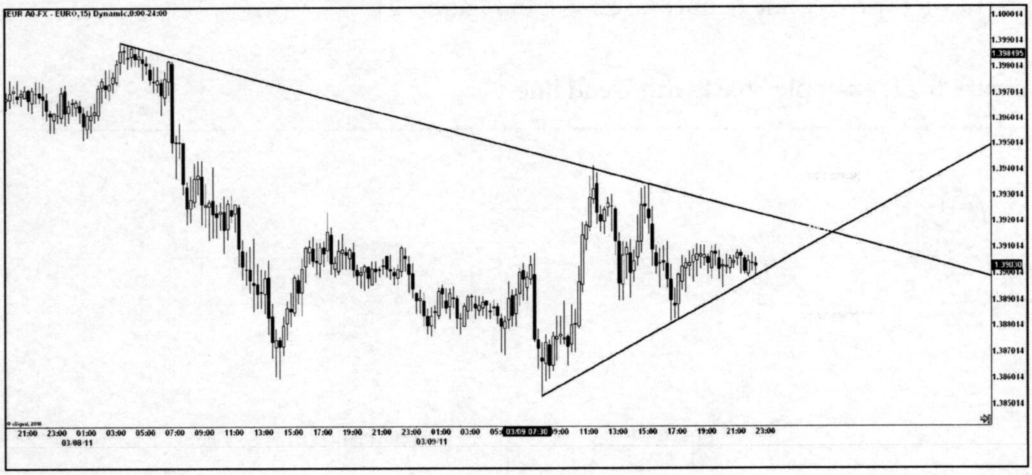

We now have three different ways to execute this trade, if indeed the price action does retrace back toward our point of entry. We can trade this as a trend line bounce, a symmetrical triangle bounce or as a Fibonacci bounce. All three strategies point to a similar entry price.

The question is which strategy should we use?

To decide we need to ask ourselves the three questions from the beginning of this section. First, which strategy is the most objective? Second, which strategy do we feel most comfortable with? Finally, which strategy would give us a more efficient entry?

In this example, we are going to go with the Fibonacci retracement strategy. The fact that the entry on this strategy is more efficient holds a lot of value for this trade. The Fibonacci bounce strategy tells us that we enter the short position once the price action retraces back to the 78.6% level, a candlestick touches this level and then closes below it. The stop loss on this strategy is 5 pips above the 100% retracement level. The target for this strategy is the 38.2% Fibonacci retracement level.

Figure 5.24 zooms in to show the continuation of the price action and the outcome of the trade.

Figure 5.24: the trade outcome

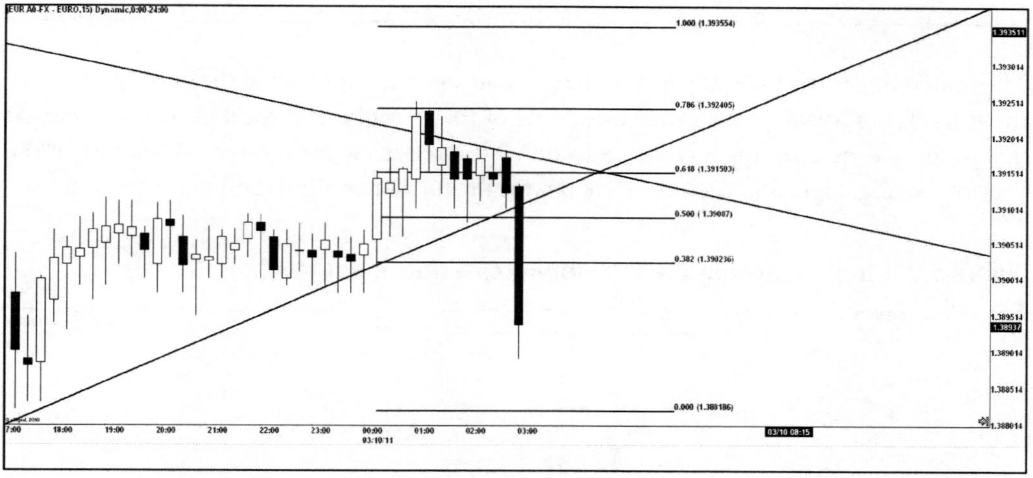

The price action moves rather quickly, hitting the target of the 38.2% Fibonacci retracement level.

Before moving on, let's look at a few of the other options that we could have exercised for this trade. Consider one of the targeting methods for the symmetrical triangle. According to this strategy, when the price action reaches the bottom trend line of the triangle, we move our stop loss to a breakeven position. By doing this we could have possibly let the Fibonacci trade run a bit further, knowing that the trade is risk free with the stop loss at breakeven. If we took this approach we could easily justify allowing our trade to run down to the 0% Fibonacci retracement level as this is the previous low of the price action. Figure 5.25 zooms in even further to demonstrate this.

Figure 5.25: another option of how to manage this trade based on Fibonacci retracement levels

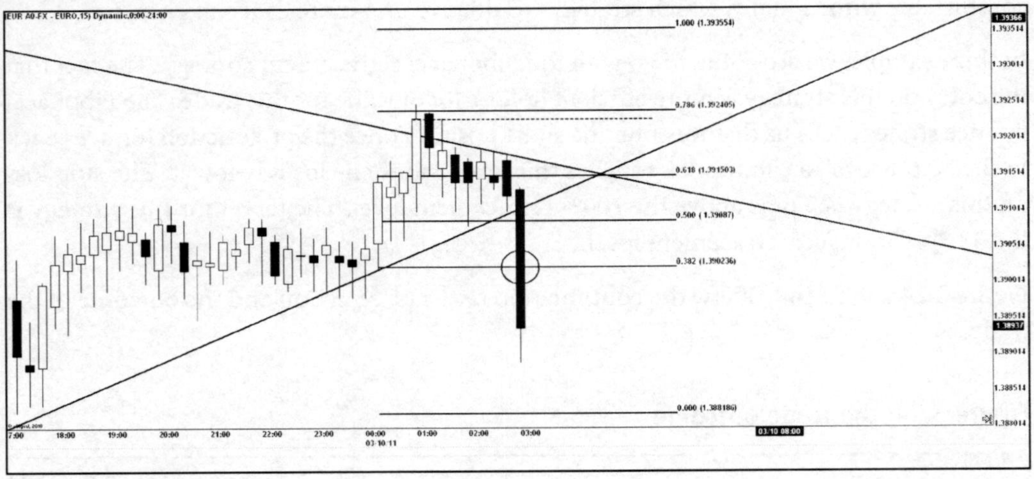

The dotted line is the new stop loss which was brought down to equal the entry point once the price action reached the lower trend line of the triangle, as indicated by the circle. At this point, we are running a risk free trade with a relatively large target at the low of the previous swing. Figure 5.26 zooms back out for the further continuation of the price action.

Figure 5.26: trade reaching the 0% Fibonacci retracement level

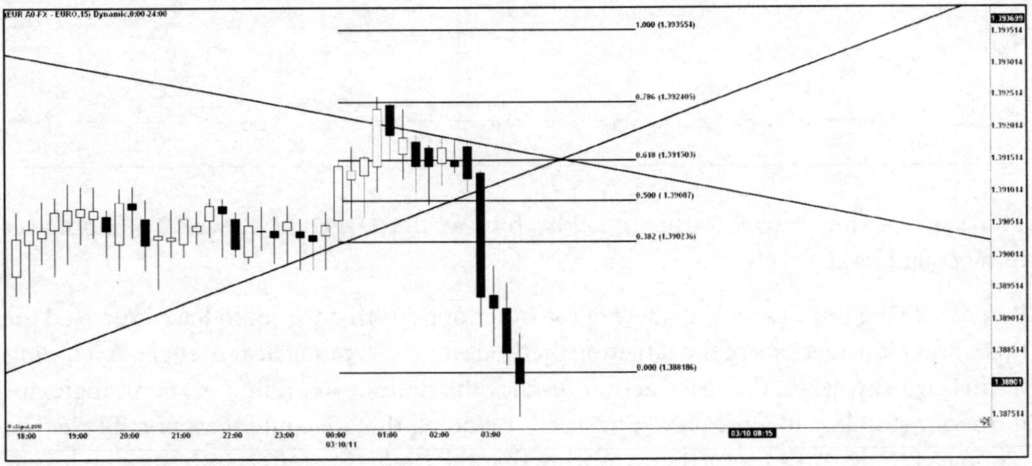

Once the price action reaches the 0% retracement level, we should be out of the position.

We could also have used some of the management rules from the trend line bounce strategy. One targeting scenario for this strategy tells us to take profit when the price action reaches a level of support. Figure 5.27 shows the earlier price action and shows the support level with a dotted line.

Figure 5.27: another option of how to manage this trade based on support principles

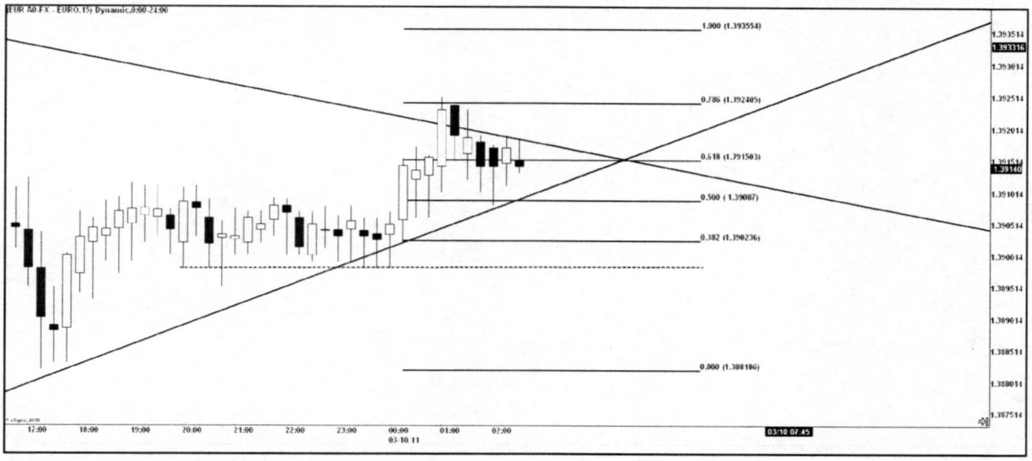

We could have used this level of support to target the trade or as an indication of when to bring our stop loss to a breakeven level.

In this example, we explored not only the power of multiple key confirmations, but the process of working through such a trade. Although more thought is required when several key strategies occur at the same time, it is positive as the setup will most likely be very solid.

This example highlights the importance of understanding each of our strategies and currency pairs. There will be times when we must make quick decisions. The ability to utilise concepts from each strategy will take our trading to the next level.

CONCLUSION

There are very few shortcuts when it comes to learning how to trend trade the foreign exchange market. The best way to have a profitable trading experience is to consistently use the four keys explained in this book. Practice implementing these keys and executing the eight strategies which are related to them. The goal is to develop the subconscious skill of making sound trading decisions on a consistent basis. When you are able to do that you will have grasped the ultimate foreign exchange trading key - a reliable intuition.

Combining the ability to trend trade the currency pairs that exist in the foreign exchange market, an understanding of trend lines, channels, Fibonacci retracement levels and symmetrical triangles and an experienced, mature intuition is the most effective way to sustain long-term trading success.

I wish you the greatest success as you unlock the power of trend trading the most dynamic financial market that the world has ever known – the foreign exchange market.

INDEX

D

E

F

H

I

K

L

M

N

O

P

R

S

T

U

V

Z

Lightning Source UK Ltd.
Milton Keynes UK
UKOW02f2344131013

219006UK00004B/32/P

9 780857 190895